Schools Council
Research Studies

Conceptual Powers of Children: an Approach through Mathematics and Science

As certain diagrams may not have reproduced clearly, these outline drawings are provided as an extra aid.

p. 89   item 6: 2 blue oblongs, 2 blue triangles

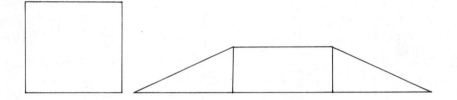

p. 164   item 10: 1 set of 5 wooden blocks painted blue;
          another set of 4 wooden blocks painted red

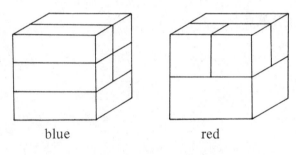

blue   red

p. 165   item 10a: first
          reconstruction
          of blue cube

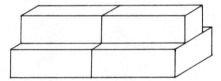

p. 166   item 10b: second
          reconstruction
          of blue cube

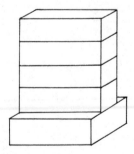

Schools Council
Research Studies

Conceptual Powers of Children: an Approach through Mathematics and Science

Eryl Rothwell Hughes
in collaboration with Joseph Rogers

A report from the Schools Council project on the
Development of Scientific and Mathematical Concepts
(7–11), based at University College of North Wales, Bangor

M
Macmillan Education

First published 1979

ISBN 0 333 24832 5

Published by
MACMILLAN EDUCATION LIMITED
Houndmills Basingstoke Hampshire RG21 2XS
and London
Associated companies in Delhi Dublin
Hong Kong Johannesburg Lagos Melbourne
New York Singapore and Tokyo

Text set in 10/12 pt IBM Press Roman, printed by
photolithography, and bound in Great Britain
at The Pitman Press, Bath

British Library Cataloguing in Publication Data

Schools Council Project on the Development of
Scientific and Mathematical Concepts (7—11)
Conceptual powers of children. — (Schools Council.
Research Studies; 0306-0292).
1. Schools Council Project on the Development of
Scientific and Mathematical Concepts (7—11)
I. Title II. Hughes, Eryl Rothwell
III. Rogers, Joseph IV. Series
372.7'3'0942   QA135.5
ISBN 0-333-24832-5

Contents

Preface

The Schools Council project on the Development of Scientific and Mathematical Concepts was directed by Dr Joseph Rogers and based at the University College of North Wales, Bangor, from 1968 to 1974. It covered the age range 7–11. This book is an account of the project's research to find out more about the ways children think and react, when facing practical problems concerned with the fundamental concepts of area, weight and volume. The study followed lines laid down by the researches of Professor Jean Piaget and his co-workers, but as it differed in a number of respects from the type of investigation normally carried out in this field, the report also discusses fundamental issues and problems in Piagetian theory and test design.

Our present state of knowledge of the way children between the ages of seven and eleven form these concepts relies on a type of practical investigation developed by Piaget and repeated, in many versions, by research workers over the last twenty years or so. Before designing the research reported here, it was necessary to analyse and evaluate previous studies with two aspects in mind: first, issues and problems concerned with Piaget's theory of conceptual development and, secondly, issues and problems concerned with the designing of tests which provided the evidence for the theory. In practice, it is difficult to isolate these two areas of discussion, as one is dependent on the other. However, it is important that such a detailed appraisal should appear in the reporting of any fairly large-scale research in this field. Research is not often published in full and it is more likely to emerge in the form of a summary in one of the various educational journals or, in a more complete version, as an unpublished thesis deposited in a university library. With one or two exceptions (e.g. Hyde's cross-cultural study of number and quantity, 1970, or Wallace's study of stages and transition in conceptual development, 1972), it is not possible for the general student of Piagetian research to read a summary of current issues and problems with special reference to a particular research programme. For this reason, and in order to place the present study in its context, the first part of the book discusses at proportionally considerable length the relevant points of issue in current Piagetian research.

When reading and writing about studies in the field of conceptual development, one suspects that the method of reporting is often responsible for giving the impression of neat clearcut design and execution. As a result, the reader is led to believe that designing Piagetian-type research and carrying it out in the company of lively, free-thinking eight-year-olds is very much akin to designing scientific experiments in the laboratory. Nothing could be further from the truth; this being so, we have to question — to a higher degree than those scientists, tightly controlling all the variables in their investigations — the reliability of such Piagetian investigations and, in particular, the interpretations and conclusions which emerge.

Comment is also made, therefore, on the trials and tribulations that appeared during the design and execution stages of the work. In this way it is hoped that the reader will become aware of the shortcomings and be able to decide for himself how reliable are the findings and interpretations. It is also hoped that a report written in this fashion will enable other teams of researchers as well as individuals to avoid the many pitfalls that can lie in their path.

As a Schools Council sponsored project our consultative committee asked us to be concerned with the implications that this work, as well as other Piagetian researches, has for the teacher in the classroom. As a result, the project progressed beyond the research stage and produced a guide book for teachers, *Area, Weight, and Volume* (published by Nelson in 1975) and a range of related practical materials (available from Taskmaster, Leicester). It is hoped that teachers will be encouraged to read this research report too, and for this reason passages which are concerned with the implications for the researcher and teacher have been inserted at appropriate points.

Any worthwhile research should encourage others to replicate and explore further the procedures used and the interpretations made. The work of Piaget has achieved this. On a smaller scale this book, together with the teacher's guide, provides sufficient detail for students and teachers to replicate the studies and to observe for themselves the way children think about the concepts of weight, area and volume. If readers are encouraged to observe children in this way, then this report will be considered to have achieved its main aim.

Introduction

Individual differences between children of the same age are so great that any class, however homogeneous it seems, must always be treated as a body of children needing individual and different attention.

Children and their Primary Schools
(Plowden Report, 1967, vol. 1, p. 25)

In recent years the theories of Piaget on child development have been brought to the attention of everyone concerned with education: research workers, local education authority curriculum advisers and teachers in the classroom have all been influenced by his writings. It is probable that this influence has been greatest in the field of curriculum design and although, until recently, Piaget has not been directly concerned with teaching methods the trends towards teaching 'by discovery' and open-plan schools have undoubtedly been influenced by his theories of child development. This trend is summed up by Cockcroft (1968, p. 1) writing in the parents' guide to the Nuffield Mathematics Project, *Your Child and Mathematics*:

Their aim [the writers of the teachers' guide], and the aim of those who have supported them, has been to base the education of five to thirteen year olds on class activity in which the children can join, learning from their own experience, *understanding by doing*. The changes involved in this newer approach are revolutionary when viewed in terms of the older one in which children were expected to accept passively facts and processes imposed upon them, often irrespective of whether their natural interest had been roused or a measure of real understanding obtained.

This child-centred curriculum, as it is often termed, contrasts strongly with the older subject-centred one and its successful implementation demands that information is available on the way children think, the misconceptions and misunderstandings that they often display and, more particularly, the way they develop concepts that are considered fundamental for the learning process.

Arguments for such curricula have, quite rightly, found considerable favour over the past few years, but it can also be argued that further major progress in such curriculum design can only occur if knowledge about children's intellectual development is increased through further research and other studies. Following the initial surge of curriculum innovation we are now probably at the stage where more work of this type should be encouraged so that the findings will further guide the curriculum planners of the future. Indeed, Piaget himself has commented on this development and in a recent publication (1969: English 1971, p. 130), referring to the training of teachers he recommends 'a close union of training and research, the students being associated with the latter right from the start'. The objective here is not to train students to become masters of a particular method of teaching but to increase their knowledge of the ways children think and to observe the stages of development of their pupils. It is only after the acquisition of such information that a teacher can practise his art and apply the teaching method that best fits his pupils's immediate requirements.

It can be argued that, to obtain such information, experiments have to be carried out with children and that this is not a role that a teacher, in his everyday work, should practise to any great extent. Piaget (1969: English 1971, p. 8) answers this argument:

It will be objected that pupils are not mere guinea pigs for us to use in pedagogical experiments but are not the many administrative decisions and reorganizations that occur at present ultimately experiments too and differ[ing] from scientific experiment only that they include no systematic controls.

Particular methods of teaching have, in their time, found favour, and arguments have been put forward for their universal adoption in the classroom. Piaget, when making his plea for the adoption of teaching methods based on knowledge of children's intellectual development, comments on many of these teaching methods when he writes (1969: English 1971, p. 8): 'We should refuse to remain content with mere opinion even when adorned with the authoritative label "according to the experts", especially since the opinions are both so numerous and contradictory' . Unfortunately our knowledge about the intellectual development of children is still somewhat hazy and no educationist advocating a particular method of teaching can be certain that his method will best meet the needs of particular groups of children and, still less certainly, the needs of individual children. Admittedly we have made considerable progress in research in this field since the days when the late Sir Cyril Burt wrote (1931) in an appendix to the Hadow Report on *The Primary School*: 'The years from seven to eleven or twelve might almost be termed the Dark Ages of childhood. Comparatively little is known of the characteristics distinguishing them.' This report stated that a considerable body of first hand data about the general character of mental growth in this age period lay scattered in the pages of periodicals and monographs, and an attempt was made to suggest teaching approaches that would be most fruitful in the various areas of the primary school curriculum. Some forty years later both the Plowden and Gittins Reports on the primary school laid considerable stress on the body of knowledge about the intellectual development of children that had been accumulated in the meantime. The work of Piaget featured strongly and the implications of these researches for the teacher in the classroom were underlined in the various recommendations concerning the form of the primary school curriculum.

Whilst this *pattern* of curriculum design is to be strongly encouraged, there is now the danger that such recommendations are likely to be adopted without further questioning. After all, it can now be said that such modern suggestions, in contrast with the previous ones, are firmly based on research evidence. It seems to the present writer, however, that we are only beginning to expand our knowledge about the ways children think and learn. Teachers and research workers need to be in close relationship if our teaching methods are to continue to improve. Hunt (1969, p. 55) has neatly summed up Piaget's work: 'Piaget's stature as the giant of developmental psychology, then, resides less in what he has completed, much as it is, than in the many beginnings his many observations and his theoretical interpretations provide'. Much then, remains to be done, and in writing this report of our own research we have attempted constantly to bear in mind the importance and value of Piaget's work but, at the same time, have tried not to accept without question the present state of our knowledge about the conceptual development of children.

In order to place our research in its context it is necessary to consider aspects of Piagetian theory and the pattern of the research studies on which this theory is based.

Acknowledgements

The project team wish to thank members of the Consultative Committee for their support and advice, and the local education authorities and schools that participated in the research (see pp. 247–9) for their willing co-operation, their hard work and the valuable feedback they provided.

1 Problems and fundamental issues

PIAGET'S INVESTIGATIONS AND EXPERIMENTAL METHOD

Piaget's investigations into children's thinking have been more extensive and
penetrating by far than those of his contemporaries, and although aspects of
his theory of cognitive development and, in particular, his practical methods
of obtaining data are open to question and criticism, the influence of his work
on any other research carried out in this field at present is dominant.

When Piaget went to Paris in 1919 to study psychology under Dr Simon, it
was suggested that he should standardize Cyril Burt's reasoning tests on
Parisian children but he did not find the task of comparing the number of
successes and failures of his subjects very interesting and thought that it would
be more interesting to find the *causes* for the failures and so analyse the verbal
reasoning of normal children. To do this he evolved what is now termed the
clinical method of examination of conceptual development. Originally this
simply meant careful observation of children's responses to test situations
arranged by the experimenter. Usually the observer did not intervene in these
situations at all but, as Piaget progressed, so he began to question the children
to try and find out the beliefs or reasoning which lay behind their responses.
These questions were open-ended, in that the answer given to a question would
govern the form of the next question. In this way Piaget tried to build up a
more complete picture of the way children think than had previously been
obtained. Sometimes a particular response would cause Piaget to add a problem
to the test situation or actually to change the materials used in the experimental set-up. This type of intervention on the part of the experimenter also had
the aim of finding out more about the way children think. In the case of the
concepts of weight, area and volume, nearly all the experimental situations
used practical materials which the children often handled, and the ingenious
design of many of these materials, enabled Piaget, through this clinical
approach, to formulate his theory of cognitive development. Elkind (1970,
p. 10) has summed up this approach admirably:

What Piaget found with this method of inquiry was that children not only reasoned differently from adults but also that they had quite different world views, literally different philosophies. This led Piaget to attend to these childish remarks and questions which most adults find amusing or nonsensical . . . he found in the 'cute' sayings of children evidence for the existence of ideas quite foreign to the adult mind.

These observations have undoubtedly enabled a more detailed picture of the child's thinking process to be obtained than previous approaches; nevertheless, the method can be, and has been, criticized for a number of reasons. Smedslund (1961, p. 12), summarized the disadvantages of the method:

Piaget's 'méthode clinique', which consists of flexible and intuitively directed conversation and play, has proved fruitful in the initial steps of research, but has the drawback that it cannot be exactly replicated, and it allows for unknown degrees of subjectivity in the procedure and interpretations.

Probably its main weakness lies in the unstructured nature of the test procedure. For example, by varying the test situation from child to child we cannot be certain that the responses of a particular child in a particular situation would be the same in another situation of a similar type. In other words, it may be difficult to assess whether the response observed is the general level of thinking of the child or whether it is a way of thinking particular to the actual test situation only. Fogelman (1970, p. 9) comments on this open-ended questioning sequence:

In this lies both the strength and weakness of Piaget's method. Its strength is that it gives much information about the child's thought. Its weakness is that the procedure is so unstructured that it leads to the suspicion that a variation in it would lead to a variation in the information obtained and the conclusions drawn.

Piaget is, of course, well aware of these criticisms and once wrote:

If one's primary concern is simply to describe and explain the variety of intellectual structures which children at different levels possess, rather than to construct rigorous developmental scales for diagnostic purposes, I believe the clinical method to be the method of choice.

Whatever the arguments for and against the approach used to collect data, it seems obvious that Piaget's clinical method is a sound way for the introductory exploration of children's thinking processes, but once a theory has been built up on the basis of such data-gathering techniques researchers that follow can do one of two things. They may replicate previous work to confirm or

question earlier conclusions, or they may attempt to refine or improve the
data-gathering procedures in order to check their reliability and hence the
truth of the resulting conclusions. Over the past few years, most researches
have tended to fall into the first category and even here, as Fogelman and
others have shown, the replication is by no means exact. Experimental and
questioning procedures often vary considerably from the original form used
by Piaget; it may not be surprising, therefore, to discover that the results differ
slightly from one to another and that somewhat different conclusions are
reached. Although these replication studies agree, in general, with Piaget's
theory of cognitive development, their variable results on different points in
this theory call for the second type of research to be developed further. There
is a need to refine and improve the observational techniques used with children
to reduce the differences between the open-ended clinical method of inquiry
used in Piagetian research and the rigid standardized testing procedures developed, in the main, for the comparison of children's performances.

When designing the present research, we debated whether such refinement
or 'tightening' of testing techniques was possible. We return to this question
in chapter 3 (p. 27).

THE PROBLEM OF COMMUNICATION AND THE USE OF VERBAL
QUESTIONING PROCEDURES

One of the main problems facing any research worker attempting to find out
the ideas or concepts held by children concerns the way he or she obtains this
information. Ultimately this problem is one of communication. Many of
Piaget's inquiries make use of talk; the experimenter asks questions and the
child answers. Whenever words are used in this fashion, the listener has to
interpret what has been said before he can respond. The child, listening to a
question, has to attempt to grasp the meaning and then answer in words which,
to him, convey the meaning of his thoughts. The questioner in turn makes his
own judgement of these answers, and may attach to the words used a meaning
not intended by the child. In other words, seeking evidence of understanding
(an internal realization) using words – questions and answers – (an external
expression) is not a particularly reliable method. Piaget, when conducting his
early experiments on children's use of language, wrote (1923: English 1926,
p. 131) 'We only hope that in the circumstances we shall not be blamed for the
method we have adopted. It is not a method at all. We have simply made
experiments "just to see".' More recently, Wallace (1972, p. 17) summed up
this difficulty: 'By making frequent use of verbal stimuli the experimenter
becomes involved simultaneously with the problems of the conceptual process

and the equally difficult questions posed by the relationship between language and conceptualisation'. Research workers have attempted to eliminate verbal factors by careful design of the tasks used to test children's understanding of concepts but, in the main, these have not been successful, as the same difficulties emerge whatever form of communication is used between the questioner and the child.

When considering the design of the concept assessment materials, we were at first tempted to follow other experimenters who attempted to purify the research design by minimising verbal factors; after all, the elimination of an unwanted variable is a fundamental feature of any good scientific piece of research. It quickly became clear, however, that in dealing with young human beings such a design was artificial by nature. We concluded that we should consider the world around the pupil as it really exists. In the classroom the teacher *does* use verbal methods of teaching; the pupil hears, interprets and responds. It is on this real platform that the teacher operates, evaluates and takes action. It is impossible to divorce language and communication from the process of concept formation. We remembered Vygotsky's words (1962, p. 51):

Thought development is determined by language i.e. by the linguistic tools of thought and by the sociocultural experience of the child . . . the development of logic in the child . . . is a direct function of his socialised speech. The child's intellectual growth is contingent on his mastering the social means of thought, that is, language.

The use of the spoken and written word, then, is closely linked with the understanding of concepts and for this understanding to be judged correctly it is important that the questioner, at least, should use unambiguous words, terms or sentences in his questioning procedure. If he or she is satisfied that this has been done to the best of his ability, he has then to judge whether the answers of the child provide evidence for misunderstanding of the concept (what he actually thinks) or evidence for misuse or misunderstanding of the words (what he hears and says). In practice, it is often difficult to decide which of these is the correct solution. When considering our interpretation of our own research findings or of other researches, the reader should always bear in mind this dilemma, and should be particularly wary of those studies which make firm interpretations based on 'evidence of poor development of a concept' when, in fact, there is a high degree of verbal communication involved. We have tried to qualify our interpretations with these factors in mind but, unlike Euclidian geometry, we cannot suffix our remarks with *quod erat demonstrandum.*

We therefore asked ourselves if we could design assessment procedures

which used verbal methods and gave good *indications* of pupils' conceptualization and misconceptualization. Evidence of good understanding of a
concept presents no problem of interpretation but, unfortunately, simply
listening to children's responses is not an altogether effective way of ascer-
taining whether they have a *poor* understanding of a concept. Indeed, Braine
(1962) believes that it is almost impossible to study conceptual development
in children if verbal questioning procedures are used. He argues that, if a child
understands the verbal cue, then he already has the concept; if he fails to
respond then very little can be gleaned about the child's understanding of the
concept. Although we would agree with this argument, our observations show
that few children fall neatly into these two extreme cases. The majority of the
children in our sample did respond in various ways to the situations we presented to them, and we believe that, on the whole, these responses did give us
indications of the understanding and misunderstanding in their minds. However, Braine's point is a valid one and we have to consider the main obstacles
and difficulties before adopting a verbal approach.

One difficulty is that children listening to a question or statement may not
have understood the speaker's meaning but may nevertheless respond to their
own conceived meaning. The children may use relevant words or phrases contained in the question but this need not necessarily imply that the child's
meaning is identical with that of the speaker. Piaget describes his early
observations on the children's use of language (1923: English 1926, p. 130):
'Once we had entered upon these investigations moreover the conviction grew
upon us that in daily life the child often hears phrases, thinks he understands
them, and assimilates in his own way, often distorting them'. When a child
responds in this fashion, he is not necessarily called upon to demonstrate his
understanding of the concept under investigation. He attaches another meaning
to the question and its true purpose eludes him. A good example of this occurs
in the Piagetian situation when houses (in the form of blocks) originally spread
out over an area (a piece of card) are subsequently pushed together (but not
stacked) and the question asked, 'Is there the same or a different amount of
room left on the card now?' The object is to discover whether the child con-
serves area on the basis that 'nothing has really changed, nothing has been
removed'; but if a pupil interprets the question in the form of 'making more
room to move about in' or 'a more convenient area to move about', then he or
she would respond in quite a different manner, not considering that the
questioner was asking anything about conservation of total area in the absolute
sense. The argument that such a response is evidence for lack of development
of the conservation of area is obviously not strictly true.

Another difficulty encountered in a verbal questioning procedure lies in the
Piagetian idea that the live development of language is 'from the whole to the

part'. That is, when the child is confronted with a sentence which he does not fully understand, he does not analyse the sentence, seeking out the difficult words and attaching a meaning to these, but rather he attempts to obtain a meaning by a general overall observation of the sentence — a scanning process. Unfortunately, in the Piagetian type of questioning used for concepts such as weight, area or volume, understanding of a statement or question often hinges on a clear understanding of a single word or short term. For example, the understanding of words such as 'amount of surface' or even 'area' is necessary if questions exploring the concept of area in all its aspects are to be understood. If this particular question was of the form 'Does this shape have the same amount of area as that shape?' the child, in scanning the whole, might pick out a general meaning of the sentence as associated with the word 'same' and give an answer accordingly. He would merely look for similarities in the shapes and not necessarily look at their areas at all.

In our own research design we have tried to structure the assessment materials. Considerable thought was given to the wording of the questions and the words used by the children in reply. We have tried to think in terms of a 'method' of assessment, but at best we sought for *good indications* of the form of understanding or misunderstanding displayed by the pupils. When making our own interpretations we constantly bore in mind that at present no researcher can claim to have made an *absolute* measurement of conceptualization in children. A research worker designing a verbal questioning procedure should therefore consider the form and presentation of his questions very carefully; be an astute listener to the responses in order to determine the type of misunderstanding or understanding displayed by the pupil; and, above all, temper his interpretations of such responses with a note of caution.

Piaget, in summing up this dilemma of the relationship between language and thought (1964a: English 1968, p. 98), writes that they 'are linked in a genetic circle where each necessarily leans on the other in interdependent formation and continuous reciprocal action. In the last analysis, both depend on intelligence itself, which antedates language and is independent of it'.

We decided, therefore, that the exploration of children's understanding of questions using the technical terms and expressions commonly employed in the classroom is part and parcel of the development of conceptualization, and whilst we may be unable to pinpoint the exact nature of any misunderstandings displayed, we believe that it is possible to obtain information from such questioning procedures which provides good indications of the type of misunderstanding likely to be in the child's mind. In an attempt to achieve this objective, however, the questioning procedures and associated practical materials were presented in a particular manner. This design procedure is discussed in chapter 3.

PROBLEMS ASSOCIATED WITH TESTS OF A PRACTICAL NATURE

Number of tests required

Most of the researches which have replicated, to a lesser or greater degree, the test materials devised by Piaget have used only one or two practical tests. That is, the child faces and responds to only one or two practical situations and general deductions about conceptualization are made from the children's responses in these limited situations. Beard (1963) repeated some of Piaget's experiments on number concepts and devised additional experiments to assess the responses of English school children between the ages of 4y 10m and 7y 2m from different areas of the country. Although the general design and questioning procedures of this research are open to some criticism, an attempt was made to use more than one practical situation to examine a particular level of conceptualization. Beard concluded not only that the children differed to some degree in the order in which they understood concepts but also (p. 116) that 'there was a greater variety in the kind of answer given than Piaget describes. Children differed a little in the order in which they achieved number concepts and more considerably in the order in which they understood any one concept in different situations'. Uzgiris (1964) also considered this problem of test design and, after referring to earlier work by Beard, Hyde, Lovell and Ogilvie, examined the effect of varying the materials used to test for the conservation of substance, weight and volume. In other words, a number of practical situations were presented to the children but all examined the depth of understanding of conservation. Whilst the questioning procedure also varied from one kind of material to another, the finding that the conservation responses of the children differed significantly when different materials were used caused us to conclude that one cannot rely on interpretations made on the basis of a single practical test situation. As Uzgiris has mentioned, a number of practical situations should be devised, all exploring the same level of a concept. The responses to all these situations taken together are likely to afford stronger indications of the child's level of thinking than is the case in the single practical item situation.

Sample size

Related to this interpretation is the question of sample size. Piagetian test situations are normally restricted to a one-to-one confrontation (one person testing one pupil at a time) and, as replication studies of this type are usually carried out by a single person, the time factor does not allow the researcher to carry out questioning procedures with a large sample. Even in a single practical item test, a total sample of 100 children represents a considerable period of testing, and when it is remembered that for analysis purposes such a sum total is broken down still further into four or five age groups, the sample size per age group is often pitifully low (15 is a common figure in such categories). Further, as the researcher normally works in a single school, individuals within a group may differ considerably in ability; as age (and sometimes sex) is the only variable the research worker can handle in the time at his disposal, the reliability of the research findings must often be open to question. On the whole, it is surprising that so many researches confirm one another's findings; one has either to admit to the general order of Piagetian theory or consider whether the truth about children's thinking processes lies hidden within the tangle of uncontrolled variables in these studies.

Analysis of the replication studies over the last two decades leads us to suppose that the former conclusion is the more favoured of the two, but it seemed to us that further refinement concerning sample size and number of practical test items was possible and, indeed, advisable if our objective of 'good indications' of depth of understanding was to be achieved.

REPLICATION OF RESEARCH AND CONSISTENCY

One of Piaget's most frequently quoted conclusions concerns the problem of conservation. He carried out a number of experiments to determine how, and at what age, or 'stage' in their mental development, children began to realize that when the appearance of objects changed it did not necessarily mean that all the properties of those objects had also changed. The properties with which Piaget first concerned himself were those of mass (or substance), weight and volume (1940). To test for conservation he used the now famous plasticine ball and sausage experiment. After elongating the ball into a sausage he, in effect, asked the children whether the plasticine had the same mass or substance, the same weight and the same volume. Piaget found that the understanding of conservation followed a regular order that was related to age. Conservation of substance occurred at about seven or eight years of age, weight at nine or ten, and volume last at about eleven or twelve. Piaget interpreted these findings theoretically and his conclusions have had far-reaching effects on the teaching of these concepts in our modern primary school. In the main, the balance and weighing of objects appears in the infant classroom whilst the concept of volume is rarely touched upon until the child reaches the end of his primary schooldays.

These experiments have been replicated in various forms by others. Uzgiris (1964) generally confirmed Piaget's theory of sequential attainment of conservation of substance, weight and volume, but it was noted that this sequence was not always constant when different materials were used for testing purposes. Elkind's (1961b) study also agreed with Piaget's findings with regard to sequence; and the ages at which the children conserved agreed with Piaget's figures. Lovell and Ogilvie, in Britain, used Piaget's plasticine test to examine children's conservation of substance and weight (1960, 1961a) and also unit blocks to examine how children at different ages conserved volume (1961b).

Their findings were at variance with some of Piaget's, and their accounts touched upon the many variable factors which could affect the children's answers and the interpretations that could be made of these answers. Their investigations showed a natural development from the somewhat simpler replication study of Lunzer (1960b), for example, which was carried out a little earlier and, in particular, showed that alterations in procedure 'yielded findings that were not brought out either in the work of Piaget or Lunzer' (1961b, p. 119). Analysis of all such experiments raised questions concerning the reliability of the experiments themselves.

MENTAL AGE AND CONCEPTUALIZATION

The question of mental age and its relationship to conceptualization did not feature strongly in the main stream of Piagetian researches. Stages were often reported in terms of chronological age, and questions concerning the order of attainment of the various stages dominated the research scene up until the early sixties. Recently, however, a number of workers (Beard, 1960; Carpenter, 1955; Dodwell, 1960; Elkind, 1961a, b; Goldschmid, 1967; Hood, 1962; Keasey and Charles, 1967; Lister, 1969 and 1972; Peel, 1959; Mealings, 1963; Wells, 1972 and Woodward, 1972) have incorporated this variable into their research design. All seem to bear out Hood's (1962, p. 276) conclusion that 'it is not age however, but mental stature which is primarily important' in the attainment of concepts.

An examination of the design of many of these researches shows that the method of assessment of mental age was suspect. Teachers were sometimes asked to select 'good', 'average' and 'poor' ability pupils from particular age ranges but it is extremely difficult to determine the basis on which such choices were made. In an effort to increase sample size, one or two of these researches asked a number of teachers to participate in their selection procedure, and one is never certain that the three-group sample selected by any one teacher actually matches the groups selected by any of the others. However, without exception, the overall pattern of the findings of these studies was clear and cautious statements, characterized by Beard's (1963, p. 115) conclusion that 'on the whole children rated as having good intelligence did better in everything', appear in the interpretations of these researches. A small proportion develop this inquiry further and give a standardized intelligence test to a wide range of pupils (for example Carpenter, 1955, and Hood, 1962) and statistical techniques are also applied to their results. In general the findings of these more carefully designed studies agree with earlier work, and it would seem that a study of the relationship between the ability to conceptualize and mental age is a worthwhile exercise. It was decided, therefore, to select our sample carefully from a much larger number of children who had been given a standardized non-verbal intelligence test and to analyse the responses in terms of the pupils' mental abilities as indicated by this test.

THE QUESTION OF TRANSFER OF IDEAS FROM ONE CONCEPT TO ANOTHER

A common topic of inquiry and discussion is the comparison of stage of conceptualization in different concepts. It has long been recognized that pupils may be at a more advanced stage in one concept than in another. Pupils may, for example, be able to conserve in situations involving one concept but unable to conserve when a similar situation concerning another concept is presented to them. In simple terms this seems to indicate that stages in some concepts are harder to grasp than similar stages in others. The rank ordering of concepts and their understanding is a common field of inquiry but the results do not always agree with one another. Piaget refers to the acquisition of the concepts of substance, weight and volume in that order but replication studies do not agree firmly with this series. Beard, in her studies, for example, concludes (1963, p. 237) that:

Piaget's order of achievement of concepts of conservation of substance and weight is, on the whole, not borne out. Success in these sections is greater for items where the materials used are familiar. Although concepts of conservation of volume are achieved later this appears to result from lack of relevant experience.

Lister (1969, 1972) carried out research with educationally subnormal (ESN) children and, although mainly concerned with the possibility of training techniques, makes the point (1972, p. 20) that at the pre-training stage

there was a clear developmental sequence in the appreciation of conservation – number came first, then substance and length, then weight, then volume and area. This particular sequence differed somewhat from that reported by Piaget (Piaget, Inhelder and Szeminska, [1948]; Piaget, [1941]; Piaget and Inhelder, [1941]) and again from that reported by Goldschmid (1967). The sequence agrees with those reported by Piaget and Goldschmid with regard to substance, weight and volume but differs with regard to the other attributes and the order in which their conservation is recognised.

Lister's words summarize the types of variation observed in the different researches, and whilst it is difficult to pinpoint reasons for these variations, both Beard and Lister hint at possible explanations. Beard points out that experience and familiarity with the type of practical materials has considerable influence on the children's thinking. The pupils do not necessarily use the same thinking processes when the problem is posed using unfamiliar materials. Whilst this may be taken to indicate a limited conceptual ability on the part of the pupil, it also alerts research workers to the possibility of distorted measures of conceptual ability being obtained when the pupil is presented with a single practical test situation in any one concept.

Lister hints, indirectly, at another possibility in the thinking processes used by children. She comments of many of the children that, after teaching and training, 'having conserved volume they did transfer this to weight and/or substance situations' (1970, p. 60). In certain situations, therefore, it seemed that in this particular sample transference of ideas from one concept to another was possible. Modgil (1974) summarizes researches on this question; although only referring to three researches concerned with training and transfer of ideas to related cognitive strategies (those of Fournier, 1967; Gelman, 1969 and Goldschmid, 1967), he also mentions that their designs have been criticized on a number of points. This idea of transference of, say, conservation is obviously an important one and, in general, is not illustrated by typical Piagetian research. It is not clear whether transference of this type is an unusual feature of the child's thinking or whether it is not witnessed simply because the design of most of the researches does not allow the observer to explore this in sufficient depth. In Lister's example, for instance, it may well be that the child who has displayed conservation in the more difficult concept of volume will be able to conserve weight and substance because, from a sequential point of view, he will already have achieved the stage required for understanding these two simpler concepts.

If we examine the best known of the Piagetian researches (see Modgil, 1974), we rarely read of researchers who have asked children questions about the same level of thinking, e.g. the idea of conservation, but in different concepts, such as weight, area and volume, and also used *different* practical situations and *different* materials. In the present research, therefore, an attempt was made to incorporate into the testing procedures practical items in each of the concepts of area, weight and volume that could be termed 'parallel' items. These items had to be designed so that they would examine the pupils' understanding of conservation in each of these concepts. In addition, it was felt that the comments of earlier researchers should be heeded and that the actual design of these test items should try and avoid some of the pitfalls previously mentioned. The final versions of the assessment materials tried to incorporate a number of these parallel items so that they included tests concerned with categorization ability, perception, measurement and the use of logic as well as those concerned with conservation. This meant that each child experienced a considerable number of practical test items (a total of some 48 items) and, in effect, all the children were being examined on their responses to all these situations and not just to those concerned with one particular aspect, such as conservation.

To summarize, in analysing Piagetian researches the following questions were asked:

1. Can the research be replicated?
2. Is the questioning procedure as unambiguous as possible?
3. Is the number of practical test situations adequate?
4. Is the sample size large enough?
5. Is the interpretation of the meaning attached to a word or expression used by a child a reasonable one or is this consideration bypassed in the final analysis?
6. Is the sampling technique concentrated largely on the chronological age of the children rather than, say, their mental age?
7. To what extent does the research design allow for the use of similar tests on different concepts so that comparisons can be made between the subject's understanding of different concepts?

These, then, were the questions considered in the design of this research and it was planned, therefore, as a study, on a somewhat ambitious scale, of the general level of development reached by children in the concepts of area, weight and volume. This approach stemmed from interest in Piaget's idea of 'stages of development'.

2 Piaget's stages of development and theory of operations

STAGES OF DEVELOPMENT

One of the major features of Piaget's theory of development of intelligence is the postulating of 'stages' of development in children. By definition, this implies that children have certain ways of thinking according to their position on a scale of mental development. Much of Piaget's experimental work has been concerned with observations of these ways of thinking, together with the quest for evidence allowing him to describe in considerable detail the different gradations on this developmental scale. In the early days the broad elements of his theory could be supported by the evidence supplied by his clinical form of observational work carried out with young children. As the work progressed, the theoretical framework became more complex, and over the past few years the detailed structure of Piaget's theory has proved daunting to readers and translators of his work alike. Above all, it has formed a basis for further researches, while the quest for more detailed evidence of Piagetian 'stages' of development in children has, over the last twenty years, produced studies in the field of child development unprecedented in earlier times.

Piaget's four stages in the development of intelligence are now so well known and well described in other works (see for example Hunt, 1961, or Flavell, 1963a) that no attempt is made here to describe them in detail. Sufficient to say that we are concerned with the so-called periods of concrete operations and logical operations. Modgil has recently (1974) summarized the characteristics of Piaget's theory of cognitive development and he highlights the following points:

1. 'Each stage involves a period of formation and a period of attainment' (Inhelder, 1962, p. 22).
2. The developing process is evolutionary by nature, in that the attainment of one stage may be the starting point of the next. This implies that the boundary line between one stage and the next is ill-defined. Wohlwill (1966) has commented that this is not a rigorous enough characteristic

13

if one is postulating a theory based on stages. However, this idea
summarizes Piaget's view of child development in terms of 'equilibration', i.e. the paradox of the child's mind being in a state of constantly
changing equilibrium between what has been learnt, organized and
stabilized and what is new, unorganized and unstable.

3. 'The order of succession of the stages is constant. Ages of attainment
can vary within certain limits as a function of factors of motivation,
exercise, cultural milieu and so-forth' (Inhelder, 1962, p. 22). This, of
course, implies that the second stage must never precede the first, nor
the third the second, and so on.

4. The developing process is essentially an 'end-on' (i.e. linear) process',
in that something understood and grasped by a child at an earlier stage
is incorporated in some form or another into his way of thinking at a
later stage even though there is an addition to his thinking so that the
child 'develops mentally'. In other words, the child never just substitutes
a more advanced or different way of thinking for his earlier view and
discards this earlier way of thinking altogether; rather he modifies the
earlier view so as to include his new interpretation.

Essentially Piaget's theory implies a sequential development; that children
must understand certain fundamental experiences before they can understand
more complex ones. Furthermore, his theory suggests that experience alone
may not be sufficient for understanding to take place, even though such
experiences may be graded according to his theory. Other factors, such as
maturation − a natural physical growth − and the child's general view of the
world governed by the surrounding environment, also determine the depth of
his understanding. The theory has, by now, been built up into an elaborate
structure and there is no doubt that Piaget's work will be recognized as pioneer
studies in the field of research into children's thought processes. However,
Pinard and Laurendau, in an essay devoted to a study of 'stage' in Piaget's
cognitive developmental theory, identified a danger likely to result from the
impact of Piaget's work when they wrote (1969, p. 121): 'Piaget's difficult
system has been enveloped in an aura of prestige irreconcilable with the
critical spirit necessary to avoid confusion between hypothesis, opinions and
facts'.

Recently the complex notion of stages has been questioned, and research
workers have attempted to proceed beyond the replication of experiments of
the 1950s and 1960s and to explore in greater depth the various implications
of the idea of Piagetian stages. In a recent work, for example, Wallace writes
(1972, p. 21): 'The question of the existence of stages in the development of
conceptualization has attracted a great deal of attention from researchers and

yet, to a large extent, remains as baffling as ever'. He refers to the methodological weaknesses of Piaget's experimental approach and comments on the
problem of using verbal methods of questioning children (p. 23):

Piaget [in 1926] discussed the dangers involved in detecting the cognitive developmental implications of children's verbalisations but there is little evidence
in his practice that he has coped successfully with them. In particular he
appears to have failed to resist the supreme temptation of capitalizing on the
ambiguity of verbal responses to derive support for his preconceptions.

Bryant too (1971a, b) has made the point that in the field of his particular
inquiry (conservation principle), Piaget's experiments may not have been
refined to a degree high enough to warrant their use as pure evidence for a
particular interpretation of a child's way of thinking.

This problem of matching a *theory* of cognitive development with the
evidence of the actual behaviour of children seems, at present, to be the
fundamental issue in Piagetian research, and we shall return to this point
when considering the concrete and formal stages of operations in the next
section.

Perhaps the most important implication of Piaget's theory is that it strongly
indicates a general path along which the thinking powers of children develop.
The majority of the experiments carried out try to determine whether a *number* of children at different ages tend to follow this general path. As the method
of carrying out these researches has improved over the last few years, in-
vestigators have found considerable overlap in their findings, so that the main
features of the theory have been accepted. However, there have also been many
conflicting results and interpretations on research details sufficiently important
to warrant a more careful scrutiny of the evidence and a more cautious application of Piaget's theory to the level of understanding of any *particular* child.
A theory generally applicable to a number or group of children roughly
defined according to age cannot at present be guaranteed to apply to all
individual children, as insufficient work has been carried out on large numbers
of children; in short, the sample sizes of most researches are too small. Furthermore, a study of individual children requires longitudinal as well as cross-
sectional researches, i.e. children need to be re-tested after periods of time to
see how individuals develop. Longitudinal studies are not easily carried out by
individual research workers; such work requires a team operation, considerable
resources, tenacity and, obviously, time. The last factor is not readily available
and has, no doubt, prevented the launching of much-needed longitudinal
studies.

This dichotomy between a general theory applicable to children as a whole

and the level of understanding of a particular child has recently aroused considerable interest, especially as teaching in general has veered towards the
child-centred approach referred to earlier. Piaget has commented on the recent
findings in this area of study; whilst arguing strongly for a 'structural trans-
formation of thought with age' (1969: English 1971, p. 170), he agrees that
this does not warrant an extreme view that the stages are inflexible and are
characterized by invariable chronological age limits and fixed ways of thinking.
He acknowledges the presence in reality of overlaps between one stage and the
next (1969: English 1971, p. 171): 'These overlaps . . . probably exclude the
possibility of establishing generally applicable stage limits'. Indeed, in a recent
publication (1972: English 1974, p. 53), Piaget actually writes: 'I would like
to insist on the notion of lag [of operations] for it can create an obstacle to
the generalization of stages and introduce considerations of caution and
limitation'. Flavell (1972) also comments on Piaget's theme of sequential
development of thought processes and pleads for recognition of the possibility
that sometimes children 'may exhibit significant asequential features in
addition to the obvious sequential ones' (p. 279). He argues the case for a more
balanced view of mental growth in children. This is a valid argument especially
when we realize that Piaget's 'generally applicable theory' already admits that
the position of a child in this sequence of thinking ability may vary from
concept to concept — the generalization already has to be applied to each
concept in turn.

To date, then, Piagetian stages and, in particular, the sequential pattern
related to age of such stages are by no means firmly established and more
information is required on the responses of children to practical situations
which may be described as characteristic of each stage.

Our research, then, had to undertake two further functions. One was to
incorporate a longitudinal survey and the other to observe, record and interpret the responses of the children to a number of practical problems ranging
through a Piagetian sequence. In other words, we tried to make the different
tests characteristic of particular Piagetian levels of development. The research
design did, in fact, incorporate both these aims and a smaller longitudinal
survey was built into the larger cross-sectional study, but in the interests of
brevity, and in an attempt to retain some orderliness in this account, the
results and interpretation of the longitudinal survey will appear separately.

Our second objective, therefore, was to try and discover whether children
in our survey followed a sequential path. If this general pattern did emerge,
we wondered to what degree individual children varied from this pattern. We
also wondered how the performances of the children in such a sequence in a
particular concept would vary from their performances in the corresponding
parallel items in the other two concepts.

THEORY OF OPERATIONS

Before describing our practical test items and analysing the results, it is necessary to remind ourselves of the main elements and properties of Piaget's theory of 'operations'.

Piaget has been concerned, in all his work, with questions of genetic epistemology. His co-worker Inhelder (1962, p. 17) has described this approach as a method seeking 'to analyse the mechanisms of the growth of knowledge insofar as it pertains to scientific thought and to discover the passage from stages of least knowledge to those of the most advanced knowledge'; it is an explanation of thinking processes from the simple to the complex. In following this approach, Piaget has refrained from considering that human intellectual development is so intricate and complex that it defies an orderly description but has assumed that such growth of thinking powers can be described in terms of a well-regulated scientific theory and a relatively neat, although complex, pattern. He has used the idea of stages to explain this growth and his theory has been described by Kessen (1962, p. 68) as 'a segmented treatment of intellectual development'.

During his early observations of the responses of children, Piaget considered the possibility that the observable reactions of his subjects to his test situations followed an organized path of development that could be explained logically, and it was not long before he extended this idea and proposed that such logical structures or models could also be used to describe the growth of the thinking processes that were slowly developing in the child's mind as he matured and gained further experience of the world. In Flavell's words (1963a, p. 169):

[Piaget] believes that certain logico-mathematical structures make very good models of the actual organisation and process of cognition in middle and late childhood. They constitute, he feels, ideal patterns which the living operational systems in the subject closely approximate; they give us a useful image of how the cognizer is organised.

In other words, the description of patterns in the disciplines of logic and mathematics can be used to explain the pattern of the development of human thinking powers.

From this point Piaget's work in this field followed two paths simultaneously. The first involved observation and analysis of children's responses to many original and ingeniously devised stimulus situations; these experiments have been replicated in some form or other by many research workers over the last twenty-five years or so. The second path sought for a rational description of the 'structural properties of thought' — the construction of a theory which could be used to describe how concepts are developed in the mind. Mays

(1953, p. 2) has described this approach as the study of the 'application of symbolic logic and logical techniques to the psychological facts themselves, and especially to the thought structures found at different levels of intellectual development'. To the reader of Piaget these two paths tend to cross and re-cross as he reads first a description of children's responses in an experimental situation and then an interpretation of this response in terms of the logico-mathematical theory. The theory describes a pattern and the responses are interpreted within this framework. Over the years Piaget has developed this pattern into a complicated mesh of theoretically possible relationships and interrelationships, which has by now advanced quite independently of experimental observations with children. In other words, to read the theory does not necessarily imply that such thought behaviours can or have been actually witnessed in experimental situations. Again, to quote Flavell (1963a, p. 170): 'Logic and mathematics are, of course, purely formal systems which need no recourse to experimental fact, psychological or other.'

The foundation of Piaget's theory lies in his idea of an 'operation'. By this term he means the way the mind absorbs all the facts presented to it — what is seen, what is heard, the results of taking action, etc. — and, more than this simple absorption, the way the mind digests this material and organizes it into a framework or structure which can be termed 'knowledge'. All the nuts and bolts and pieces are assembled in the mind and the resulting structure is then used to form that person's eventual response. By observing the responses we attempt to identify the main features of these *operational structures.* To Piaget operational structures constitute the basis of knowledge, and the central problem in the study of the development of knowledge is understanding the formation, elaboration, organization and functioning of these structures. Whilst an English translation often fails properly to convey the original meanings expressed by Piaget, perhaps the best summary of the idea of an operation is expressed in his own words when he wrote (1964b, p. 176):

Knowledge is not a copy of reality. To know an object, to know an event, is not simply to look at it and make a mental copy or image of it. To know an object is to act on it . . . it is an interiorized action.

For instance, joining objects in a class to construct a classification, or ordering or putting things in a series, or counting and measuring are all operations. In other words, mere observation is not an operation but the ordering of observations into a structure in the mind is. An operation also has the property of totality. The framework or structure built up in the mind is linked to other operational structures. For example, a class of objects is not just based on the objects themselves, it is based on the *idea of classification* which exists in the mind. Similarly, the putting of objects into a series does not depend on the simple observation of the objects singly or altogether, it depends on the total idea of what is meant by a series.

Operational structures do not exist in the mind simply to be tapped off when practical experiences designed to stimulate such thought processes are presented to the child. They develop from the simple to the complex and, if the presented situation involves parts of an operational structure which is too complex and far ahead of the child's level of development, he cannot absorb and truly digest his experiences as he is unable to develop the right structure to operate correctly on the information. As Hunt remarked (1961, p. 200): 'His interaction with that situation has no more effect upon his conceptual structures than does the proverbial "lecturing a pig about Sunday" '.

If this theory of development of knowledge is analysed, it is clear that the process of elaboration in the mind depends on activity. Two types of activity may be witnessed in the young child: one is logico-mathematical – the all-mental type – ordering, counting, sorting, and so on; the other explores the objects themselves, physically examining the weights, volumes and other properties of the material. This second type of activity allows the child to develop an increasingly complex conception of the properties of the objects. Both types interact with one other and the combination of direct action and mental analysis allows the child to build up his concept of the topic under study.

As a result of this idea of development, Piaget naturally develops the theme of operational structures into a linear or end-on sequence of development, and the various series of structures in the sequence are called 'stages'. As mentioned earlier, this step in the theory implies that there is a series of structures which is indispensable for subsequent intellectual stages. In our research we are mainly concerned with one stage or period – that of concrete operations – although we also consider the beginning of the following stage – that of formal operations.

The period of concrete operations

Children in the concrete operational stage demonstrate a complicated process of elaboration of thinking powers; their mental performances begin to demonstrate considerable flexibility and they are continually adapting to new situations. They also produce evidence of elementary logico-mathematical thought structures but, in contrast with the stage that follows, they must have objects to manipulate before they can demonstrate these ways of thinking. It is the close association with actual activity in concrete situations that gives this stage its name. It should be emphasized, however, that the concrete stage does not imply that the children can only carry out simple measurements or direct comparisons with real objects or apparatus without thinking about their actions. The use of logic *is* demonstrated but it is of a type that is distinguishable from that used in the stages of formal operations. Piaget (1972:English 1974, p. 21) contrasts these two forms of logic as follows:

This period [of concrete operations] is that of a logic which is not based on verbal statements but only on the objects themselves, the manipulable objects. This will be a logic of classifications because objects can be collected all together or in classifications; or else it will be a logic of relations because objects can be combined according to their different relations; or else it will be a logic of numbers because objects can be materially counted by manipulating them. This will thus be a logic of classifications, relations and numbers, and not yet a logic of propositions.

It is at this point that Piaget uses his theoretical model to describe the thought structures characteristic of this stage, and it is necessary briefly to describe their properties so that we can return to this form of analysis when discussing the results of our observations. What follows is an abbreviated account of theory and for greater detail the reader should refer to more rigorous accounts, such as Flavell (1963a) or Hunt (1961).

The intricate model used by Piaget describes the fully developed concrete operational thinking process in terms of the ability to use nine types or 'groupings' of thought operation. Four of these can be described in mathematical terms and five in logical terms. These may be summarized under five headings.

Combinativity or transitivity
In mathematical terms this means that any two classes or more can be combined into one total class which embraces or embodies them all. For example, the separate classes 3, 7 and 8 can be embodied in the total class 18 (3 + 7 + 8 = 18). In logical terms this occurs in expressions of the type 'all boys and all girls' which is embodied in 'all children'. This form of logic, where two classes can be combined to give a total or third class, also occurs in propositions such as 'If A is greater than B and B is greater than C' when a total class would be 'then A is greater than C'; this last statement contains both the others.

It can be seen that although A, B and C may represent an actual property (say weight) of real objects, a simple measurement of these weights in pairs, A and B, B and C does not give by direct observation alone the idea that 'therefore A is heavier than C'. The child has mentally to operate on his observations and he can only come up with the conclusion 'A must be heavier than C' if he already has the structure or idea of combinativity or transitivity in his mind. He can, of course, check this type of logical deduction by weighing A directly against C, but the child who has fully developed this type of thinking sees no need to do this — his thought structure tells him that it must be so.

In a similar way we can describe the other groupings in the concrete operational stage.

Reversibility

This means that every mathematical or logical operation is reversible, i.e. there is an opposite operation which can cancel it. Thus $2 + 7 = 9$ but also $9 - 7 = 2$ or, in logic terms, 'all men and all women' is embodied in the expression 'all adults' but also, reversibly 'all adults except men' is embodied in 'all women'.

To Piaget this idea of reversibility is an important one. The development of this way of thinking enables the child to go over the separate bits of information in his mind, and he can retrace or check all the steps he has taken before arriving at a conclusion. A good example of this type of thinking occurs in the well-known Piagetian test where two balls of plasticine are demonstrated to be of equal weight and the child is then asked to roll one of them into a long sausage shape, or to flatten it into a pancake, or to break it into pieces. He is then asked whether the weights of the two balls are still equal or whether one weighs more than the other. Inhelder has pointed out (1962) that two forms of reversible thought allow the child to arrive at the correct conclusion. In the first thought process the child relates the increase in one dimension to the corresponding decrease in another dimension — a compensatory reason ('When it gets longer it gets thinner and it still weighs the same'). In the second thought process the child reverses the action in his mind ('You only have to make the sausage into a ball again and you can see right away that nothing is added and nothing is taken away'). For Piaget the ability to express this idea of reversibility must occur before the child can proceed to more advanced ways of thinking. 'For Piaget', writes Flavell (1963a, p. 189), 'reversibility is not merely one of five grouping properties, it is *the* core property of cognition in a system — the one from which all others derive.'

Associativity

This means that when operations are combined, the order of the combination process has no effect on the final result or conclusion. This grouping stems from reversibility. Thus, $(7 + 6) + (3 + 2) = 3 + (2 + 7) + 6$. In logic terms this means that the child can combine a number of ideas or operations in a variety of ways and realize that the final deduction always remains the same, as in: 'A is the uncle of B and B is the father of C; then if A is the only brother of D, then D must be the grandfather of C'. This way of thinking allows the child to explore alternative ways of working things out and marks an advanced stage in the concrete operational period.

Identity

This is the simple idea that when an operation is combined with its opposite nothing is altered. Thus, $(+7) + (-7) = 0$ or, in logic terms, the idea is expressed in statements such as 'If I walked 10 miles north and then 10 miles south I will be back where I started'. This ability to cancel an earlier idea by a later one is again seen by Piaget as an important development in the thinking process.

Tautology or iteration

The fifth type of grouping has two versions, one for classes and relations and the other for numbers.

Tautology means that when a classification or a proposition is repeated, no more information is added. Repeating a message, for example, may help the listener to absorb and digest the information but the repeats give no more information than that expressed in the first statement.

Iteration applies to numbers and means that when a number is combined with itself it gives a new number. E.g. $4 + 4 = 8$ or $5 \times 5 = 25$, etc.

These logico-mathematical structures provide the core groupings of thought operations and Piaget maintains that, in theory, all forms of arranging classes or relationships fall into variations of these. This theory is purely an exploration of possibilities, but it does not say that children actually think in this way. What is maintained is that, if a child in this concrete operational stage fully grasps the basic nature of classes and relations and the possible operations one can perform upon them, then it is reasonable to suppose that his way of thinking fits into the basic pattern of the groupings outlined above.

When interpreting the responses of children in our test situations, therefore, we continually bear in mind this Piagetian model, and in studying the development of the concepts of weight, area and volume we have tried to plan practical situations which incorporate some of the thinking processes outlined above.

The period of formal operations

From what has been said already we see that children at an advanced level of development in the period of concrete operations can 'think about' their actions; they are not limited to simple observation or repetition in a stimulus-response type of reaction. In other words, they do think in a sort of logical fashion. However, they still fall short of the type of thinking processes which are demonstrated in the reasoning powers of adults. Children in the concrete operational stage may display all the operations outlined earlier but they only do so when they are handling concrete objects; they need the prop of a real visible aid before they can demonstrate such ways of thinking. They are quite unable to display the same forms of logic when confined to verbal propositions — they cannot think in the abstract.

Berlyne (1957, p. 8) has summarized the stage of formal operations:

The child no longer needs to confine his attention to what is real. He can consider hypotheses which may or may not be true and work out what would follow if they were true. Not only are the hypothetico-deductive procedures of science and mathematics and logic open to him in consequence but also the role of would-be social reformer. The adolescent's task for theorizing and criticizing arises from his ability to see the way the world is run as only one out of many possible ways it could be run and to conceive of alternative ways that might be better.

In other words, not only can the adolescent in this stage operate or think about all the facts that he sees in the real world about him, but he can also operate on what he imagines could possibly be true. He can think in the abstract.

For this stage, too, Piaget has considered in logico-mathematical terms the types of operational structure that could be displayed. He once more uses the model of propositional logic and he used the mathematical notion of 'lattices' and the logician's 'calculus of propositions'. The model explores all the possible ways of thinking in this hypothetico-deductive fashion and attempts, as before, to categorize the possibilities into 'groupings'. Because of the more varied ways of thinking open to the adolescent at this stage, the model too becomes more complex than the one applied to the concrete operational stage. No further analysis of this model is given here, as its framework did not feature strongly in our actual test situations. However, realizing that the most important general property of formal-operational thought concerns the possible or hypothetical rather than just the *real*, we attempted to plan our sequence of practical situations so that, in the later items, the pupils had to use this deductive form of reasoning to obtain correct answers: they had to think in the abstract and consider possible ways of solving the particular problem and, in turn, mentally eliminate some of the possible actions or solutions before actually manipulating the materials.

The designing of assessment materials which explore this type of reasoning power in adolescents makes use of experimental situations where a number of factors could affect the outcome of the investigation. A pupil at the formal operational stage is capable of organizing his experimental procedure, of considering all the possible combinations, and of determining the importance or otherwise of each contributing factor. Piaget and his fellow researchers have made use of a number of investigations which incorporate such factors and, as an illustration of this type of investigation we quote Inhelder's summary of the candle, screen and ring experiment (1962, p. 25).

The adolescent is given a candle, a projection screen, and a series of rings of different diameters; each ring is on a stick which can be stuck into a board with evenly spaced holes. The instructions are to place all the rings between the candle and the screen in such a way that they will produce only a single 'unbroken' shadow on the screen — the shadow of a ring. Gradually the adolescent discovers that 'there must be some relationship' and he tries to find out what relationship it is by *systematic attempts* until finally he becomes aware that it is a matter of proportionality.

A pupil demonstrating the thinking powers characteristic of this stage is capable of categorizing the materials in a mentally complex manner, of forming hypotheses which he can test, of considering all possible explanations before arriving at a conclusion, and of predicting outcomes as a result of his earlier deductions.

Our research did not incorporate practical situations of this complexity and, although the later assessment items do call on the pupil to make deductions and to consider, in abstract thinking terms, the solutions to the problems, we did not use experiments which called on the pupil to form a hypothesis, control variables, or carry out a detailed investigation of the candle, screen and ring type.

Our assessment items, then, covered the range of thinking operations from the stage where the children rely heavily on the real, observable situation and where their powers of reasoning depend almost entirely on the immediate appearance of things, through the concrete operational stage where the ideas of conservation, reversibility, etc. are displayed, to the stage where the children begin to display the ability to work out possible procedures and solutions in their minds — abstract thinking — before handling the material.

Note: Smedslund (1977) and Brown and Desforges (1977) have recently discussed this crucial issue of stages. Their arguments reinforce the summary presented here, but as these articles were published after the main part of the present account was written, they are not considered in detail in this chapter.

3 Designing the assessment materials: aims, objectives and problems

It is not an easy task to design a test situation using practical materials and an oral method of questioning which can be replicated in a more or less unvarying manner and which, at the same time, allows the pupil a degree of freedom to express his reasons for his answers or selection of material.

The purely clinical approach used by Piaget to discover the reasoning behind his subjects' answers is probably a suitable but time-consuming method for studying the responses of a relatively small number of children placed in a fairly simple practical situation, but it has several serious disadvantages when applied individually to a large number of children. Smedslund (1961, p. 12) sums up the disadvantages of this approach:

Piaget's 'méthode clinique' which consists of flexible and intuitively directed conversation and play, has proved very fruitful in the initial steps of research, but has the drawback that it cannot be exactly replicated, and it allows for unknown degrees of subjectivity in the procedure and interpretations.

A number of research workers have commented on the intuitive approach to diagnosis used by Piaget — who has himself remarked (Piaget and Szeminska, 1941: English 1952, p. 149): 'Statistical precision could no doubt easily be obtained, but at the cost of no longer knowing exactly what was being measured'. Braine, in a critique of Piaget's method of inquiry, has pointed out that if Piaget modified his methods he might feel that this would only make the diagnosis more difficult; he would be in danger of losing contact with the processes he wanted to study: 'For his own formulation of his research goals, Piaget is probably right; a mere standardisation of his tasks would lose the flexibility which is one of their virtues' (1962, p. 44). Unfortunately, as Fogelman's (1970) analysis of researches of this flexible type so clearly shows, when replication of Piaget's experiments is attempted, there is considerable variance in the results. It is often impossible to isolate the true reason for a child's misconception. To return to Braine's point that standardization may make the diagnostic problem more difficult: he maintains that

the straightforward recording of correct and incorrect responses in a standardized form may cause the research worker to fall between two methodological
stools 'with the result that Piaget's research goals — the study of developing
intellectual processes — may be cast out along with some of his methods'
(1962, p. 45). Braine argues that such a standardized procedure using a fixed
questionnaire and analysis of correct and incorrect responses distracts the
research worker from '[the main problem] — what has developed that determines the correct responses of the older children — to one which is not central
for Piaget (i.e. what determines the wrong responses of the younger children)'
(p. 45).

It is clear that the problem of methodological approach is not an easy one
to solve. In attempting a solution we had the following aims in view:

1. We had already decided that the problem of communication could not
   be divorced from the learning process and we therefore wanted to find
   out how children responded to verbal questioning procedures. In doing
   this, however, we looked very carefully at the type and form of question
   that we used.
2. We wanted to test a large number of children but on a one-to-one basis,
   i.e. each pupil was to be tested in turn. We felt that, as other researches
   had clearly shown that the responses varied according to the test
   materials, the way it was handled (or not handled) by the testee, the
   wording of the questions and other factors, it was important that we
   should attempt to standardize our procedure so that the test situation
   could be replicated satisfactorily.
3. We did not entirely agree with Braine's view that the main issue was the
   determining of the way older children had arrived at correct responses.
   We felt that it *was* important to try and find out the reasons for
   children's misconceptions, since only when a teacher was armed with
   this type of information could he help the young learner overcome his
   difficulties. Piaget's theory of stages is developmental in character and
   we felt that, if the common misconceptions could be identified in our
   research, there was the possibility of also organizing a teaching approach
   in sequential fashion. Bearing in mind Ausubel's words (1965b, p. 114)
   that 'Sequential organisation pre-supposes, of course, that the preceding
   step is always clear, stable and well organised. If it is not, the learning of
   all subsequent steps is jeopardised', we felt that such steps could only be
   well organized if we first clearly identified typical misconceptions held
   by children. We wanted our research to be of some value to the practising
   teacher.

4. We agreed with Braine's view that a simple analysis of correct responses
to single practical test situations would not supply us with very much
useful information, and we felt that interpretations based on isolated
'tests' of this type were not particularly reliable. We decided, therefore,
that more useful information could be gleaned if we had a number of
test items in our assessment procedure. An attempt was made to
arrange these items in two ways. First, when examining a typical
Piagetian thought operation such as reversibility or conservation, we
tested the children using more than one practical situation; the materials
varied but all tested the same thought operation. We wanted to find out
if, in general, the children consistently thought in the same way even
though the test materials were different. Secondly, the test items were
devised so that the thought operations involved varied from the more
basic concrete operations to the more complex abstract thought processes. In this way we hoped to observe in every child tested the powers
and limitations of his thought processes. We wondered if we could obtain
an overall picture which would show that if children failed, say, to show
the ability to conserve or reverse their thought processes, then those
same children would not be able to carry out more complex tasks using
thought operations higher up on the Piagetian scale.

As a first step, therefore, we aimed to produce practical materials that
could be used quickly and simply in the test situation and, above all else,
allowed the tester to replicate the situation exactly over and over again. A
number of points have to be made about the design of such materials.

(a) Visual distractors and other complicating features
Sometimes the children had to examine the materials visually but were not
allowed to handle anything — a 'subject passive' situation. On other occasions
the children were instructed to handle the materials before answering questions
— a 'subject active' or 'dynamic' situation. If the children were placed in the
passive situation and had to make visual comparisons between objects, then it
was important that such comparisons could clearly be made; that is, the
materials had to be so designed that no other confusing visual element was
accidentally built into the situation. For example, a child might be asked to
compare the interior volumes of two boxes where the external volumes and
internal depths were different but the interior area of cross-section was the
same. The aim was to see if the child focused his attention on the three
interior dimensions rather than confining his attention to insufficient or
irrelevant visual information (the exterior dimensions or the area of cross-
section alone, for example). Therefore it was important that the interior

depth of the boxes could be clearly compared while, to avoid right answers to be given for wrong reasons, the box of larger exterior volume had to have the smaller interior depth. Further, to avoid confusing visual effects, the interiors of both boxes had to be the same colour. Such attention to design was essential if we were to be fairly confident that the child could focus his attention on the meaningful observations. If the pupil gave wrong reasons for his answers, we wished to be fairly certain that the reasons were the result of an inadequate development of the concept on his part and not the confusing design of the practical materials.

Similarly if the child was placed in a dynamic situation and asked to use the materials to find something out, we wanted to be fairly certain that, if he failed to carry out the task, the failure could be attributed to poor understanding of the principle behind the task rather than simply to poor manipulative skill. For example, when we asked children to compare the areas of two irregular shapes by using transparent grids for measurement purposes, we wished to see if they realized that the various 'half-units' had to be added to the whole square 'units' (see Area, item 12, p. 111) before they could arrive at an answer. We had to be certain, therefore, that the irregular units could not simply be compared visually, that the transparent grids were placed over the shapes by the tester (avoiding simple manipulative difficulties), and that the units and half-units could be counted fairly easily (avoiding sheer counting difficulties). In practice, a few children were baffled by the sheer counting task, i.e. they may have realized the concept of half- and whole units but simply could not count the units in any logical fashion, even though the number of 'squares' to be counted were relatively few. They often counted squares more than once or missed squares out. When designing equipment for such dynamic situations, we had to be constantly aware of the danger of introducing complicating features which would have prevented us from observing the conceptual features we had in mind.

(b) Channelling of thought and response

We also believed that some of the practical materials used in the more common Piagetian situations tended to encourage the children to adopt a particular viewpoint. We wondered whether such practical tests tended to channel the thoughts of the pupils so that they would adopt certain reasons and give answers accordingly, and would disregard other reasons which they might have been *able* to apply in these situations. For example, in the classic plasticine ball and sausage test, the child first sees that the two balls weigh the same and is then usually asked, in effect, if they both have the same weight after one of the balls is elongated into a sausage form. For Piaget, a pupil at an early stage in concept development would focus his attention on the visible alteration of length and would associate the increase in length with increase in weight. The logic of the child would be related to the concrete visible world, and the more advanced thought processes of reversibility — causing the pupil to give answers of the form 'It must still weigh the same because nothing has been added or removed' or 'It must still weigh the same because I can change it back into the ball' would not occur. Unfortunately, analysis of the actual form of the questions appearing in researches clearly shows a number of these replications to have doubtful questioning procedures in that they tend to channel the thoughts of pupils along certain lines. For example, a question in the form 'Who [of tester and pupil] has the most plasticine now?' implies that a choice of one or the other should be made and that possible equality is not to be considered. Similarly, 'Is there *still* as much plasticine in the sausage as there is in the ball?' strongly suggests a positive (and, in this case, the right) answer.

It is extremely difficult to decide on the best form of question but, in the above example, for instance, the form used by Smedslund (1961, p. 154) in his classic experiment could be considered as best: 'Do you think this contains more, or the same amount or less clay than the ball?' The child now has to choose one of three possibilities. Further to such choices, the question 'Why do you say that?' demands a response which may give a clue to the misconception or conception formed.

To carry the analysis further, it seemed to us that not only could the form of the questions prompt certain responses but so could the visual appearance of the materials. To return to the ball and sausage experiment, for example, by elongating the ball into a sausage we were strongly orientating the child's thought processes towards considering actual physical change. As adults trained as scientists, we considered what our views would be of this situation if we had no knowledge, based on experience, of the conservation of weight. We felt that we would have to choose between one of two possible reasons before giving an answer. The first would be 'logical' and based on reversibility or the fact that nothing has been removed; the second would be 'concrete' and based on the certain knowledge that a physical change (length) had taken place and that there was, therefore, a strong possibility that the weight had changed (a perfectly sound scientific notion). We argued, like Piaget, that for the child the argument based on perception would tend to dominate until experience (or maturation) enabled him to make an alternative suggestion. Indeed, we wondered, as conservation is by no means a common phenomenon in nature, whether the argument based on perception and therefore on likely change was not a more reasonable probability in this situation. After all, it could be considered that adults only chose the concept of weight in the previous example because it *was* conserved; had we chosen, say, the 'diameter' of the plasticine we could not have applied a conservation principle to the change from ball to sausage shape.

It is possible that the ability to conceptualize lies in the ability of a person to resolve this dilemma of choice between a reason based on 'logic' and one based on 'concrete' appearances. If this is so, then there is no need to assume that thought based on perception always precedes thought based on logic. It could be that, because a person has two possible forms of reasoning open to him, he has in any given situation to choose between them in order to arrive at an answer. Consequently, it can be argued that if a practical situation emphasizes the perceptual element, it is very likely that reasons based on perception will be selected by the subject. Bryant (1972b, p. 79) discusses this issue of conflict between two judgements and writes: '[The subject] can only adopt one of these two incompatible judgements and realises that one of them must be wrong . . . Faced with this dilemma he falls back on the more recent of the two'. Bryant suggests that even young children have two possible reasons on which to base their answers and choose the one supported by the more recent cues.

Lunzer (1972), criticizing this study, points out that there is little evidence to show that these two ways of thinking do indeed co-exist and conflict in the child's mind. He argues that children at early Piagetian stages do not consider the logical form of reason for conservation at all. Maturation and experience would cause both ideas to emerge; conflict would result only at transition stages and be resolved with increasing powers of conceptualization so that, in the end, logical answers would be used consistently. However, the ability continually to consider and debate possible answers is one of the key characteristics of advanced conceptualization, and this is exactly what Piaget meant when referring to his stage of formal operations. Simply witnessing an answer based on logic, as opposed to an answer based on perception, does not by itself confirm that the subject is necessarily at an advanced stage of conceptualization; it simply demonstrates that he can use logic. The key question is whether the subject has debated possible answers in his mind and used the correct form of reasoning for his answer. Very often tests used in research do not consider this latter point; often the mere recording of a logical thought operation is taken as evidence of conceptualization.

Beard (1963) indirectly refers to this problem when discussing the Piagetian test for understanding conservation of volume. In this particular test the subjects are asked whether the total volume of sugar and water remains the same when the sugar is dissolved in the water. As scientists we know that conservation in such situations is extremely unlikely and that the volume of solution is less than that of the water and undissolved solute. Beard writes (p. 236):

It follows that children who argued 'logically' that the volume should remain unchanged were ignoring some aspect of the situation and were, in fact, wrong . . . Reasoning logically the child may make the hypothesis that the volume should be unchanged when a solute dissolves, but this does not represent the highest level of thinking in relation to conservation of volume; he must proceed from there to verify or reject the hypothesis. Although Piaget and Inhelder chose a substance which would behave according to most people's expectation it would appear that, even in this case, a more sceptical attitude would show a higher stage of thinking. It is curious that these children who believed the volume to be conserved, who were at the highest stage were among the oldest children questioned whereas those who showed reasonable doubt, who were placed at a lower stage were, in general, several years younger.

Two points emerge from Beard's comments. First, older children were placed at a higher stage simply because they gave a 'logical' answer. There is no evidence that they had in fact analysed the situation and resolved the conflict between two possible answers. They had plumped for an answer based on logic — and were in fact wrong; appearances did not encourage an answer based on perception. The only correct answer was 'I cannot tell until I have checked by measurement'. The conflict cannot be resolved by thought alone. In other words selection of one reason (say, logical) rather than another (say, based on perception) does not provide absolute evidence of the stage of conceptualization reached by the subject.

Secondly, Beard expresses curiosity that the correct answer, reasonable doubt, was expressed by the younger children. Again, there is no evidence that this choice of answer, which happens to be correct, follows on a consideration of all possible answers, those based on perception *and* those based on logic. There is no evidence to show whether the children were attempting to resolve a conflict in their minds or whether their choice of answer was based on perception alone and doubt expressed simply because the children 'couldn't tell'.

In order to examine these points further, tests should place the children in a conflict situation and should not just simply encourage one type of answer rather than another. We decided, therefore, to design two types of assessment item which would examine the stage of development of conservation. The first type, repeated with different materials, was constructed so that the pupil saw and agreed that the properties (weight, area or volume) of a pair of weights, shapes or volumes were identical in magnitude. One of the materials was then altered so that a dimension (such as length) was increased to a degree which encouraged the pupil to 'centre' or focus his attention on this change. The pupil was then asked a standard form of question (following Smedslund) to see whether he realized that weight (or area or volume) was conserved regardless of the other physical change. From Piagetian theory we expected three forms of answer. One would be an answer based on the observable physical change, and no conservation would be admitted. A second would be an answer which indicated that conservation was recognized on the basis that, as one of the dimensions had increased, the other had decreased — a compensatory reason. In most Piagetian researches this is taken to be evidence of conservation but the mere recognition that as one dimension increases the other decreases is not a sound reason for concluding that the property in question has been conserved. It is often impossible to judge in terms of actual magnitude whether an increase *exactly* compensates another decrease — a necessary judgement if a sound conclusion is to be possible.

A good example of this judgement difficulty, in exact magnitude terms can be seen in the experiment (Volume, item 8a, p. 161), which uses two obviously equal volumes of water in identical flat containers. One is poured into a tall narrow container and the other into a wide-based beaker. These latter containers are chosen so that the level of liquid in the narrow container is much higher than in the beaker. Children often focus their attention on this irrelevant dimension and thus conclude that the tall container now contains more water. Others give an answer based on compensation: 'They both have the same amount of water as this container is narrower and that one is wider'. Whilst these children are obviously grappling with more than one dimension at a time, and are therefore at a more advanced conceptual stage than the first group, neither they nor adults, for that matter, can be certain that such differences are, in magnitude terms, exactly compensated; as a result, conservation is not a conclusion made with absolute certainty. On the other hand, of course, a pupil giving this answer may *have* the concept of conservation and realize, *as a result*, that if one dimension increases then the other must have decreased by a compensatory amount. The third form of answer is one based on reasoning of a reversible nature and, in this case, is always given with absolute certainty: 'There is still the same amount of water in both containers because the water can be poured back into the flat dishes and the levels would be the same again'. Another form of the answer is that of the type 'Nothing has been added or removed' (operation of identity), and again the pupil giving this answer is certain that he is right.

It is usually concluded that children who give this third form of answer have the notion of conservation, but we wondered what would happen if we designed a second type of assessment item where the pupil once again observed a change in a dimension and was thus encouraged to focus his attention on what, in reality, was a change which did not alter the magnitude of the concept in question (say, area or volume). He was also given or clearly saw all the necessary steps to encourage him to think about and express the final logical step which was the correct answer. In other words, the pupil was placed in a situation where he had to choose between two possible explanations, one based on the observable change and the other on concrete logical operations. We wondered whether conservers in the first type of assessment item would maintain their logical form of answer in this second type of item, where they were in a situation providing a degree of conflict. We argued that only strong conservers would answer correctly in both situations and that there would be a number who conserved in the first situation but who would revert to arguments based on perception in the second situation. The two types of test would supply us with more detailed information on conservation than was usual in researches using only single item tests.

(c) Understanding of oral questions
General comment has already been made on the problem of oral questioning techniques but in terms of our actual assessment items two further points emerge.

Before using certain words or phrases in the concept assessment items, preliminary tests had to be built into the sequence to establish whether the children understood the adult meaning attached to the words or phrases used. For example, in the sequence on the concept of area the words 'surface' and 'amount of surface' were used in certain items to denote area. The children had therefore first to be questioned, using practical materials, to see whether they understood these words. We wondered if an analysis of their understanding of these fundamental phrases would cause us to reflect on the wisdom of using such oral techniques in concept assessment items.

We had realized in our pilot survey (see p. 37) that the problem of understanding a question was likely to be related to the nature of the terms used. For example, much work has been concerned with the so-called conservation of substance or quantity, and in this context the question often contains the word 'amount', which is not further qualified but which, to the experimenter, is specifically substance. The child, however, may take this word to mean volume, weight or even length, and answer the question according to his interpretation. Other words such as 'bigger', 'smaller', 'size', 'large', etc. could similarly be interpreted in various ways; when adults ordinarily use these words with alternative meanings, we can hardly expect to use them as strictly definitive in the test. To use the word 'size' to indicate volume, for example, must be extremely confusing to the child handling materials designed to encourage conceptualization of volume when he has earlier been constructing a block graph concerned with size of shoes, i.e. length.

A further problem was related to the degree to which the word or phrase used in the question was of an 'abstract' or 'concrete' nature. Braine (1962) has again commented on this feature, instancing the difference between the two words 'cars' and 'vehicles'. He points out that the abstract word calls on the listener to recognize a class of objects (or even class of classes), e.g. Fido— Dog—Species moves from the concrete to the abstract. Recognizing this difficulty, we asked ourselves whether the Piagetian questioning procedure contained words or phrases of this more abstract kind and, as a result, made it difficult for the pupil to understand the meaning of the question. Again Braine asks whether the classic question 'Are there more poppies than flowers' is incorrectly understood by children simply because 'poppy' is a more con- crete word than 'flowers'. 'It is not certain that there would have been errors', he writes (p. 51), 'if, instead of using the words "poppies" and "flowers", Piaget had asked "Are there more of these (pointing to the poppies) or more of these (pointing to all the flowers)?" thus indicating the class members osten- sively rather than by name'. Donaldson (1978) discusses the weaknesses of Piagetian questioning procedures involving abstract phrases and produces evidence to show that the addition of single 'real life' adjectives to the wording of questions often enabled children who had previously given incorrect answers to grasp the meaning intended by the questioner and to correct their answers. For example, in the standard Piagetian sub-class/total class question 'Are there more black cows or more cows?' accent is placed on the identification of the sub-class through the use of the adjective 'black'. When the question was re- worded (p. 44) as 'Are there more black cows or more sleeping cows?' (all the cows were laid on their sides), the children were better able to identify both sub-class *and* total class and answer accordingly.

In a similar fashion we wondered whether questions relating to conservation of area, for example, were easier to understand when a word such as 'fields' was used as an indicator of area rather than the more abstract 'amount of sur- face', even though the pupils might have been tested earlier on their under- standing of 'surface' and 'amount of surface'.

We decided to try to avoid the use of ambiguous words (a difficult task); to make a preliminary check on the children's understanding of key words or phrases used in the concept tests; to incorporate words or phrases of a concrete nature and compare responses to such questions with responses to similar ones using words of a more abstract nature; and, finally, to build into our standard questioning procedure instructions to the tester on the use of hand indications to convey extra meaning to the pupil.

This design process is a complicated and forbidding task, and it is not sur- prising that most researches and the resulting interpretations are based on, at most, one or two practical test situations examining one aspect only of concept development. In constructing our range of items to cover more than one aspect of conceptualization in the concrete operational stage and, in addition, studying three fundamental concepts, we recognized with increasing conviction as our work progressed that this field of inquiry into children's understanding of concepts has as its weakest link the form of communication used between the tester and the child.

4 The sample: selection procedures

One of the main problems that emerges when children are tested one at a time is that of sampling. Most Piagetian research is based on examining the performance of children of different ages, and it is only on rare occasions that the tester also carefully selects his sample on the basis of another variable such as ability.

Usually the research worker is limited in his choice of schools and very often relies on the teacher to supply him with children at certain ages and of 'average' ability. Criteria for 'average' ability are rarely described, and even in the case of selection by age, it is not always clear whether the children's ages fall within well-defined limits at the time of testing or whether they are selected from age groups. For example, a child may be selected from a year group or class on the basis that he is of 'average' ability and from a class with an average age of, say, nine. The child's age may differ considerably from this average age. When one examines the responses of some twenty children of a certain stated age obtained from one or two classes in a single school it is important to remember that all the children are, in fact, unlikely to be of the same age and that the resulting spread could affect the picture obtained of the children's conceptual abilities at that age. The time of year when the research is carried out could also affect the interpretation of the test results, especially if the study concentrates on younger age groups. It is now well recognized that children of slightly different ages could have experienced up to one year's difference of schooling, which would obviously affect researches intended to measure conceptual abilities at certain ages.

As stated earlier, the main criticism of this type of research is that general interpretations on conceptual ability are made from testing a small sample of children on one or two practical test items and, up to the present time, methods of overcoming this problem have not been very successful.

The sample size may be increased by using more research workers and spending more time on the research; in economic or time terms this cannot be considered as a practical proposition. The sample size may also be increased by using a more structured form of test procedure and also by limiting the number of practical tests used. This is usually achieved by a pencil and paper form of objective testing. The interpretations of these researches attract the criticisms that the information on which they are based is of an extremely limited nature and that the advantages of the clinical approach — inquiry in depth into each individual's responses — cannot be achieved in this fashion.

The sample size may be increased, too, by using single practical test situations so that the time spent testing any individual is relatively short. This is a common way of conducting Piagetian research but, as has been argued, the interpretation of the results cannot be generalized to all similar situations. The sample size may be increased by training temporary testers (e.g. college students) and by duplicating the test materials. This approach suffers from the disadvantage that the Piagetian testing procedure becomes very unreliable, as the form of the questions and manner of presenting the test materials may vary considerably from one questioner to another. The cost of duplicating the materials may also preclude this approach.

Realizing that this problem of sample selection in Piagetian research could not be entirely overcome, we adopted the following procedures in the present study.

THE PILOT SURVEY (1970–72)

A pilot study was first carried out with the following objectives.

1. To devise and try out a number of practical test items for each of the three concepts — weight, area and volume. These tests were to be of a sequential nature so that typical Piagetian stages of development could be observed.
2. To devise the tests so that they could be presented in a fixed, structured form, i.e. in a standard way to each child.
3. To examine the problem of communication and to standardize the questioning procedure.
4. To test children between the ages of $7\frac{1}{2}$ and 11 with six-month gaps between the selected age groups. The children had to be within one month of the selected age at the time of testing.
5. To select these children from a number of schools so that it would also be possible to make a preliminary study of the relationship between their responses to the Piagetian test situations and their ability as measured by an independent test.
6. To select the children to be tested from a much larger group who had been given a well-standardized intelligence test. In this way it was intended that the children would fall into one of four well-defined ability bands (varying from high ability to low). In other words, the selection was not on a random basis, as it was intended to examine the

performances of *a number* of high and low ability pupils in addition to the performances of pupils of average ability.

7. To test as many children as possible but using only test administrators who were very familiar with the materials, so that they could interpret the answers of the children and hence measure both the effectiveness of the standard test procedure and the design of the tests themselves. In this way it was hoped to be able to improve the tests and, in particular, the method of recording the responses, so that it would be possible to instruct teachers, quickly and effectively, in the use of the materials.

8. To examine a small proportion of those children on a longitudinal basis. The children were to be examined a number of times at six monthly intervals.

This pilot survey was carried out between 1970 and 1972 in thirty-six north Wales schools. Two research workers, aided by three part-time assistant researchers, tested over 350 children between the ages of $7\frac{1}{2}$ and 11. These children were selected from a total of 1500 children who had been given one of two non-verbal intelligence tests from the National Foundation for Educational Research (1954 and 1964): *Picture Test A* (up to 8 years) and *Nonverbal Test BD* (8–11 years). The choice of these tests is discussed on p. 41 in connexion with the main survey. The schools were selected by consultation with educational advisers in the six north Wales counties (prior to the 1974 reorganization of local government) and, through the co-operation of the headteachers, a reasonably even distribution of rural and urban schools was achieved. Following this survey, the tests published in this report were developed.

All the children's responses were recorded and categorized; as a result it was possible to devise a recording system enabling the test administrator to identify the main types of response in a fairly easy practical manner. This recording system appears, in modified form, in the separate teachers' guide, *Area, Weight and Volume* (see p. viii above). Although a number of test items were rejected during this pilot stage, a total of 48 test items (13 for weight, 18 for area and 17 for volume) were incorporated in the major survey, which was carried out between 1972 and 1973.

Practical procedures which were generally understood by the children were also recognized; a standard procedure for administering the tests could then be refined for the main survey. Although it was realized that such a standard procedure had its limitations (see earlier discussion, p. 25) it was felt that the relatively large number of tests and large sample in the main survey, together with the detailed pilot survey, would enable meaningful interpretations to be made.

THE MAIN SURVEY (1972–73)

As the test procedures had been devised in a standard form and the system for recording the children's responses was also of a fixed pattern, it was decided to aim for a sample of 1000 children between the ages of $7\frac{1}{2}$ and 10 years of age. (Since the pilot survey had shown that only a relatively small proportion of the test items were suitable for the eleven-year-olds, an increase in sample size to cover this age was not justified.)

The sample was obtained by following the normal Schools Council procedure and inviting schools and teachers to participate in the project. In this way the teachers' views of the materials could be evaluated and, from the researcher's point of view, the often neglected relationship between teachers and educational research workers who were interested in children's conceptual development could be fostered. This task involved the teachers as test administrators of a rather unusual kind and, although the period of participation was relatively short — six to eight weeks, the extra load that the teachers had to add to their day-to-day work was considerable. In addition to these practical difficulties, the test materials had to be duplicated (30 sets of each concept kit) within a short period so that adequate time would be available for in-service training sessions for the teachers.

Eighty-eight schools joined the project for this phase of the work and, in order that teachers should not work in isolation in any one school, two teachers from each school were invited to participate. The schools were selected from nine widely differing geographical areas within the local education authorities (LEAs) shown in Table 1.

Table 1   Sample details for main survey

Region	Schools	Teachers	Children intelligence tested	Children selected
Cheshire	10	20	328	104
Shropshire	10	20	521	110
Glamorgan	10	20	555	115
Monmouthshire	10	20	551	116
Newport (Mon.)	10	20	492	105
Wiltshire	9	18	354	108
Manchester	10	20	474	111
Lancashire:				
Lancaster	9	18	418	92
Blackpool	10	20	495	61
Totals	88	176	4188	922

Method of teacher participation

After consulting LEA advisers, the research team met the twenty or so
teachers from each area at a local teachers' centre for a two-day familiarization
course. Each school then received a complete set of the three concept assessment kits and it was suggested that one teacher should be responsible for
testing children in the concepts of area and weight, and the second teacher for
testing with the volume concept kit. During a fortnight or three-week trial
period the teachers tried out the materials in their own schools, involving
children outside the age range required by the research. During this time, too,
they administered the two non-verbal intelligence tests (see p. 38) to the
children whose ages would fall within a month of the required ages during
actual testing. These tests were marked and scored by the main research team
and from these results the children actually required for the study were
selected.

After the trial period the research team again met the teachers and discussed
problems relating both to test administration and to the recording of responses. The testing of the children on the three concept kits took 6–8 weeks
– considerably longer than anticipated from the results of the pilot survey,
but the reactions of the children and the efficiency of the teachers allow the
writer to feel confident that the answers of the children recorded and reported
upon here reflect a survey which has to a large extent overcome the methodological weakness with which this type of operation is so often associated.

At the end of the six- or eight-week period of testing, the research team and
teachers met to exchange their findings. As a result of these consultations, and
following the suggestions of the project consultative committee, it was decided
to produce not only this report, but also a teachers' guide on the classroom
use of the assessment materials, and other materials produced (see p. viii).

The selection of the children

It had originally been decided to obtain some 150 children from each of the
age groups 7y 5m; 7y 11m; 8y 5m; 8y 11m; 9y 5m; 9y 11m and, in the light
of the indications obtained from the pilot survey it was also decided to select
these children within four bands of ability as indicated by the non-verbal
intelligence tests.

Most researches obtain their sample by a random technique, in order that
the relatively small number in the sample may approximate to the population,
which is assumed to have a normal distribution. This practice enables the
research worker to use many statistical techniques on his results and to report
accordingly.

For this research, however, such an approach was not desirable since the main point was to discover how high ability pupils at a given age fared on the concept tests by comparison with lower ability children. It was decided, therefore, to select equal, or nearly equal, numbers of children from each of four ability ranges and to do this by using the intelligence test scores. The ability bands selected (Table 2) were: score 89 and under; score 90—99 inclusive; score 100—109 inclusive; score 110 and above.

Table 2   Distribution of selected children by ability band

Age	Score band				Totals
	⩽89	90—99	100—109	⩾110	
7y 5m	34	40	35	37	146
7y 11m	38	36	36	40	150
8y 5m	31	42	37	40	150
8y 11m	38	42	36	39	155
9y 5m	37	39	40	39	155
9y 11m	37	35	41	36	149
Totals	215	234	225	231	905*

* 17 of the 922 selected children failed to complete all the test items.

The points of division (89/90; 99/100; 109/110) thus divided a normally distributed population into approximately equal proportions (e.g. assuming a normal distribution of scores about a mean of 100 with a standard deviation of 15, from a score range of 9·5 we obtain 9·5/15 = 0·633, representing, from standard tables, 24% of the population). Although the application of statistics is thereby limited, it was felt that such selection procedures would produce more evidence than hitherto on the relationship between conceptual development and ability as measured by a non-verbal intelligence test.

Two further points need to be made about the selection of the intelligence tests.

First, to avoid the problem of communication, non-verbal tests were selected. Furthermore as the manifestation of intelligence identified by these picture and pattern selection tests was the ability to categorize, it was hypothesized that a meaningful relationship might be recognized between scores on these tests and performances with the concept assessment kits.

Secondly, there was no intelligence test available that satisfactorily covered the entire age range involved in the research. A compromise had to be made; the NFER *Picture Test A* was selected for the 7y 5m and 7y 11m children and the NFER *Non-verbal Reasoning Test BD* for all the older children.

To avoid the problem of selecting children of a given age at the same time of year and to make the main survey feasible in practical terms, it was also decided to stagger the time of involvement of each of the participating areas, over a period of a year. Whilst this overcame some of the disadvantages referred to earlier, it did mean that schools lacking an infant section might be unable to provide seven-year-olds at certain times of the year. This practical difficulty was encountered to a certain extent and did result in a bias towards a selection of seven-year-olds from regions that participated in the project towards the end of the school year. As the results, in general, conform to the findings of the pilot survey, this bias is not considered to affect their nature to a high degree. The regional distribution, by age, of children in the sample is shown in Table 3.

Table 3   Regional distribution of selected children in each age range

Region	Age						Totals
	7y 5m	7y 11m	8y 5m	8y 11m	9y 5m	9y 11m	
Cheshire	11	19	15	20	19	20	104
Shropshire	21	19	18	18	17	17	110
Glamorgan	11	21	23	20	20	20	115
Monmouthshire	0	22	26	22	22	24	116
Newport (Mon.)	14	16	19	19	19	18	105
Wiltshire	32	21	10	14	19	12	108
Manchester	22	18	17	17	19	18	111
Lancashire:							
Lancaster	29	12	14	12	14	11	92
Blackpool	10	7	10	12	10	12	61
Totals	150	155	152	154	159	152	922

In the following chapters, it should be borne in mind that the sections covering the separate concepts of area, weight and volume only deal with the responses of children of average ability (score bands 90–109), whilst chapter 8, comparing the numbers of correct responses across the three concepts, deals with all the children studied. These numbers, as stated earlier, do not represent a normal distribution but are obtained from a total made up of equal numbers of children in each of the selected ability bands. Chapter 9, relating concept attainment to intelligence, refers to these four ability bands.

Finally, it should be remembered that all the children studied in this survey completed all the practical tests (905 children completed each of the 48 practical tests, a total of 43,440 test administrations).

5 The concept of weight

The concept of conservation of weight has been explored by many research workers after Piaget and Inhelder (1941) had suggested that their researches showed that children attain conservation of substance at about the age of seven, conservation of weight at about the age of nine and conservation of volume at about the age of twelve (Piaget, 1972). In Britain Lovell and Ogilvie have conducted similar tests (1960, 1961a, b). They tested 322 children between the ages of 7y 8m and 10y 8m (1960) using the single test situation of the plasticine ball and sausage type, concluding that, in general, performance of their subjects was similar to the Genevan sample. However, they questioned Piaget's conclusions on a number of points. They argued that the children's thinking was frequently dominated by perceptual 'centring', usually on single dimensions − 'It's more because it's longer' (p. 112) − and that a considerable proportion of their subjects were at the transition stage between conservation and non-conservation. Furthermore they noted that, in contrast to Piaget's thesis, 'reversibility does not necessarily produce conservation in spite of the fact that it is given as a reason for conservation among conservers' (p. 114). Lovell and Ogilvie carried out supplementary experiments where they varied the materials (using rubber bands instead of plasticine) and demonstrated that conservers in one situation may not be conservers in the other, although in both cases the materials used were continuous, i.e. did not have to be broken up before elongation. They also raised the verbalization issue. They pointed out that considerable verbal confusion existed in children and gave as an example the pupil's answer 'It'll get right long and smaller and smaller' (p. 117) and the assumption had to be made that by 'smaller' the child meant 'thinner'. They commented on this difficulty: 'Piaget, too, has read into the child's remarks what he thought the latter meant, although we cannot be sure that either Piaget or ourselves always judged correctly on this issue'. In their discussion of results they warned future workers in this field (p. 117) of 'the grave dangers involved in accepting a child's apparent understanding at face value'.

43

In 1961 too, Elkind reported his replication of Piagetian research on the concepts of substance, weight and volume carried out with some 200 children between the ages of five and eleven (1961a). For the age range studied his results closely agreed with Piaget's findings, and there was a regular age-related order in the discoveries of the conservation of quantity, weight and volume. Again the research was based on a single test situation. In a second study published in the same year (1961b) he administered similar tests to some 470 12—18 year-olds in Massachusetts. In a discussion of the results, he pointed out that conservation of volume appeared after that of weight and also that, in this research, failure was mainly attributable not to verbal misunderstanding but to the subjects often focusing their attention on the observable dimensions or physical changes of the material rather than relying on logical mathematical conceptions. Elkind also raised the question of the relevance of variables other than age to conservation ability; in particular he wondered whether intelligence was an important factor which had not hitherto featured strongly in replication studies of this type.

Beard (1963) carried out the plasticine ball and sausage experiment on a sample of about 350 children between the ages of 4y 10m and 8y 10m. Although concerned with conservation of substance rather than weight, she added to the experiment by breaking the plasticine into smaller pieces, i.e. changing it into a discontinuous object and asking 'Is there still as much plasticine in the ball as there is in all the pieces?' This test was seen as being more difficult than the straightforward continuous elongation of the ball into a sausage shape. This research clearly showed that slight variation in procedure and form of question produced very different responses by the same children.

Undoubtedly the most intensive research on the concept of weight has been carried out by the Scandinavian Smedslund, who published his findings in a series of papers in 1961—2. In the main these researchers were concerned with the question of concept acquisition and training and, although not directly relevant to our study, they refer to one or two factors which appear to affect the children's ability to conserve weight. First, the acquisition of the belief in conservation is not related to practical experience alone; it also involves the children in a mental conflict between thought processes based on visual deformation or other physical changes and those based on logical thinking. Belief in conservation seems to appear when this mental conflict is resolved. Secondly, in an experiment using continuous material (plasticine) and dis-continuous material (many pieces of linoleum) he found that 'subjects rarely acquire conservation of continuous quantities before they have acquired conservation of discontinuous quantities' (1961, p. 206).

The research of Uzgiris (1964) has been referred to earlier but two points about this study need to be emphasized here. First, the conservation tests used four different materials (plasticine, metal nuts, wire coils and plastic covered wire) and a standard set of questions. It was found that the conservation of substance, of weight and of volume was acquired in the same sequential order, regardless of material, but it was also found that consistency of responses to a fixed set of questions across the range of materials fell considerably when the subjects showed that conservation was only in the process of being achieved. Secondly, this research agreed with Smedslund's study that conservation with discontinuous materials seems to be easier to acquire than with continuous materials.

Fogelman (1970) has summarized the results of the main replication researches and as it may be of interest to compare this with our results we reproduce his summary in Table 4.

Table 4   Plasticine ball and sausage (or equivalent) test
in conservation of weight (average ability)

Age	Percentage showing conservation according to:				
	Beard	Lovell	Smedslund	Elkind	Uzgiris
5	33·3	–	–	21	–
6	45·0	–	20	52	–
7	48·9	–	–	51	20
8	29·2	4	–	44	35
9	58·3	36	–	73	65
10	–	48	–	89	65
11	–	74	–	78	75
12	–	–	–	–	85

Source: Fogelman (1970, p. 41)

It can be seen that there is considerable variation between the different researches. It appears that the many variables in the different experiments affect the responses considerably. The wording of the questions, the way the materials are used and the selection of the sample all affect the results sufficiently to make the task of interpretation in terms of concept formation a very difficult one indeed. Perhaps the fundamental difficulty is related to the selection of the samples; it is not known whether the different groups are all of average ability or, indeed, of comparable ability.

In designing our materials, therefore, we attempted to reduce some of these confusing factors and also tried to explore further some of the pointers provided by the earlier researches. It was clear that a number of test items had to be designed, and that each child had to experience each item regardless of his success or failure in some of them. In addition to replicating and redesigning some of these Piagetian test materials, we also included other items which seemed to us to follow a progression in the acquisition of the concept of weight. In this way we attempted to discover if our tests could indicate a sequence in the development of children's ability to understand the fundamental ideas about weight.

It will be noted that our tests do not explore the concept that weight is the force of attraction exerted on a body by the earth. We felt that this involved further work on the concept of forces in general and although we had hoped to proceed to this path of inquiry, time did not allow us to pursue this approach any further.

The concept of weight assessment kit consisted of twelve items grouped under the following headings: 'Things heavier and lighter', 'Conservation of weight', 'The simple use of units' and 'The use of logic'. Most of the items depended on an understanding of the use of the balance and, because of this major feature, it can be argued that the concept of weight in terms of a force is insufficiently explained in this series of tests. Whilst recognizing this criticism, we felt that pupils in the primary school first come across the concept of weight through direct comparison of the weight of two objects by holding one in each hand and then by using a mechanical device which indicates the same thing. We know from other Piagetian researches that children in the age range under study are unlikely to understand the concept behind the balance as such (i.e. the Law of Moments) but such an understanding is not required to realize that an equal arm balance can be used as an indicator for equal and unequal weights. As this is more often than not the starting point for practical comparisons of weights in the primary school, it was also reasonable for us to use it as a basis for explaining the children's understanding and misunderstandings of the concept of weight.

THINGS HEAVIER AND LIGHTER

Assessment items 1–3 correspond to *Area, Weight, and Volume (AWV)*, Tests 1–3 for weight.

Item 1: red wooden ball; blue wooden ball

Give S a ball to hold in each hand.
> *'Which is the heavier of these two balls?'*

Item 2: green wooden ball; orange wooden ball

Give S a ball to hold in each hand.
> *'Which is the lighter of these two balls?'*

Item 3: pale blue wooden ball; yellow wooden ball; balance clearly displayed in front of S

Give S a ball to hold in each hand.

3a   *'Which of these balls weighs more?'*

3b   *'What would happen if the blue ball was put in this pan* [indicate] *and the yellow in that pan* [indicate] *?'*

3c After S has replied, place one ball in each balance pan.
'What would happen if they were of equal weight – if they weighed the same?'

In these introductory items we attempt to find out if the pupil understands the words or phrases 'heavier', 'lighter', 'weighs more' and 'of equal weight'. In addition, we check that the use of the balance is accepted to compare weights so that we can proceed to further use of the balance in later items, knowing that the pupil will not give incorrect responses simply because he cannot use the equipment.

The weights in each pair are identical in volume but they are loaded so that children with an average sensitivity to the feel of different weights can clearly perceive the differences. On each occasion the pupil is given a loaded container to hold in each hand. Care is also taken that the balance used is sufficiently sensitive and accurate for the test requirements. (A number of typical primary school balances fail in this respect and are also, of course, of doubtful value in teaching.)

Results: items 1–3 (terms)

Table 5   Results for weight items 1–3: answers to terms using 'heavier', 'lighter', 'weighs more'

	7y 5m	7y 11m	8y 5m	8y 11m	9y 5m	9y 11m
	%	%	%	%	%	%
Correct	92	97	96	98	95	97
Incorrect	8	3	4	2	5	3
Sample size, N (= 100%)	146	150	150	155	155	149

Most of the children answered these questions correctly (Table 5). They related the terms 'heavier', 'lighter' and 'weighs more' to their comparisons of weights by feeling. It seemed, therefore, that the majority of the children associated these words with the basic concept of weight in terms of feeling the downward force of the objects on their hands. As each pair of objects was of the same volume it was not possible at this stage to determine whether the children also associated weight with volume. Complexities of this nature appear in a later item.

Results: item 3 (balance)

Table 6   Results for weight item 3: understanding the use of the balance

	7y 5m	7y 11m	8y 5m	8y 11m	9y 5m	9y 11m
	%	%	%	%	%	%
Correct	88	90	93	96	95	95
Incorrect	12	10	7	4	5	5
Sample size, N (= 100%)	146	150	150	155	155	149

Again the majority of the children understood the use of the balance (Table 6). They realized that the pan holding the heavier weight would go down and that if both pans held equal weights then the arm of the balance would remain level. It was, of course, important to test that the children could relate this technique of weighing to the concepts of equal and unequal weights before more penetrating questions could be asked. It was interesting to observe that when balances using a centre pointer were used the children became very particular about the position of exact balance. As the balances generally used in the primary school have neither the sensitivity nor the accuracy to warrant such an exact pointer device perhaps one could infer that pupils at this stage should not be encouraged to focus their attention on a pointer but allowed to judge for themselves the horizontal level of the balance arm. Piaget has shown that, in related studies on levels of water in containers tipped at different angles, children often have a poor notion of the horizontal level, and as it is the fundamental observation for the judgement of equality of two weights with the balance, attention should be focused upon it.

After completing these initial assessment items with the pupils, it was feasible to use these words and the balance for the tests dealing with the children's concept of conservation of weight.

CONSERVATION OF WEIGHT

Assessment items 4–6 correspond to *AWV*, Tests 4–6 for weight.

Item 4: 2 plasticine balls of equal volume and weight (about 5 cm in diameter); balance

Place the balls on the table in front of S. Use the balance to demonstrate that the balls weigh the same.

> *'Are they the same weight?'*
> *'Watch carefully'*

4a Roll one ball into a sausage shape (about 10 cm in length).

> *'Does the sausage weigh the same as the ball or is it different in weight?'*

If S answers *'the same'*,

> *'Why do you say that?'*

If S answers *'the same because one is fatter but the other is longer'* or similar compensatory reason,

> *'Is there any other reason why they weight the same?'*

If S answers *'different'*,

> *'Which weighs more?'*
> *'Why do you say that?'*

4b Roll the sausage until it is longer and thinner (about 20 cm in length).

> *'Does the sausage weigh the same as the ball or is it different in weight?'*

If S answers *'the same'*,

> *'Why do you say that?'*

If S answers *'the same because one is fatter but the other is longer'* or similar compensatory reason,

> *'Is there any other reason why they weigh the same?'*

If S answers *'different'*,

> *'Which weighs more?'*
> *'Why do you say that?'*

Item 5: 2 Russian dolls; balance

Place the two dolls on the table in front of S and demonstrate, using the balance, that they are of equal weight.

> *'Do the two dolls weigh the same as each other?'*
> *'Watch carefully.'*

Remove the dolls from the balance pans. Place one doll in front of S. Open the other one and take out the three smaller dolls.

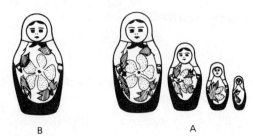

B   A

'*Do all these dolls together* [indicate group A of four dolls] *weight the
same as this doll* [indicate doll B] *or are they different in weight?*'
If S answers '*the same*',
'*Why do you say that?*'
If S answers '*different*',
'*Which weighs more?*'
'*Why do you say that?*'

Item 6: **1 yellow Lego block; 1 red Lego block (of equal weight and dimensions); balance**

[NB the various coloured blocks in this item are made up from dissimilar sets
of smaller pieces.]

'*Watch carefully*'
Use the balance to demonstrate that the two blocks weigh the same.

'*Are they the same weight?*'

6a Change the shape of the red block into an elongated stepped form.

8 of eight-dot Lego   4 of eight-dot and 4 of   1 eight-dot
fixed together in pairs   six-dot Lego fixed together   Lego

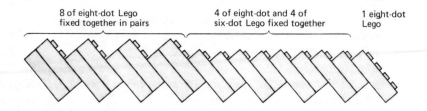

'Does the red shape weigh the same as the yellow block or is it different in weight?'
If S answers *'the same'*,
    'Why do you say that?'
If S answers *'they weigh the same because one is longer but the other is thicker'* or similar compensatory reason,
    'Is there any other reason why they weigh the same?'
If S answers *'different'*,
    'Which weighs more?'
    'Why do you say that?'

Item 6 (cont): 1 yellow Lego block; 1 blue Lego block (of equal weight and dimensions); balance

    'Watch carefully'
Use the balance to demonstrate that the two blocks weigh the same.
    'Do the blocks weigh the same?'

6b Separate the blue block into 7 pieces.

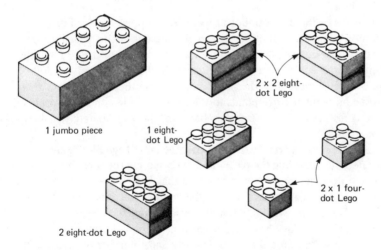

1 jumbo piece   1 eight-dot Lego   2 x 2 eight-dot Lego   2 x 1 four-dot Lego   2 eight-dot Lego

    'Do all these blue pieces together [indicate] *weigh the same as this yellow block* [indicate] *or are they different in weight?'*
If S answers *'the same'*,
    'Why do you say that?'
If S answers *'different'*,
    'Which weighs more?'
    'Why do you say that?'

In all these items concerned with conservation the pupil remains in the 'passive' situation, i.e. he does not actually manipulate any of the materials himself. Previous research has shown that there is a tendency for more children to give correct responses when they actually handle the materials and we argued that only if the children had clearly grasped the idea of conservation would they give correct responses when in a passive situation. Therefore we deliberately selected the more difficult situation for our measure of conservation.

The form of the questions in all of these items is such that the pupil is asked whether a pair of objects weigh the same or whether they are different in weight, i.e. he always has to select one of two possibilities.

Item 4 is the usual plasticine ball and sausage experiment and, although it is the only one of the continuous material type, it is repeated twice by further elongating the sausage to check whether the children's responses are consistent. Other researches have often shown that, as the sausage is further elongated, some children who have earlier admitted conservation revert to responses based on the visual appearance of the material. As the sausage gets longer so this perceptual feature dominates the reasoning of the child.

Item 5 is of the discontinuous type; here the pupil is placed in a conflict situation in that either he can give reasons of the reversible type and thus conclude that weight is conserved, or else he can centre or focus his attention on the number aspect and conclude that the spread out dolls together weigh more than the single doll 'because there are more of them'. This centring on number corresponds to the centring on length which occurs in the previous test item. Both reasons are based on the immediately visual aspect of the materials.

Item 6 is in two parts. In the first part the large Lego blocks are elongated by separating the pieces and reassembling them in a line form as shown in the diagram. It should be noted that Lego pieces of different volumes are used as the separate parts so that the number factor is eliminated as far as possible. We did not want children to simply count the pieces and give a 'correct' answer ('They both weigh the same') simply because two numbers were the same ('because they both have the same number of pieces'). This number feature is more important in the second half of the test, where the pieces forming the second block are completely separated. Here the numbers of pieces in the two large blocks are made obviously different, one block consisting of two pieces and the other of seven. Other researches have tended to show that children are more likely to give correct responses when the pieces are entirely separated. When the pieces are joined together to form an elongated block the length feature appears to dominate the thinking of a child at the pre-conservation stage. Once more, therefore, the more difficult situation is given first in order to discover the firm conserver. Finally, it should be noted that in all these test items it is important that the pupil should first see and agree that the two identical objects weight the same as one another before any changes in their shape or dimension occur.

Results: item 4

Table 7   Results for weight item 4a: plasticine ball and sausage (average ability)

Answer and reasons given	7y 5m	7y 11m	8y 5m	8y 11m	9y 5m	9y 11m
	%	%	%	%	%	%
a. Sausage & ball same weight as were same in beginning	44	58	56	62	72	71
b. Sausage & ball same weight as nothing added or removed	9	6	7	11	17	13
c. Sausage & ball same weight as sausage longer but ball fatter	4	3	3	5	1	2
d. Sausage heavier as is longer	15	8	8	9	3	3
e. Ball heavier as is fatter, wider	15	13	21	10	2	6
f. Any other answer, no reason or guess	13	12	5	3	5	5
Summary						
Correct (a, b)	53	64	63	73	89	84
Uncertain (c)	4	3	3	5	1	2
Incorrect: centring (d, e)	30	21	29	19	5	9
Incorrect: other	13	12	5	3	5	5
Sample size (= 100%)	75	72	79	78	79	76

In general the figures for item 4a (Table 7) are higher than those quoted by Lovell and Ogilvie (1961a) and are not in accord with Piaget's recent summary (1972: English 1974, p. 4) that 'the notion of conservation of weight is not acquired until about the age of nine or ten for about 75% of the children'. The figures do, however, agree fairly closely with those given by Elkind. When asked to give reasons for their answers, the children's responses fell quite neatly into one of four types of explanation. Children who conserved fully gave answers based on reversibility of thought (a and b in Table 7). They analysed in their minds the entire sequence of observations and they were able to apply logical thought to these concrete situations. A much smaller number of children concluded that the ball and sausage have the same weight but their reasons were based on compensation (c in Table 7) or, as Piaget terms it, co-ordination of relations, e.g. breadth makes up what is lost in length. Piaget has stated (1947) that this form of analysis by the child is necessary before conservation comes about but, for reasons given earlier (p. 32), we do not entirely agree with this argument. Very few children gave this explanation for their answers and, from comparison with similar items in the other two concepts (see later), we tentatively suggest that an explanation of this type merely affords us evidence that the pupil is grappling with more than one dimension at once and is at a transition stage. In the case of the concept of weight, we doubt whether it is a necessary transitory explanation, as very little evidence for its use by the pupils was obtained.

The third type of explanation, however, was much more common. It fits into the type of thinking dominated by perceptual centring, on a single dimension. Children who gave this type of explanation (d and e in Table 7) usually gave immediate and confident responses and they obviously understood the question. It is clear that they believed a change in a dimension of an object affects the weight of that object.

The fourth type of answer was based on guesswork; sometimes children gave nonsense explanations for their choices but more often no explanations were forthcoming. Only a small number of children gave this type of answer although the figures were higher for the seven-year-olds.

On the whole, then, Piaget's categories of answers are clearly observable in our sample and, at first sight, his orderly theory of conceptualization seems to be followed by our pupils. However, two further observations may be made from our results. First, it will be remembered that each age group is made up of children of average ability as measured by a non-verbal intelligence test and also that each age group falls into a fairly narrow age bracket. It can be seen that the performance of the groups does improve with age as Piaget maintains, but between the age limits of our sample (7y 5m and 9y 11m) there is a wide variation in the performance of individuals. Of the children aged 7y 5m

53% gave correct reversible reasons for concluding that weight is conserved but a considerable proportion of children who were two years older failed to conserve weight in the same test.

Secondly, the researches previously quoted (Hyde, 1959; Beard, 1957) have pointed out that children who are conservers in one situation are not invariably conservers in another. As this finding is somewhat at variance with that of Piaget, we now examine the results of test items 4b, 5 and 6.

Results: item 4b

Table 8   Results for weight item 4b (average ability)

Answer	7y 5m	7y 11m	8y 5m	8y 11m	9y 5m	9y 11m
	%	%	%	%	%	%
Correct: reversibility	36	54	57	67	87	82
Compensatory reason	13	14	10	6	4	1
Incorrect: centring	39	32	33	27	9	11
Incorrect: other	12	0	0	0	0	6
Sample size (= 100%)	75	72	79	78	79	76

In item 4b the sausage is made longer and the same questions are asked as before. By comparison with the results of the first part of this item (4a) it can be seen (Table 8) that up to the 9y 5m age group the number of correct responses falls but this is only significant for the 7y 5m age group. It appears that a few of these pupils who had earlier given reasons based on reversibility now abandoned this reasoning and, because the visual element was more pronounced, they now believed that the weight of the plasticine had altered. Others now gave a compensatory reason − 'The sausage and ball have the same weight as the sausage is longer but the ball is fatter' − and it is impossible to ascertain whether the children had really changed their reasons or whether they were merely giving an alternative explanation for their belief in conservation. On the whole we can conclude that a few children who have previously given reasons based on reversibility do change their minds when the distracting visual increase in length is accentuated, but the number is on the whole small. For the two highest age groups there is hardly any change in the performance figures; around 85% of the children of average ability in this age group continued to give reasons based on reversibility. One in six of the older children, however, continued to maintain that the weight of the plasticine had changed.

Results: item 5

Table 9   Results for weight item 5 (average ability)

Answer	7y 5m	7y 11m	8y 5m	8y 11m	9y 5m	9y 11m
	%	%	%	%	%	%
Correct	44	42	56	81	78	74
Incorrect: group of 4 dolls heavier because more of them	25	24	16	8	4	3
Incorrect: other	31	34	28	11	18	23
Sample size (= 100%)	75	72	79	78	79	76

The results of this item (Table 9) vary somewhat from those of 4a; with the exception of age group 9y 11m, the numbers of correct responses are always lower in this item. We shall return to this point later. Those absolutely correct again gave reasons based on reversibility of thought — 'They still have the same weight as they weighed the same at the beginning, nothing has been added or removed'. With the incorrect answers the majority in the three youngest age groups focused their attention on the increased number of dolls and gave an answer based on this. A considerable proportion of children in all the age groups did not give either reason for their choices. These children provide us with little evidence of the thinking behind their choices. Some merely use imagination — 'There are dolls inside the unopened one as well' — whereas others appear to make a random selection simply in order to give an answer of one form or another. At best we can only conclude that their concept of conservation is not securely developed and the reason for the continuing equality of the weights is not firmly in their minds.

One other point needs to be made. In this item the pieces constituting the two weights are discontinuous, i.e. they are separated one from another during the test. For example, the dolls which were originally stacked together are spread out. As we have pointed out, other researches indicate that more children conserve weight when discontinuous objects are used; the very act of breaking up the original object into its constituent parts seems to encourage the children to reverse their thoughts. Comparison of the results in this item with those of the previous one does not demonstrate this effect of a discontinuous object, but the design of this particular item has one major difference from those used by other researchers. The separate pieces were not at first clearly observable; the dolls were stacked one inside the other and they eventually appeared 'by magic', as one pupil expressed it. In this particular case some children may believe that if the smaller dolls are inside the big one then their weights are supported or carried inside the big one and effectively 'disappear'. To them such weights may only reappear and affect the total weight when the dolls are separated and stand on their own feet. This hypothesis, however, was not explored any further. The encouragement of reversible thought by the use of discontinuous objects may therefore only apply if the pupils can see the separate pieces throughout the operation; first joined together and then separated. We probed this point further with item 6.

Results: item 6

Table 10   Results for weight item 6 (average ability)

Answer	7y 5m	7y 11m	8y 5m	8y 11m	9y 5m	9y 11m
	%	%	%	%	%	%
Correct	63	64	82	91	92	91
Incorrect: centring	20	15	10	4	4	9
Incorrect: other	17	21	8	5	4	0
Sample size (= 100%)	75	72	79	78	79	76

For item 6a (Table 10) the numbers of correct responses with answers based on reversibility are now consistently higher for all the age groups than in the previous items. As before, the most common reason given for concluding that one of the blocks has greater weight when it is elongated was that based on physical appearance alone: 'The red shape is now heavier because it is longer than the yellow shape' or 'The yellow block is heavier than the red one because it is fatter and wider'; reversibility of thought and analysis of the objects before they were physically altered does not appear to enter into the thoughts of these children. There were a considerable number of children, however, particularly in the two lowest age groups, who again merely chose one shape or another and were unable to give reasons for their choice or else gave reasons of the 'imagination' type. It appears that discontinuous objects of this type do encourage pupils who earlier did not use a reversible thinking process to use this form of reasoning now and thus demonstrate that they are able to conserve weight. To check this, we wondered what would happen if we continued this item further and separated the pieces from one of the blocks — making sure, however, that the children could not equate the two blocks by simply counting the number of pieces in each block.

Table 11 Results for weight item 6b: Lego blocks (average ability)

Answer	7y 5m	7y 11m	8y 5m	8y 11m	9y 5m	9y 11m
	%	%	%	%	%	%
Correct	73	69	82	87	94	92
Incorrect: centring	11	17	10	5	4	4
Incorrect: other	16	14	8	8	2	4
Sample size (= 100%)	75	72	79	78	79	76

Once more, the numbers of correct responses (Table 11) are higher than in any of the previous tests and for the three lower age groups separation of the pieces does cause a number of non-conservers to change their minds and give correct answers based on reversibility. Some form of learning has taken place. For the higher age groups no further improvement is observed and we see that, in our sample, nearly 10% of the children of average ability between the ages of nine and ten still failed to appreciate that weight is conserved when the physical dimensions of an object are changed, although they clearly saw that nothing has been added or removed.

Summary of test results: conservation of weight

We may summarize our interpretations of the results of the tests concerned with conservation of weight. For children of average ability, as measured by a non-verbal intelligence test, we found that:

1. In general, our pupils gave answers which fitted into the typical categories outlined by Piaget. The pupils appeared to demonstrate the thought structures he describes.
2. In general, performance does improve with age, although our figures vary from those quoted in other researches.
3. Whilst performance trends for groups of children seem to follow a pattern, it is clear that extrapolation from this pattern to the performance of individual children at any age is not an entirely reasonable step to take. There are wide variations in performance levels across our age range; a considerable proportion of the younger children conserved whilst some of the older children failed to conserve in any of our tests.
4. Performance varies considerably if the test materials are varied, and no sound deduction can be made about general patterns of performance from the evidence produced by single test items alone. This is especially

true if the questioning procedure is not carefully studied at the test design stage.

5. As our pupils' performance varied so much from test item to item, it seems clear that a high proportion of the children in our sample (at all ages) were at transition stages; they were uncertain of their own conclusions. It is clearly impossible for the researcher to categorize these pupils in one developmental stage or another. It is noted, however, that the progression of the pupils' thinking is always from reasons based on perception to those based on logic dependent on concrete operations. We consider that this supplies ample evidence of the need for teaching programmes which are sequential and carefully related to purpose-designed practical materials, and matched to the observed developmental stage of the individual child. The age range 7–10 years is clearly one where teachers should explore each pupil's understanding of the concept of weight and give guidance to those who are at the transition stage; further practical experience to those whose reasoning is based on appearance 'at first sight'; and further challenges of a concreto-logical nature to those who have clearly grasped the idea of conservation of weight.

It is to an analysis of these more complex ways of thinking that we must now turn.

THE SIMPLE USE OF UNITS

One of the fundamental steps in the growth of understanding the nature and properties of most physical quantities is the ability to measure and make comparisons. If children can carry out such observations in a logical fashion, they have collected, stored and categorized information in a particular way which enables them to think about it and arrive at conclusions which can increase their knowledge of the concept studied. For Piaget simple measurement alone is not sufficient to guarantee that the child can carry out this mental process. Instruction on a technique of measurement will not necessarily encourage the child to sort out and categorize his measurements, nor will it automatically encourage the child to question and probe for the implications of such measurements. As an introductory exploration of the growing ability of the pupil to use this type of logic, assessment item 7 attempts to examine the ability to use simple units.

Assessment item 7 corresponds to *AWV*, Test 7 for weight.

Item 7: 2 cylinders of equal volume painted orange and green; 10 yellow unit weights (cubes); balance

[NB the orange cylinder has a weight equal to 7 units.]

Place the orange cylinder and unit weights on the table in front of S.
> '*Weigh this* [indicate orange cylinder] *for me using these* [indicate unit weights] . *Find out how many of these* [indicate unit weights] *weigh the same as the orange.*'

If S is unable to operate, end item. Otherwise proceed.

7a   '*How many of these* [indicate unit weights] *weigh the same as the orange?*'

Point to the green, heavier cylinder.

7b   '*This weighs twice as much as the orange; how many of these* [indicate unit weights] *will weigh the same as the green?*'

If S is hesitant repeat the question once. If S gives an incorrect or no response, end item.

Otherwise proceed.

7c   '*Use the balance to find out whether you are right. Find out if the green does weigh fourteen.*'

If S is hesitant repeat the question. If S is unable to operate, end item.

If S operates successfully by placing the green cylinder on one pan and the orange cylinder and 7 units on the other balance pan,
> '*Does the green one weigh twice as much as the orange one?*'

If S answers '*no*', end item.

If S answers '*yes*',
> '*How do you know?*'

Here, for the first time, the pupil is in an active situation. The first part of the item simply tests the ability of the child to use a balance to find the weight of a loaded container. It should be noted that the units of weight that are used are arbitrary, i.e. no attempt is made to direct the pupil's attention to any particular standard unit. Further, to avoid confusion likely to be caused by counting, only a small number of units are used (7 units being the answer in this case).

The second part of the item tests for the understanding of the term 'weighs twice as much' and for the ability to double the answer obtained in the first part. The containers used are identical in volume.

The third part goes one step further. Here the pupil is asked to check his previous verbal answer but, to do this, he must reorganize in his mind all the previous information, as he is only supplied with 10 units, i.e. he must make use of the knowledge that the first container is equivalent in weight to 7 units. This calls on the pupils to think in a deductive fashion — a logico-mathematical operation — as thinking based on perception alone does not supply an obvious answer.

Results: items 7a and 7b

When asked to find out how many of the unit weights weighed the same as the object of unknown weight, nearly all the children, regardless of age, were able to carry out the direct comparison. At seven years of age 87% of the pupils and at nine and ten all the children were able to perform this task, which did not require them to form conclusions; it was a direct physical operation and, as such, presented few problems. When, however, we asked them to use this information to tell us the weight of a second container, given the added information that it weighed 'twice as much' as the first, the responses were very different (Table 12).

Table 12   Results for weight item 7b (average ability)

Answer	7y 5m	7y 11m	8y 5m	8y 11m	9y 5m	9y 11m
	%	%	%	%	%	%
Correct: 2nd container would weigh 14 units	12	28	47	71	76	82
Incorrect	88	72	53	29	24	18
Sample size (= 100%)	75	72	79	78	79	76

Two conclusions could explain these results. Either the children who failed did not understand the term 'twice as much', or else they fully understood the question but did not possess the mental ability which would have allowed them to use the known information to solve the problem. It has been stated earlier (p. 3) that the problem of language and communication looms large in researches of this kind and, as Piaget maintains that language can constitute a necessary condition for the *completion* of mental operations without being a sufficient condition for their *formation*, we decided to explore further the pupils' reasoning powers based on manipulation of weights. We argued that if a number of such items could be presented, a performance pattern would emerge which would allow us to see whether structures of logical thought were gradually developing in the children in our age range or whether poor responses were simply due to misunderstanding the questions, i.e. a communication barrier.

THE USE OF LOGIC

In the main, our tests examine the ability of the children to use logic in concrete situations. It is only in the last item that we ask questions related to propositional logic, that is, to an analysis of possibilities. The assessment items depend, in the main, on the concept of reversibility being firmly grasped by the child. With this mental process he can proceed to demonstrate the thought structures of seriation, classification, transitivity, etc. and it is this mental ability that we attempt to examine next.

All the following test items call on a more advanced mental ability on the part of the child than has been demonstrated so far. As the number of manipulations of the weights increases, the pupil has to memorize a number of steps. Since it is not intended that these items should simply test the pupil's ability to recall events, care has been taken not to overstress this memory aspect. Nevertheless, it is obvious that memory does play a part in the conceptualizing process, and in all these items it is considered a necessary feature of the design.

In a number of items the pupil is placed in a conflict situation, in that he has to decide whether to base the reasoning for his final answer on the visual appearance of the materials or on a logical thinking process based on the information he has received in the earlier part of the item. It is argued that a pupil at a more advanced conceptual level will use logic and disregard distracting visual effects whilst the pupil at a simple stage of conceptualization will, more often than not, focus his attention on the visual appearances of the material.

Results: item 7c

Item 7c tests the children's ability to work out a procedure to check their answer to item 7b. Once they have mentally solved this problem, the resulting action is merely a check which confirms their thoughts. The tester simply has to observe this practical action *to know* that the children have carried out the mental process. According to Piaget such thinking processes are only displayed by children well advanced in their conceptual abilities.

Table 13   Results for weight item 7c (average ability)

Answer	7y 5m	7y 11m	8y 5m	8y 11m	9y 5m	9y 11m
	%	%	%	%	%	%
Correct: use of logic	7	10	30	37	52	57
Incorrect	93	90	70	63	48	43
Sample size (= 100%)	75	72	79	78	79	76

The results (Table 13) clearly demonstrate that this task is beyond the ability of most of the children in the sample. In order to explore the pupil's ability to think in such a logical fashion the following items examine this stage in more detail.

Assessment items 8–13 correspond to *AWV*, Tests 8–10 (item 11 does not appear in *A VW*), 11 and 12 for weight.

Item 8: 3 balls – green, red and yellow – of equal weight but dissimilar volumes; balance

Place the three balls on the table in front of S, with the red ball in the middle.
    'Watch carefully.'
Place the green and the red balls on the balance, one on each pan.
    'Is the weight of the green ball the same as the weight of the red ball?'
Place the green ball on the table in front of S, leaving the red ball on the balance pan.
    'Watch again.'
Place the yellow ball on the empty pan of the balance.
    'Is the weight of the yellow ball the same as the weight of the red ball?'
Place the yellow ball alongside the green ball, leaving the red ball on the balance pan. S is not allowed to handle the balls.
    'Does the green ball weigh the same as the yellow ball or is it different in weight?'
If S answers *'the same'*,
    'Why do you say that?'
If S answers *'different'*,
    'Which is the heavier?'
    'Why do you say that?'

Item 9: 3 boxes of equal volume painted gold, green and silver; balance

[NB Descending order of weights is gold, green, silver.]

Place the three boxes on the table in front of S, with the green box in the middle.
> *'We are going to find out which is the heaviest box.'*

Give S the green and gold boxes.
> *'Use the balance to find out which is the heavier box, the green or the gold.'*
> *'Which is the heavier box?'*

Replace the boxes on the table. Give S the green and silver boxes.
> *'Use the balance to find out which is the heavier, the green or the silver.'*
> *'Which is the heavier box?'*

Place the boxes in front of S with the green in the middle.

9a Pointing to the gold and green boxes,
> *'Can you remember which was the heavier, the gold or the green?'*

9b Pointing to the green and the silver,
> *'Which was the heavier, the green or the silver?'*

If S gives incorrect answers to (a) and/or (b) repeat item *once* more. If S gives incorrect answers to either (a) or (b) a second time, end item. Otherwise proceed.
> *'Point to the heaviest box of the three.'*
> *'Why do you think that is the heaviest box?'*

Item 10: 4 boxes of equal volume painted yellow, white, green and red; balance

[NB Yellow and white weigh the same, red is heavier, green lighter.]

Place the four boxes on the table in front of S.
> *'Watch carefully.'*

Place the yellow and white boxes on the balance, one on each pan.
> *'Are they both the same weight or are they different in weight?'*

Place the boxes in the following order in front of S: red, yellow, green, white.
> *'Use the balance to put these boxes in order of weight, that is, find the heaviest box and put it here* [indicate] *and then the next heaviest, and so on.'*

RECORD WEIGHING SEQUENCE ON RECORD SHEET AS FOLLOWS:
e.g. R/Y, W/G, etc.

After S has finished weighing and has put the boxes in order:

'*Point to the heaviest box.*'

If S chooses the red box proceed, otherwise end item.

'*Point to the lightest box.*'

If S chooses the green box proceed, otherwise end item.

Remove the green box.

'*Which is the lightest of these three?*'

If S chooses the white or yellow box:

'*Is the white/yellow box lighter than the yellow/white box?*'

Item 11: 2 blocks equal in volume painted dark blue and pale blue; 3 smaller blocks of equal volume painted pale blue, yellow and orange; balance

[NB The 2 pale blue blocks together weigh the same as dark blue, orange same as yellow.]

Place the blocks on the table in front of S.

'*Watch carefully.*'

Place the 2 pale blue blocks on one balance pan and the dark blue on the other.

'*Do the pale blue blocks together weigh the same as the dark blue block, or are they different in weight?*'

Remove the blue blocks from the balance and place them in front of S.

'*Watch again.*'

Place the orange and yellow blocks on the balance, one on each pan.

'*Does the orange block weigh the same as the yellow block or is it different in weight?*'

Hold the smaller pale blue block above the yellow block as if to place it on the balance pan.

'*What would happen if I put this pale blue block on the pan with the yellow one* [indicate] *?*'

'*Why do you say that?*'

Hold the 2 pale blue blocks above the yellow block, and the dark blue block above the orange block as if to place them on the balance pans.

'*What would happen if <u>both</u> pale blue blocks were added to this pan with the yellow block* [indicate] *and the dark blue block was added to this pan with the orange block* [indicate] *?*'

'*Why do you say that?*'

Item 12: 3 cylinders painted fawn, blue and green; 4 smaller cylinders painted red; balance

[NB 3 red weigh the same as green, fawn same as blue.]

Place the cylinders on the table in front of S with the red ones stacked in pairs.

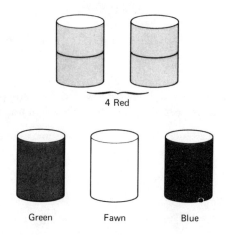

4 Red

Green   Fawn   Blue

'Watch carefully.'
Place the green cylinder on one balance pan and the 3 red ones, one at a time, on the other pan (2 red cylinders stacked, one separate).

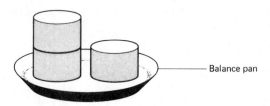

Balance pan

> *'Does the green one weigh the same as these red ones* [indicate] *or is it different in weight?'*

If S answers *'different'*,

> *'Why do you say that?'*

End item.
If S answers correctly, proceed.

Replace the green and red cylinders on the table in front of S (2 red cylinders stacked, the other 2 separate).

Place the fawn and blue cylinders on the balance, one on each pan.

> *'Does the fawn one weigh the same as this blue one* [indicate] *or is it different in weight?'*
>
> *'If I placed the green one on this pan with the fawn one* [indicate] *how many red ones would I need to add to the blue to make the pans level, so that they weighed the same?'*
>
> *'Why do you say that?'*

If S answers *'because they are equal in weight'*,

> *'How do you know that they are equal in weight?'*

Item 13: 4 blocks of equal volume painted black, green, pale blue and brown; balance

[NB Green weighs the same as black, blue twice black.]

Place the 4 blocks on the table in front of S.

> *'Use the balance to find out whether these two blocks weigh the same as each other* [indicate green and black blocks] *.'*

If S is unable to operate, end item. Otherwise proceed.

> *'Are they equal in weight? Does the black block weigh the same as the green block?'*

If S gives an incorrect response, end item. Otherwise proceed.

Ensure that the black and green blocks remain on the balance pans.

> *'One of these blocks* [indicate pale blue and brown] *weighs twice as much as the black block. Can you find out which one it is?'*

If S is hesitant repeat the question. If S is unable to operate, end item.
If S operates successfully by placing the pale blue block on one balance pan and the green and the black blocks on the other balance pan,

> *'How do you know that the pale blue block weighs twice as much as the black block?'*

Comments on items 8–13

Item 8: The containers have the same weight but different volumes and different colours, so that they can be easily identified. The pupil remains in the passive situation in this item but, before answering the final question, he first sees and agrees that container A is equal in weight to container B and that container B is equal in weight to container C. To answer the final question he has to make use of this pereliminary information; to help him recall all this, the materials are placed in front of him as a memory aid.

Item 9: Again the pupil is placed in the passive situation. There are no distracting visual features in this item; the containers of different weights are identical in volume. The memory factor dominates here; as a preliminary step, therefore, this ability to memorize is tested first and, to help the pupil, the first part of this item may be repeated once. Again deduction forms the only base on which a correct solution can be given.

Item 10: For the first time in this series the pupil is in an active situation and is asked to place four containers of identical volume in order of weight. This is a more complex task than item 9 but, to reduce the problem of memorizing the separate weighings, the pupil first sees and agrees that two of the containers are equal in weight. One of the other containers is heavier than this pair and the fourth is lighter. Again each container can be clearly identified by colour. In order that the tester may analyse the thinking processes that cause the pupil to select particular containers, the weighing sequence must be carefully recorded.

Item 11 examines the pupil's ability to relate a balancing of the objects in the balance pans to the idea of equality of weights in the two pans and not to the relative volumes of the objects or to the numbers of objects on each pan. We suspected that, if the children had earlier based their reasons on the immediately visual aspect of the materials, then they would probably first favour similar reasons in this item. We also suspected that comparison based on counting was one of the earliest types of classification to be used by pupils and that this too would be used as a reasoning platform.

Item 12: In this item the pupil once more has to use logic in order to arrive at a correct solution but a degree of conflict is introduced, as it can be seen that for the two balance pans to carry equal weight, the total volume of containers on one pan is greater than on the other; the number of containers on one pan is also different from the number on the other. A pupil at a simple conceptual level would be expected to focus attention on these distracting visual features.

Item 13: Although this item once more makes use of the idea 'weighs twice as much', the thought processes needed to arrive at a correct solution are more complex than those required in the earlier items. The pupil has now to consider all possible ways of arriving at a solution before taking any practical action. The item uses a thinking operation in Piaget's formal operational stage. Although the final action gives a strong indication that the thinking behind the activity is correct, the pupil is also asked to explain, in words, the reasons for his actions.

Results: item 8

Table 14   Results for weight item 8 (average ability)

Answer	7y 5m	7y 11m	8y 5m	8y 11m	9y 5m	9y 11m
	%	%	%	%	%	%
Correct answer and reasoning	39	33	58	63	82	84
Correct answer but subjects unable to explain how arrived at answer	37	26	16	15	7	8
Incorrect	24	41	26	22	11	8
Sample size (= 100%)	75	72	79	78	79	76

Performances which produce correct responses and evidence for correct reasoning (A = B, B = C, therefore A = C) generally show a steady improvement with age (Table 14) but are not as good as in the earlier tests concerned with conservation. The task, demanding the knowledge of transitivity, appears harder than those demanding only reversibility of thought. However, a considerable proportion of children, especially at the lower ages, stated the correct answer although quite unable to explain in words how they arrived at it. This point is worth noting, as it would be tempting neatly to categorize these children as either passes or failures according to the predetermined judgement of the research worker, whereas it is clearly impossible to decide whether they have used the thought structure dependent on transitivity. If transitivity has been used by the majority of these pupils then the figures for correct responses can be equated to those of the earlier tests on conservation. At least, it seems reasonable to suggest that this type of concreto-logical thought closely follows the establishment of the idea of conservation and reversibility in the child's mind.

Of those who failed, the majority based their reasons on the appearance of the objects ('That one is heavier because it is bigger') but the numbers, at all ages, who used this form of argument are consistently, though not significantly, less than in the tests on conservation.

Results: item 9

In this item the pupil is called upon to place three objects of identical volume
in order of weight. To do this he sees that object A is heavier than object B
and also that B is heavier than C. Memorization of the two observations is
necessary before the pupil can use the information to place the containers in a
serial order, and the tester checks that the pupil does remember before asking
the final question 'Point to the heaviest box of the three . . .'. From the
results (Table 15) we see that serial ordering, even of this simple type, is a
much more difficult task than the earlier items dealing with transitivity.
Furthermore, the pupils find it more difficult to explain the reasons for their
choices. As before, of those who were 'incorrect' a small number who chose
the correct box were unable to give reasons for their choice or gave incorrect
reasons. Here we conclude that these pupils have not yet formed sound

Table 15   Results for weight item 9 (average ability)

Answer	7y 5m	7y 11m	8y 5m	8y 11m	9y 5m	9y 11m
	%	%	%	%	%	%
Correct answer and reasoning	31	32	54	56	66	72
Incorrect	69	68	46	44	34	28
Sample size (= 100%)	75	72	79	78	79	76

principles for serial ordering; although they may, in their minds, be beginning
to carry out the correct thought processes, they are quite unable to express
these thoughts and give any other reason simply in order to answer the
question. As Piaget points out, this development of thought structure is internal
within the mind, and it does not necessarily follow that a pupil beginning to
use this way of thinking is capable of explaining or analysing his thoughts to
anyone, particularly to a research worker hoping to observe and establish neat,
orderly developmental stages.

Item 9 does not ask the pupil to work out a practical method in order to
place the three objects in order of weight; all the necessary observations are
presented to him by the tester. Next, therefore, we presented the children with
a more open-ended serialization task.

Results: item 10

Table 16 Results for weight item 10 (average ability)

Answer	7y 5m	7y 11m	8y 5m	8y 11m	9y 5m	9y 11m
	%	%	%	%	%	%
Correct	13	4	16	24	24	36
Incorrect	87	96	84	76	76	64
Sample size (= 100%)	75	72	79	78	79	76

The pupil has now to work out a sequence of weighing operations before he can operate mentally on the information he has gathered. The problem has a dual nature; not only has the pupil to work out logically how he could possibly arrive at an answer, but he must also decide on the practical measurements that have to be taken. For a sound concept of the serialization task the pupil must think about these procedures before carrying out the actual practical measurements. Logical thought must precede practical operation. This, perhaps, is a boundary line in the sequential development of concept formation. In the earlier test items children carried out observations first and thought about them afterwards, and we therefore expected item 10 to present greater challenges to our pupils.

From the results (Table 16) we see that this is clearly so. Even the older primary school children found this task difficult, although they had only to compare the weights of three objects (the fourth container was equal in weight to the middle container and could be eliminated from the ordering process). At all ages over 90% of the children failed to eliminate the fourth container from their observations, still including it in their practical manipulations. If they had thought of the necessary weighings beforehand, they would have realized that it was an irrelevant observation. Two types of correct weighing sequences were observed. First, 2% of the 7y 5m group and 5% of the 9y 11m group worked out the correct order with the minimum number of weighings. Pure concreto-logic was demonstrated. Secondly, the rest of the children who were correct carried out weighings based on successive elimination. One object would be weighed against the rest, then another, and so on. Those who failed merely resorted to random trial and error weighings, although it was clear that many of these pupils were attempting to work out a sequence of weighings and, indeed, the majority of these 'failures' were perfectly satisfied and confident that they had placed the weights in the correct order.

Serial ordering of weights, even though the containers were of equal volume, was a difficult task for most children in our age range and presented thinking operations considerably more advanced than those tested for earlier. It should be emphasized that in this ordering task the children were not asked to compare each weight in turn against a set of standard units. Undoubtedly this latter task would be found much easier, as it is reduced to the serial ordering of numbers.

As we had not introduced any situations where a number of distracting elements were built into the test we next gave the pupils 'logic' tasks on weight where the distracting features of different volumes and different numbers of weights were introduced.

Results: item 11

Here we tested for the logical operation that because weights A + B = weight C, and weight D = weight E, therefore weights A + B + D *must be equal* to weights C + E. However, volumes A + B + D were greater than volumes C + E.

Table 17   Results for weight item 11 (average ability)

Answer	7y 5m	7y 11m	8y 5m	8y 11m	9y 5m	9y 11m
	%	%	%	%	%	%
Correct	32	35	32	43	66	64
Incorrect: reason based on centring	39	37	28	18	22	16
Incorrect: other	29	28	40	39	12	20
Sample size (= 100%)	75	72	79	78	79	76

These results (Table 17) may be compared with those for item 9. Item 11 is not as difficult as the open-ended serialization task in item 10. The children who were judged correct were those who were capable of explaining their answers; they stored information of the separate observations in their minds and used this to give the final logically correct answer. Once more the pupils were in the passive situation, watching the tester carrying out the preliminary manipulations. Of those who failed, a considerable number centred or focused their attention on the greater volume of one set of blocks or on the fact that one balance pan contained more blocks. The immediate appearances of the objects still dominated their thinking. The responses of the remainder who failed appeared to be haphazard and based on guesswork. Yet again the task shows the wide variation in the ability of the children at all ages. For example, 32% of the average ability $7\frac{1}{2}$ year-olds gave correct answers whilst 36% of the average ability 10 year-olds failed completely to provide the correct solution to what, at first sight, appears to be a fairly straightforward logical operation. We explored this type of task further with item 12.

Results: item 12

This test is essentially similar to the previous one. The distracting elements of volume and number are again introduced. We wished to see if the responses would be similar if slightly different materials were used. We wanted to see if variations in performance would occur in this type of task as well as in those concerned with conservation.

Table 18   Results for weight item 12 (average ability)

Answer	7y 5m	7y 11m	8y 5m	8y 11m	9y 5m	9y 11m
	%	%	%	%	%	%
Correct	33	36	56	64	80	76
Incorrect: centring	51	33	27	23	14	11
Incorrect: other	16	31	17	13	6	13
Sample size (= 100%)	75	72	79	78	79	76

For the two lowest age groups (Table 18) the figures for correct responses closely matched those of the previous item, although of those who failed more focused their attention on equality of volume or equality of number of containers. In the higher age groups the performances improved. A number of children who had not previously demonstrated this type of logic now explained their reasons correctly. Either a measure of learning had taken place as a result of the previous task, or possibly the fact that the pupils had to deduce how many containers would be needed to balance the weights on the pans was a greater challenge to their thinking powers and, in effect, forced them to analyse the task in more detail than in the earlier item, when they simply explained what would happen if objects were placed on the pans. Certainly, a proportion of the children are, once more, at a transition stage and, although a general performance pattern for the group as a whole emerges, it is obviously extremely difficult to predict the performance of individual children on the basis of single test items.

Finally, we wanted to find out if some of our pupils were capable of working out methods of solving a problem using logical thought within the formal operational stage.

Results: item 13

In the first part the children have to check, using the balance, whether two blocks have the same weight. With isolated exceptions all the children at all ages succeeded in this task. The second part of the test, however, required them to use this knowledge to find out which of two other blocks had twice the weight of either of the first pair. It will be remembered that item 7b had tested the children's responses to the term 'weighs twice as much' and, although there were few correct responses (12% and 28%) for the two youngest age groups the majority of the older children had answered correctly. In this item the number of correct responses was considerably lower (Table 19).

Table 19   Results for weight item 13

Answer	7y 5m	7y 11m	8y 5m	8y 11m	9y 5m	9y 11m
	%	%	%	%	%	%
Correct: operation and reasoning correct	1	1	2	9	19	20
Incorrect: unable to operate	99	99	98	91	81	80
Sample size, N (= 100%)	146	150	150	155	155	149

The pupils cannot, in this item, carry out a practical operation until they have logically worked out the steps to prove whether they have found the correct block. The final practical step merely confirms their thinking. This capability of examining all possibilities and logically using arguments of the type 'If so and so is true then it must follow that . . .' characterizes the child at Piaget's formal operational stage. In this particular test, at least, the majority of our sample could not sort out these steps at all; the given information and knowledge of the terms simply could not be used as they had not reached the stage of mental development which would have allowed them to think about the task in the correct logical fashion.

Summary of test results: the use of logic in relation to the use of the balance and the concept of weight

For children of average ability it was found that:

    1. Nearly all the children in the sample, regardless of age, could carry out

weighing tasks of a simple one-to-one comparison, e.g. they could find the number of unit weights equal in weight to a given object. Immediately the problem involved the use of simple logic combined with practical weighing operations, a wide range of performances with age resulted. This was true even when the necessary weighing activities were carried out by the tester.

2. All the items concerned with the use of simple logic proved to be more difficult at all ages than earlier items concerned with conservation. It would appear, therefore, that conservation and reversibility of thought do precede the ability to use logic of the type described and both abilities improve with age.

3. As with the results of conservation tests, these later items also demonstrate that a considerable proportion (around 30%) of the seven-year-olds *were able* to answer correctly. In contrast, a roughly similar proportion of the ten-year-olds were *unable* to solve many of the items, although the logic that they should have applied was of a relatively simple type.

4. A number of the younger children giving correct answers to these later items were unable to explain their answers. This would seem to indicate that mental ability may not be matched by communication ability. The testing procedures did not probe this hypothesis further.

5. As in the case of the earlier items, it was consistently observed that, when irrelevant visual features were introduced and accentuated (e.g. number of containers, volume of containers, etc.) so that reasons based on simple perception were alternative answers to choose, then many of the children gave answers based on appearances alone. However, this single alternative was not the sole basis for wrong answers. A considerable proportion of children sometimes gave answers based on reasoning rather than perception but the reasons were, in adult terms, illogical (see Tables 17 and 18 (items 11 and 12) for proportions of wrong answers not based on visual centring). These children were obviously grappling with the problem in an abstract thought fashion but had not yet hit on the logical reason which would fully explain their choices.

6. When the children faced a more open-ended problem (e.g. the serial ordering item 10, and items 12 and 13) where they had to work out procedures in their minds before taking practical action, the numbers of correct responses at all ages fell dramatically. The results support Piaget's view that this thought operation appears at a later stage than the form of logic described earlier. Once more, however, the results also show that a fair proportion of the younger children have the ability to reason in this fashion and age is not a sound guide for predicting the performance of individual children.

For the research worker and teacher these interpretations raise a number of issues. It is possible to distinguish between two types of test design. In the first the pupils remain passive, watching the tester demonstrating all the practical tests, they merely have to store all this information and think about the observations. In the second type of test the pupils have to work out the necessary practical procedures to obtain the information which will enable them to answer correctly. It could well be that the actual form of logic that should be used on the information will be the same in both cases, but the second type of test calls on other mental qualities — the ability to anticipate all possible observations, and to consider alternative actions if the early observations show that the practical procedures used have no meaningful outcomes. This form of thinking and operating is not simply trial and error. It is a mental analysis in depth of the problem. Designers of tests on the use of logic do not, in the main, categorize their test design in this fashion but interpret the results in terms of the form of logic used, without sufficiently taking into account the procedures that the pupils have to experience before they are able to use the appropriate logic.

Analysis of test design in this fashion has direct relevance for the teacher in the classroom. It would seem to indicate sequential features that need to be considered when designing learning situations for the pupils. A task where the children are given specific instructions on the observations to be made followed by questions on these observations should precede tasks where the children are asked to *work out* procedures before answering questions about their observations. The latter type of task requires the teacher to think carefully about the form of questions he needs to ask in order to guide the children to work out procedures for themselves. In other words, questions have to be designed which guide but do not 'give the game away'. *Area, Weight, and Volume,* the teachers' guide allied to this report, enlarges on this theme and attempts to illustrate the need for carefully designed sequential learning situations which progressively challenge the mental and manipulative skills of the pupils.

Once more, too, the question of communication skills on the part of researcher, teacher and pupils emerges from the interpretations of the research results. Time and again children gave correct answers but could not explain their reasoning. Our tests failed to provide further information on the thinking abilities of this sample. Perhaps future research could identify such pupils in a preliminary set of tests and, by carefully designing further test items of a non-verbal variety, examine the thinking powers of these children more closely.

If teachers involve the children in more practical tasks than hitherto, it follows that many children may develop the ability to solve the set problems in their minds and through resultant action; but if the allied vocabulary and communication skills are not carefully built into the learning situation, they may never be called on to explain, in oral or written terms, the mental steps they have used. A well designed task would have the development of communication skills as a necessary objective. It is therefore suggested that an appropriate learning task would have questions for the pupils embodying:

1. guidance on the practical procedures to be encouraged;
2. the form of logic to be used to solve the set problem;
3. the further development of the appropriate vocabulary;
4. encouragement to explain or analyse the mental steps taken in arriving at answers.

6 The concept of area

The growth of the concept of area is commonly said to precede that of volume and it is certainly true that, in the main, the concept of volume rarely receives as much attention in the primary school as that of area. Research seems to indicate that a teaching sequence based on 'topic' sequences (i.e. area before volume) is not entirely warranted and it can be argued that the development of these topics in a parallel fashion could have material benefit for the growth of understanding of both concepts.

Piaget has discussed the development of these concepts by children in *The Child's Conception of Geometry* (1948) and distinguished a number of levels of achievement. At the first level, the ability to match shapes in terms of areas and volumes slowly develops. Then recognition that objects and surfaces may be reorientated and have their shapes changed without changing their areas or volumes occurs, and with this recognition comes the realization of the notion of conservation of area and volume.

Fundamental to this understanding is the growth of the idea of reversibility. Piaget maintains that, at a second level, the pupils develop the ability to measure length and gradually, through the use of appropriate units in practical, concrete form (an area shape or volume block), they develop the ability to measure areas and volumes. At a final stage comes the realization that areas and volumes can be calculated, i.e. the pupils are capable of grasping that multiplication of certain linear dimensions achieve the same purpose as simple direct measurement using units of a concrete nature.

It is also accepted that the different facets of the concept of volume — such as exterior volume, interior volume, volume of a solid object, volume of space, displaced volume etc. — imply that very wide practical experience is required for a full understanding of this concept. On the other hand, the concept of area, although embodying all the levels previously described, is by comparison relatively limited in range. Practical 'shapes' and associated units are easily made by the teacher, and sums using the concept of area at the level of multiplication of length and breadth have, by tradition, appeared as a fundamental ingredient of primary school mathematics syllabuses.

In our research, recognizing that these levels of conceptual development occur, and arguing that children are more likely to have everyday experience of volume in its solid and spatial forms than of the possibly more abstract idea of an area, we probed the depth of understanding expressed by children of both these concepts.

A consideration of previous studies showed that nearly all had more limited objectives. Most examined one concept and made use of only one or two practical items with the result that, in the main, only one or two of the Piagetian levels of achievement were examined. Following the pattern of the study of the concept of weight, it was therefore decided to test the same children on both area and volume and to incorporate, in both concepts, items examining the main levels of conceptual achievement described by Piaget.

In an attempt to order the discussion of children's responses, all the tests dealing with the concept of area and with volume are considered in separate chapters. Chapter 8 relates the responses of the children to the similar levels of achievement in all three concepts: weight, area and volume.

SORTING AND MATCHING

When children were tested on their understanding of conservation of area in the pilot survey, there were clear indications that a considerable proportion were giving wrong answers as a result of poor manipulative skill or because they failed to grasp the meaning of key terms used in the questions. Those children who appeared to fit into these categories could not be examined further on the concept of area because it was impossible to determine exactly what they were trying to convey in their answers.

In the main survey, therefore, it was decided to build into the test sequence a number of items which explored children's manipulative skills and their understanding of key expressions that would be used in later items. The problems of communication and use of verbal expressions were explored in some depth in the series of tests on the concept of area, and an attempt has been made to analyse the children's responses by taking into account both their understanding of the expressions used and their concept of the properties associated with area.

Assessment items 1–5 correspond to *AWV*, Tests 1–4 and 6 for area.

Item 1: plastic shapes of assorted colours

[NB 7 different kinds of shape are used, as follows: 3 triangles (2 identical,

the third generally similar); 5 triangles (3 identical); 4 oblong/rectangles
(3 identical); 6 rectangles (4 identical); 3 other shapes, dissimilar to the above.]

Place the shapes at random on the table in front of S.
 'Pick out those shapes that would fit over each other exactly.'
If S does not understand 'fit over', demonstrate using two pieces of paper of
identical dimensions, and then repeat the instructions.

Item 2: 15 orange shapes; 1 large blue square

Arrange the shapes on the table in front of S.

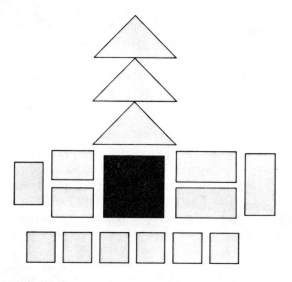

Point to the large square.
2a   *'What is this shape called?'*
Point to an oblong.
2b   *'What is this shape called?'*
If S answers *'oblong'* please use this term for the rest of the Area Test.
If S answers *'rectangle'* please use this term for the rest of the Area Test.
Point to a triangle.
2c   *'What is this shape called?'*

2d   *'Now I want you to make as many squares as you can from these
        orange shapes* [indicate] *which would exactly fit over this blue square*
        [indicate] *.'*

Item 3: 1 square-based pyramid

Give the pyramid to S.
> *'How many surfaces has this pyramid?'*

If S begins to count,
> *'Show me as you count.'*

Item 4: 2 yellow rectangles of equal dimensions

Place the two rectangles on the table in front of S.
> *'This is a surface* [indicate one rectangle] . *Does it have the same amount of surface as that shape* [indicate other rectangle] *or does it have a different amount of surface?'*

If S answers *'the same'*,
> *'Why do you say that?'*

If S answers *'different'*,
> *'Which has more surface?'*
> *'Why do you say that?'*

Item 5: 1 large circle; 1 small circle; 2 squares

Place the four shapes on the table in front of S.

> *'Which shape has the most surface?'*
> *'You can move them around if you want to.'*

Remove the shape chosen.
> *'Which of these three shapes has the most surface?'*
> *'Why have you chosen that one?'*

If S compares the chosen shape with only one other shape,
> *'Why do you think that it has more surface than this one* [indicate remaining shape] *?'*

If S indicates that two or more shapes are equal in area,
> *'Why do you say that these two have the same amount of surface as each other?'*

Results: item 1

The pupils handle the shapes and are free to manipulate them in any way they wish. The key expression is the statement 'fit over each other exactly', and the test explores the children's ability to pick out shapes which are of equal area and similar shape. The concept of area does not feature strongly here, as the pupils are not called upon to pick out pieces which have equal areas but *different* shapes. In other words the matching, from a preliminary scanning process, may be based on the recognition of similar shapes rather than of equal areas.

Table 20   Results for area item 1 (average ability)

Answer	7y 5m	7y 11m	8y 5m	8y 11m	9y 5m	9y 11m
	%	%	%	%	%	%
Matched all possible shapes	52	53	63	54	53	80
Matched some but not all shapes	41	37	33	45	47	20
Failed to operate	5	8	4	1	0	0
Sample size (= 100%)	75	72	79	78	79	76

It can be seen (Table 20) that, even at the older ages, this task was by no means an easy one for the children. Often three shapes were similar, and it was noticeable that many pupils simply picked out pairs of shapes and did not explore further possibilities; *one-to-one* matching seemed to dominate the minds of many of the pupils. Another reason for failure was that pupils were often satisfied that matching and fitting only needed to be approximate.

Even in this preliminary test, therefore, both the problems of understanding terms ('fit over each other exactly') and the ability to manipulate materials emerge.

Results: item 2

Over 90% of all the children recognized the square shape and the triangular shape. The results for the rectangular shape are given in Table 21. The word 'oblong' is obviously the commonly used term, whilst a considerable proportion of younger children failed to describe the shape at all.

Table 21   Results for area item 2b (average ability)

Answer	7y 5m	7y 11m	8y 5m	8y 11m	9y 5m	9y 11m
	%	%	%	%	%	%
Used term 'oblong'	38	41	53	55	50	54
Used term 'rectangle'	35	36	34	37	41	42
Unable to describe shape	25	21	11	6	10	4
Sample size (= 100%)	75	72	79	78	79	76

The final part of the item (2d) called on the pupils to build up a large square by using smaller shapes. The children had to scan all the pieces before comparing and matching. A degree of analysis is required and this forms the basis for the ability to categorize materials. This ability is of paramount importance for the growth of conceptualization. Results are given in Table 22.

Table 22   Results for area item 2d (average ability)

Answer	7y 5m	7y 11m	8y 5m	8y 11m	9y 5m	9y 11m
	%	%	%	%	%	%
Successful	52	58	72	88	94	96
Unsuccessful	48	42	28	12	6	4
Sample size (= 100%)	75	72	79	78	79	76

The greatest difficulty occurred with the triangular shapes. Children who failed could not manipulate the triangles; they appeared unable to realize that the orientation of one triangle had to be different to that of the other. In attaining fit, most of the younger children concentrated on picking out shapes that fitted into the corners of the large square and filled in the 'space' left, i.e. they did not appear to scan the area as such. Even many of the older children carried this task out on a trial and error basis, especially when more than two shapes had to be picked out to make up the large square. It was particularly noticeable that even those children who had correctly made up all the possible squares, and were left with a small number of odd shapes, did not rely on their perception of this remainder. They had to test further by practical manipulation though, to the adult tester, this was obviously unnecessary.

Both mental perception and practical trial and error methods were used by the children; in the case of the shapes left over, where only one of these methods of solution needed to be used, many children could not determine which method to use, and, unable to rely on one form of reasoning only, used both. We shall return to this problem of selection of reasons in later tests.

Results: item 3

The understanding of the term 'surface' is tested in order to be certain that it can be used as a term for 'area' in later items. Although the greater majority generally understood the word 'surface' in terms of areas it was noticeable (Table 23) that the base of the object was not recognized as a surface even

Table 23   Results of area item 3 (average ability)

Answer	7y 5m	7y 11m	8y 5m	8y 11m	9y 5m	9y 11m
	%	%	%	%	%	%
Correct surfaces	28	31	44	56	65	68
Missed out base	59	61	44	37	28	28
Failed	13	8	11	6	8	4
Sample size (= 100%)	75	72	79	78	79	76

though pupils held the pyramid in their hands. This finding again highlights the problem of word or term recognition in the classroom. As three-dimensional objects were not used in the following items, the problem of surfaces and bases did not arise again and so the term 'surface' was used as the abstract term to denote area.

Results: item 4

Understanding of terminology is again examined, but this time the key statements are 'same amount of' and 'different amount of' and the pupils are asked to compare areas of rectangles. All the children agreed that the rectangles had the same amount of surface, but it was often impossible to recognize whether the reasons they gave for their choice had really been used as a basis for their deductions or were simply 'reasons' to justify a selection which had, in fact, been made as a result of a scanning or general observation and comparison of

the two areas. The explanation 'Because they both had the same shape' was a
common answer (Table 24), and it was obvious that this was judged to be an

Table 24   Results for area item 4 (average ability)

Answer	7y 5m	7y 11m	8y 5m	8y 11m	9y 5m	9y 11m
	%	%	%	%	%	%
Same amount of surface because same shape	24	22	32	35	32	43
Same amount of surface because same size	44	43	47	45	51	45
Same surface: other reasons	32	35	22	21	18	12
Sample size (= 100%)	75	72	79	78	79	76

adequate explanation by the children although they knew that different areas
could have the same shape. The word 'size' was also commonly used in a
general sense, and it was impossible to judge whether the children used this
global term to mean 'area' or some other dimension. The other common
reason given was 'They both have the same amount of surface because all the
sides are the same length' — clearly verbal description of area was not well
developed in these pupils.

Results: item 5

Again the children are tested on their understanding of 'amount of surface'
but here they have to order shapes in terms of their areas. The majority of the
children used the words 'amount of surface' to indicate area, and the fact that
they also focused their attention on the word 'more' also strongly implies that
selection and order in terms of surface is called for. Nevertheless, 32% of the
$7\frac{1}{2}$ year-olds and 14% of the 9 year-olds (Table 25) were unable to select the
correct shapes even though the estimation of area could easily be carried out
visually. Obviously the term 'amount of surface' is not an easy definition of
area for some of the children. This understanding of terminology is explored
further in the next section.

Table 25 Results for area item 5 (average ability)

Answer	7y 5m	7y 11m	8y 5m	8y 11m	9y 5m	9y 11m
Shape with most surface	%	%	%	%	%	%
Correct	90	94	91	95	96	96
Incorrect	10	6	9	5	4	4
Shape with greatest area from remaining 3						
Complete square has most surface	66	75	81	84	93	94
Both squares have same amount of surface	5	7	1	0	1	1
Incorrect: other	27	17	18	14	6	5
Sample size (= 100%)	75	72	79	78	79	76

Summary of test results: matching and fitting

1. Pupils rely to a large extent on practical manipulation in order to match and compare areas of shapes. Often this manipulative process is difficult for the seven-year-old children and for some of the older pupils. Trial and error and one-to-one matching are the sole bases for many of these operations. Mental analysis and recognition before actual practical manipulation seem to develop slowly with practical experience until the stage is reached when children scan the material and mentally sort out the shapes before *checking* through practical activity that their mental choices were correct. (This was particularly evident in item 2.)
2. Terms and expressions were often used vaguely by the children in our sample and, as the actual word 'area' was very rarely used, it was difficult to determine whether the words used in their explanations conveyed adequately what were the true mental reasons for their answers.
3. On the whole, words that have obviously been used consistently in the classroom — for example, squares, triangles, oblongs, rectangles, surfaces — are quite well understood. Familiarity and *consistent* usage is obviously a key factor for communication skills and, in turn, accurate conceptualization.

For the research worker the need for preliminary tests of manipulative skills and for the understanding of terms to be used in tests for conceptualization is strongly implied. Perhaps many researches have arrived at conclusions concerning conceptualization which are unreliable because the responses of the children are restricted to their communication and manipulative skills.

For the teacher the classroom activities should clearly involve a great deal of practical work, closely linked to the use of terms in a consistent and un-ambiguous fashion. Indeed, it could be argued that the term 'area' should be used very early in this learning process alongside the more general word 'surface' especially when the amounts of surfaces are to be compared. Here the phrase 'area of a surface' could be introduced in a meaningful way.

CONSERVATION OF AREA

Piaget, with his co-workers Inhelder and Szeminska, discussed children's growing ability to understand Euclidian geometry in *The Child's Conception of Geometry* (1948: English 1960). His ingenious experiments and somewhat unexpected findings have had considerable bearing on recently produced guides for teachers of mathematics in primary schools (e.g. Nuffield Junior Mathematics). A number of experiments were devoted to a study of conservation of area and some of these are of particular interest in the present context. In one experiment two identical cardboard 'fields' were shown to the child and he agreed that there was 'the same amount of grass to eat' on each field (p. 263). Equal numbers of houses were then successively added to each field, but in one field they were spread over the area whilst in the other they were arranged in a close group. After the addition of equal numbers of houses to each field, the child was asked whether there was 'the same amount of grass to eat' in both fields. Younger children relied on perceptual impressions and concluded that when the houses were packed together there was more grass to eat than when the houses were spread out; older children ignored this visual aspect and gave reasons based on the use of simple logic, e.g. 'No, it looks as if there's more green there – but it isn't true because there's the same number of houses' (p. 271).

Two points emerge from this experiment. First, as in the concept of weight and volume, perceptual features appear to dominate the younger children's thinking but in this particular experiment this evidence may be coloured by the fact that fields and objects in fields, i.e. areas within areas, were used. After all, the conclusion that there is more 'area' available when the houses are clustered together than when they are spread out is a fairly reason-able one when it is remembered that the teacher in the classroom may have used the very same idea when he or she has moved all the desks to the corner of the classroom to 'give us more room to move about'. In short, it is not clear whether the children are misinterpreting the point of the question or whether they are demonstrating a true misconception, honestly believing that the areas available are different in the two fields.

Secondly, it should be noticed that the questions were asked in terms of real world or concrete experience, i.e. words such as grass, houses and fields were used to denote area. Another study by Piaget used two fields of similar areas and 'potato plots'; the plots were originally seen to be of the same area but one was cut into movable sections, thus altering its shape. The children were examined to see whether they realized that, when the plots of different shape were placed on the fields, the areas of field left were identical and so were the areas of potato plots (i.e. the complementary areas also remained equal). It was found that many children would conserve the areas of the plots but at the same time deny conservation for the fields 'left over'. However, the wording of the questions in this latter experiment was often more abstract than in the earlier example, e.g. 'Is there still *as much room* [or same space] for potatoes?' was the question for the potato plots (p. 287), whereas the 'fields' question (p. 289) was of the form 'Is there still as much grass for the cows?'

Whilst the different form of the questions may have been highlighted in translation, it is clear that the wording could have considerable effect on the children's reasoning and on their eventual answers. Flavell (1963a, p. 339) expresses this criticism: 'There is always the lurking feeling that non-conservation may be some sort of experimental artifact, that if the situation were somehow made more realistic, closer to his everyday needs, the young child would not make these incredible errors in quantitative reasoning'. In Flavell's study (another of Piaget's experiments), the subject was given the task of bisecting, trisecting, etc. a circular clay 'cake' and among other things, was questioned as to the relative 'amounts to eat' in the intact whole versus the whole in pieces. The results suggested that 'non-conservation can emerge loud and clear even in situations quite close to "real life" ' (p. 339).

In another experiment by Piaget and his colleagues (1948: English 1960) children were given congruent cardboard shapes. After they had agreed that they were both the same 'size' (size being used by the questioner to denote area), a piece was removed from one of them and moved to another part of this shape. Younger children did not conserve area when such changes occurred; they often gave answers showing that they relied entirely on what they could actually see ('This one is bigger because it is longer' – p. 276). Again it is difficult to conclude what meaning the children had attached to the words 'size' or 'amount of room' used by the questioner; likewise, it is uncertain whether the word 'bigger' used by the children in their answers really indicates that they were thinking about area or whether they are trying to say 'By bigger I mean longer so since it is now longer it is bigger'.

Piaget's researches clearly showed that younger children relied heavily on reasons based on visible changes, whereas older children conserved area and gave answers based on reversibility of thought (e.g. 'It must have the same area as it can be changed back to the first shape' or 'the area must still be the same as nothing has been added or removed'). However, the problem of communication also emerged strongly in these studies; since it could well be that many of the answers given are measures of communication ability rather than measures of conception, it was decided to explore this avenue further in the present inquiry. It was not clear whether Piaget had used the same children for all his tests on area or whether his general interpretation had emerged from a study of the responses of different children in the different tests. The following tests were therefore given to all the children in our sample and, in an attempt to examine the various factors discussed above, all the test items explored the children's ideas about conservation of area but each was designed to study different facets of the concept. It must be stressed, however, that the test items should be examined and interpreted together, as it is clear that the examination and interpretation of a set of answers obtained from a single test situation give a very limited and incomplete view of the children's thoughts about conservation of area.

Assessment items 6–10 correspond to *AWV*, Tests 5 (modified), 7–8 and 10–11 for area.

Item 6: 2 blue oblongs; 2 blue triangles

6a Assemble the blue shapes on the table.
   'Does this square have the same amount of surface as that shape [indicate] *or does it have a different amount of surface? You can move the shapes if you want to.'*
If S answers *'the same'*,
   'Why do you say that?'

If S answers *'the same because one is longer but the other is fatter'* or similar compensatory reason,

> *'Is there any other reason why they have the same amount of surface as each other?'*

If S answers *'different'*,

> *'Which shape has more surface?'*
> *'Why do you say that?'*

Item 6 (cont): 3 green oblongs

6b Assemble the oblongs on the table.

> *'I want you to imagine that these are fields. Does this field* [indicate single oblong] *have the same amount of grass as those two together* [indicate two oblongs] *or does it have a different amount of grass? You can move the shapes if you want to.'*

If S answers *'the same'*,

> *'Why do you say that?'*

If S answers *'the same because one is longer but the other is fatter'* or similar compensatory reason,

> *'Is there any other reason why they have the same amount of grass as each other?'*

If S answers *'different'*,

> *'Which field has more grass?'*
> *'Why do you say that?'*

Item 7: 1 red rectangle; 2 red triangles

7a Assemble the shapes on the table in front of S.

 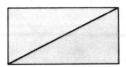

'*Does that oblong* [indicate] *have the same amount of surface as this oblong, or does it have a different amount of surface?*'
If S answers '*different*', place the whole oblong over the other one and repeat the question.
Reassemble the two triangles.

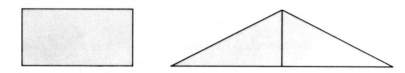

'*Does this shape* [indicate triangle] *have the same amount of surface as the oblong, or does it have a different amount of surface?*'
If S answers '*the same*',
   '*Why do you say that?*'
If S answers '*the same because one is longer but the other is fatter*' or similar compensatory reason,
   '*Is there any other reason why they have the same amount of surface?*'
If S answers '*different*',
   '*Which has more surface?*'
   '*Why do you say that?*'

Item 7 (cont): 3 yellow triangles

7b Assemble the shapes on the table in front of S.

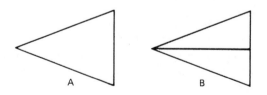

'*If I were to paint this shape red* [indicate A] *would I need the same amount of paint, or a different amount, to paint that shape red* [indicate B] *?*'
If S answers '*different*', place A over B and repeat the question.
Reassemble B.

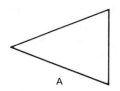 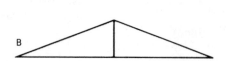

'*If I were to paint this shape* [indicate A] *would I need the same amount of paint, or a different amount, to paint that shape* [indicate B] *?*'
If S answers '*the same*',
'*Why do you say that?*'
If S answers '*the same because one is longer but the other is fatter*' or similar compensatory reason,
'*Is there any other reason why they would both need the same amount of paint?*'
If S answers '*different*',
'*Which shape would need more paint?*'
'*Why do you say that?*'

Item 8: 1 orange triangle; 1 orange square

[NB Area of the 2 shapes is the same, see p. 103.]

Give S a shape to hold in each hand.
'*I want you to imagine that these are biscuits and you are very hungry, which would you prefer to have?*'
'*Why do you say that?*'
If S gives a reason which is unmathematical,
'*Has this shape the same amount of biscuit as that one, or does it have a different amount of biscuit?*'
If S answers '*the same*',
'*Why do you say that?*'
If S answers '*the same because one is longer but the other is fatter*' or similar compensatory reason,
'*Is there any other reason why they have the same amount of biscuit?*'
If S answers '*different*',
'*Which has more biscuit?*'
'*Why do you say that?*'

Item 9: 3 identical shapes: X, Y and Z

Assemble the shapes on the table in front of S.

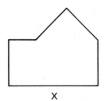 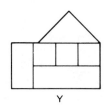 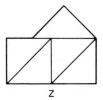

| X | Y | Z |

'*Do these three shapes have the same amount of surface as each other or do they have different amounts of surface?*'

If S answers '*different*', match the shapes by placing X over Y then X over Z, and repeat the question.

Otherwise proceed

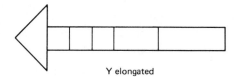

Y elongated

9a Reassemble Y as above.

'*Does this shape* [indicate Y] *have the same amount of surface as that shape* [indicate X] *or does it have a different amount of surface?*'

If S answers '*the same*',

'*Why do you say that?*'

If S answers '*the same because one is longer but the other is fatter*' or similar compensatory reason,

'*Is there any other reason why they have the same amount of surface as each other?*'

If S answers '*different*',

'*Which shape has more surface?*'

'*Why do you say that?*'

9b Separate the pieces of Z.

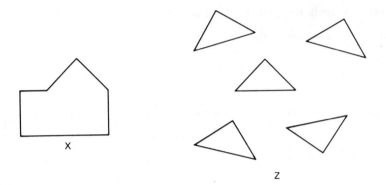

'Do all these pieces together [indicate Z] have the same amount of surface as this shape [indicate X] or do they have a different amount of surface?'

If S answers 'the same',
  'Why do you say that?'
If S answers 'different',
  'Which has more surface?'
  'Why do you say that?'

9c Place X to one side and separate the pieces of Y.
  'Do all these pieces together [indicate Y] have the same amount of surface as all of those pieces [indicate Z] or do they have a different amount of surface?'

If S answers 'the same',
  'Why do you say that?'
If S answers 'different',
  'Which has more surface?'
  'Why do you say that?'

Item 9 (alternative)

Assemble the shapes on the table in front of S.

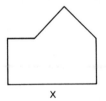
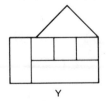
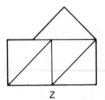

'If I were to paint these three shapes would they each need the same amount of paint, or a different amount of paint?'

If S answers *'different'*, match the shapes by placing X over Y then X over Z, and repeat the question.

Otherwise proceed.

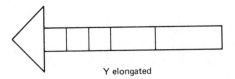

Y elongated

9a Reassemble Y as above.

'If I were to paint this shape [indicate Y] *would I need the same amount of paint, or a different amount, to paint that shape* [indicate X] *?'*

If S answers *'the same'*,

'Why do you say that?'

If S answers *'the same because one is longer but the other is fatter'* or similar compensatory reason,

'Is there any other reason why they would need the same amount of paint?'

If S answers *'different'*,

'Which would need more paint?'

'Why do you say that?'

9b Separate the pieces of Z.

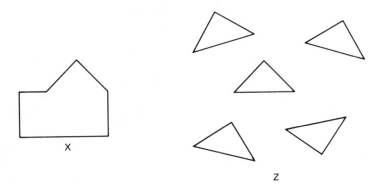

X

Z

'If I were to paint all of these pieces [indicate Z] *would I need the same amount of paint, or a different amount, to paint that shape* [indicate X] *?'*

If S answers *'the same'*,

'Why do you say that?'

If S answers *'different'*,

'Which would need more paint?'

'Why do you say that?'

9c   Place X to one side and separate the pieces of Y.

'If I were to paint all of these pieces [indicate Y] *would I need the same amount of paint, or a different amount, to paint all of those pieces* [indicate Z] *?'*

If S answers *'the same'*,

'Why do you say that?'

If S answers *'different'*,

'Which would need more paint?'

'Why do you say that?'

Item 10: 1 wooden cylinder; 2 similar cylinders which have their surfaces covered by plastic material

Give S the wooden cylinder.

'How many surfaces has this shape? Show me as you count.'

10a Remove the wooden cylinder. Place the two plastic covered cylinders in front of S.

A   B

'Does this curved surface [indicate the coloured surface of A as shown] *have the same amount of surface as that* [indicate the coloured plastic of B] *or does it have a different amount of surface?'*
If S answers *'different'*, end item. Otherwise proceed.

10b Peel off the plastic material which has a vertical join (A) and place the oblong piece of plastic on the table.
   'Does this oblong have the same amount of surface as that curved surface [indicate the coloured plastic of B] *or does it have a different amount of surface?'*
If S answers *'the same'*,
   'Why do you say that?'
If S answers *'different'*,
   'Which has more surface?'
   'Why do you say that?'

10c Peel off the plastic material from the second cylinder (B) and place it next to the oblong on the table.

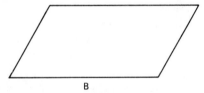

A   B

   'Does the oblong have the same amount of surface as this shape [indicate B] *or does it have a different amount of surface?'*
If S answers *'the same'*,
   'Why do you say that?'
If S answers *'different'*,
   'Which has more surface?'
   'Why do you say that?'

Item 10 (alternative)

Give S the wooden cylinder.
   'How many surfaces has this shape? Show me as you count.'
10a Remove the wooden cylinder. Place the two plastic covered cylinders in front of S.

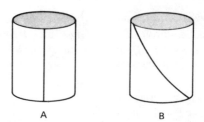

'*If I were to paint this curved surface* [indicate coloured surface of A] *would I need the same amount of paint, or a different amount, to paint that curved surface* [indicate coloured surface of B]*?*'
If S answers '*different*', end item. Otherwise proceed.

10b Peel off the plastic material which has a vertical join (A) and place the oblong piece of plastic on the table.
'*If I were to paint this oblong would I need the same amount of paint, or a different amount, to paint that curved surface* [indicate B]*?*'
If S answers '*the same*',
   '*Why do you say that?*'
If S answers '*different*',
   '*Which would need more paint?*'
   '*Why do you say that?*'

10c Peel off the plastic material from the second cylinder (B) and place it next to the oblong on the table.

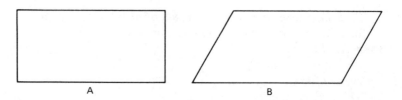

'*If I were to paint this oblong would I need the same amount of paint, or a different amount, to paint this shape* [indicate B]*?*'
If S answers '*the same*',
   '*Why do you say that?*'
If S answers '*different*',
   '*Which would need more paint?*'
   '*Why do you say that?*'

Results: item 6

In the first part the words 'amount of surface' are used; in order to arrive at the correct answer (that the areas of the two shapes are the same), the child has mentally or practically to change one shape so that it is identical to the other. In other words, the child has to realize that only by 'reversing' one shape, so that it is the same as the other, can he conclude with certainty that their areas are the same. The shapes are designed so that when they are first seen by the child one of them has a much larger dimension than the other, i.e. a perceptual feature is deliberately accentuated.

Table 26 Results for area item 6a (average ability)

Answer	7y 5m	7y 11m	8y 5m	8y 11m	9y 5m	9y 11m
	%	%	%	%	%	%
Correct	24	21	36	47	65	53
Compensatory reason	3	3	6	1	1	2
Incorrect: centring	49	38	38	29	23	27
Incorrect: other	24	38	20	22	11	16
Sample size (= 100%)	75	72	79	78	79	76

The results (Table 26) show that many children at all ages in the sample concluded that one shape was greater in area than the other although they were free to handle the shapes. Of the wrong answers, many did indeed focus their attention on the greatest dimension and gave answers of the type 'This one has the most surface because it is longer'. It should be noted, however, that other reasons for the wrong answers were also given; these were often highly individual and imaginative and did not fall into any of the Piagetian categories. It would seem that there are three possible reasons for all these wrong conclusions.

1. The child understood the meaning of the words 'amount of surface', was able to manipulate the shapes but, because he had a poor concept of area, still believed that one shape had a greater area than the other.
2. The child gave the wrong answer not necessarily because of a poor concept of area as such but because he did not understand that the words 'amount of surface' were used by the questioner to indicate the concept of area.
3. The wrong answer was given because the child could not manipulate the shapes and fell back on any reason in order to give an answer. In this

case one of the triangles had to be turned the other side up in order to make the other shape; this was obviously not realized by many of the children. (NB the triangular shape has been changed into a rectangular shape in *AWV*, test 5.)

In an attempt to explore this further, the item was in effect repeated but the more realistic or concrete 'amount of grass' was used instead of the more abstract 'amount of surface' and the shapes were simplified (as rectangles instead of triangles) so that the manipulative skill required was minimal.

Table 27   Results for area item 6b (average ability)

Answer	7y 5m	7y 11m	8y 5m	8y 11m	9y 5m	9y 11m
	%	%	%	%	%	%
Correct	65	67	84	94	86	89
Compensatory reason	1	6	5	1	8	2
Incorrect: centring	21	21	8	4	4	7
Incorrect: other	12	7	3	1	2	2
Sample size (= 100%)	75	72	79	78	79	76

On the whole there was improvement in performance at all ages (Table 27). Correct reasons were now given by the majority of the children. Even so, 33% of the 7½ year-olds and 28% of the 8 year-olds still arrived at the wrong answer and many of these did focus their attention on the visual aspect of the problem as Piaget describes.

In both parts of the test the children had to work out the possible reasons for the similarity of the areas, i.e. the tester did not first present equal areas of similar shapes and then alter the shape of one of them in a typical Piagetian fashion and in the light of the varying results obtained this was an obvious follow up item to present to the children.

Results: item 7

Here, for the first time, the questioner displays and obtains agreement that two shapes have similar areas (again using, in turn, an abstract phrase and a realistic phrase) and then changes one of the shapes by rearranging it so that one linear dimension dominates. The child no longer handles the material but has, in effect, to choose between two possible arguments before giving an answer. One argument depends on the logic of reversibility and conservation of area is concluded, whilst the other depends on immediate observation of an increased dimension together with the conclusion that this change has also increased the area of one of the shapes.

In the first part of the item the phrase 'same amount of surface' is used. The results (Table 28) fall neatly between those of the two parts of the

Table 28   Results for area item 7a (average ability)

Answer	7y 5m	7y 11m	8y 5m	8y 11m	9y 5m	9y 11m
	%	%	%	%	%	%
Correct	53	49	75	78	81	87
Compensatory reason	0	1	0	0	1	0
Incorrect: centring	37	40	16	19	14	10
Incorrect: other	10	11	9	3	5	3
Sample size (= 100%)	75	72	79	78	79	76

previous item. This can be interpreted in one of two ways.

1. A degree of learning has taken place; more children begin to use logical arguments rather than arguments based on immediate observation, and more children begin to realize that 'amount of surface' indicates area.
2. Because the necessary manipulative skill has been eliminated, one could expect the test to be easier to understand than its counterpart using the abstract phrase in the previous item.

It was obviously of interest to witness the responses of the children to this same test using the realistic term 'amount of paint needed to paint the shape' instead of the abstract phrase 'amount of surface'.

Table 29   Results for area item 7b (average ability)

Answer	7y 5m	7y 11m	8y 5m	8y 11m	9y 5m	9y 11m
	%	%	%	%	%	%
Correct	60	54	70	81	87	91
Compensatory reason	5	6	3	1	1	1
Incorrect: centring	29	31	15	13	10	3
Incorrect: other	6	9	12	5	2	5
Sample size (= 100%)	75	72	79	78	79	76

The correct results (Table 29) are again consistently higher than in the abstract (7a) version but are slightly less than the corresponding realistic version of item 6b. It could be that the use of a different shape, i.e. a triangle, together with increased focusing of attention on change of a linear dimension, encouraged some children to rely on perception rather than on concreto-logical arguments in order to arrive at their answers.

Obviously, slight changes in the presentation of the materials can have marked effects on the responses of the children. Although this point has been referred to by other researchers (see earlier discussion on this general issue, p. 44), the present results accentuate these differences and clearly show that, although some children consistently give the same reasons for their answers, many do change their reasons and argue in a reversible or concreto-logical fashion in some situations and on the basis of what they see in other situations. In the present examples, the differences in the test situation probably causing the lack of consistent responses were:

1. the degree to which realistic terms versus abstract terms were used;
2. the degree to which the children themselves had to manipulate the materials;
3. the degree to which the conflicting perceptual feature dominated the situation;
4. the nature of the shapes: it could well be that children believe that the area properties of squares or rectangles are different from the area properties of triangles, i.e. that area is conserved with change of shape in one case but not in the other.

In the present study it is clearly impossible to determine the reasons for the varying results, but it can be stated with some confidence that, whilst children in general obviously do demonstrate the Piagetian stages of thinking within this age range, a considerable proportion of children of average ability use different arguments according to the nature of the presented task. These children are capable of concreto-logical thought but on occasion prefer to rely on apparently important observations. This enables them to conclude that two areas *could* be the same because 'nothing has been removed', but they also *see* that a dimension has been increased and it is this second argument which dominates, so they answer accordingly.

Results: item 8

To probe this possibility further the children were given two shapes — a right-angled triangle and a square — so designed that their areas were equal but the height of the triangle was double the length of the side of the square, i.e. by

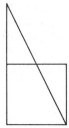

placing the triangle over the square it was fairly easy to determine that both had the same area but the dimension of one side of the triangle was perceptually much greater than the length of the side of the square. We wondered whether the children would rely heavily on perception or whether they would attempt comparisons by matching, fitting over, etc., i.e. whether the children would be capable of examining all possible ways of comparing the two areas. Although this test is more open-ended than the previous ones and therefore likely to be more difficult, nevertheless one would have expected the majority of the children who had used concreto-logical arguments in the previous examples to do so again.

Table 30   Results for area item 8 (average ability)

Answer	7y 5m	7y 11m	8y 5m	8y 11m	9y 5m	9y 11m
	%	%	%	%	%	%
Correct	9	8	18	21	30	26
Compensatory reason	4	6	1	3	3	2
Incorrect: centring	71	76	75	68	66	64
Incorrect: other	16	10	6	8	1	8
Sample size (= 100%)	75	72	79	78	79	76

There is a dramatic increase in the number of answers depending on the immediately observable (Table 30). Although, as in all previous results, there was an overall improvement with age, the majority of the children now relied on perception. Although many of these had clearly demonstrated that they were capable of using a logical argument, they did not choose to use such thinking to solve this problem.

In an attempt to eliminate the problem of understanding the question it was decided that in the following tests all children who had *continuously* answered correctly using the abstract 'amount of surface' (Table 31) should

Table 31   Proportions of children in samples tested with abstract and realistic
form of questions in later area items (average ability)

Answer	7y 5m	7y 11m	8y 5m	8y 11m	9y 5m	9y 11m
	%	%	%	%	%	%
Children giving consistently correct answers in items 1−7 using 'amount of surface'	17	11	33	35	53	45
Remaining children (given questions in 'realistic' terms for subsequent items)	83	89	67	65	47	55
Sample size (= 100%)	75	72	79	78	79	76

continue to receive this form of questioning, whereas children who had earlier
answered incorrectly in one or more of the tests using this abstract form
should have identical tests with the questions expressed in more realistic
terms. In this way it was hoped that the results would not reflect communication skills to such an extent as the earlier items and would give a fairer indication of conceptual ability.

Results: item 9

It has been mentioned earlier that it seems easier for children to grasp the idea
of conservation if the change of shape is of a discontinuous rather than a
continuous type, i.e. when the shape is broken up into separated bits rather
than changed into a continuous elongated form. It appears that breaking an
object into separated pieces encourages the children mentally to reassemble
the parts and, in effect, reverse their thoughts, whereas the continuous elongated
form accentuates the perceptual feature of elongated dimension and encourages
children to arrive at conclusions about conservation of area which are based
on appearances alone.

In item 9a one of the shapes is changed into a continuous elongated form
whereas in 9b an identical shape is broken up into five triangles of similar area.

Table 32   Results for area item 9a: continuous elongated form (average ability)

Answer	7y 5m	7y 11m	8y 5m	8y 11m	9y 5m	9y 11m
	%	%	%	%	%	%
Correct	61	67	82	87	92	92
Compensatory reason	3	3	1	0	0	4
Incorrect: centring	32	22	13	9	5	3
Incorrect: other	4	9	4	4	3	1
Sample size (= 100%)	75	72	79	78	79	76

The results for 9a (Table 32) are in close agreement with those of 5b and also generally agree with the results of item 7b. It appears that the results of these three items taken together show the average performance of our children and may be taken to represent the sort of results that might be expected if children of average ability were given a single typical Piagetian test on the conservation of area. In other words, this is the general pattern of conceptual ability indicated by other researchers who have replicated one or two of the Piagetian tests on the conservation of area. There seems to be a transition stage between 8 and $8\frac{1}{2}$ years of age. When the shape is broken up into separate pieces in 9b (Table 33) the number of correct responses, especially

Table 33   Results for area item 9b: discontinuous pieces (average ability)

Answer	7y 5m	7y 11m	8y 5m	8y 11m	9y 5m	9y 11m
	%	%	%	%	%	%
Correct	73	68	91	91	96	93
Compensatory reason	1	0	0	0	1	1
Incorrect: centring	16	18	7	4	2	0
Incorrect: other	9	14	12	5	1	6
Sample size (= 100%)	75	72	79	78	79	76

at the younger ages, increases and fewer children are deceived by appearances.

As a final step, we wondered what would happen if the continuous arrow form of the shape in 9a was also broken up and the area of all the pieces compared with the separated pieces of the shape in item 9b (the two total areas were the same and this had originally been observed and agreed by the children when the pieces had been made up into identical shapes). This time, however, the elongated arrow shape was broken up into 6 pieces (1 triangle and 5 rectangles) whereas the original separate bits were made up of 5 congruent triangles. We wondered whether some of the children who had earlier given correct reasons would now change their minds and conclude that one total area would be greater than the other because it contained a greater number of pieces or because the total length of pieces were greater in one case than the other (i.e. because of a dominating visual aspect).

Table 34   Results for area item 9c (average ability)

Answer	7y 5m	7y 11m	8y 5m	8y 11m	9y 5m	9y 11m
	%	%	%	%	%	%
Correct	61	60	89	83	96	96
Compensatory reason	0	0	0	0	0	0
Incorrect: centring	31	22	5	6	4	1
Incorrect: other	8	18	6	11	0	3
Sample size (= 100%)	75	72	79	78	79	76

This was indeed found to be the case in the two lowest age groups (Table 34); the number of children relying on perceptual aspects of the situation returned to the figures for the first part of the item. Again there appears the transition stage between 8 and $8\frac{1}{2}$ years of age.

In the study of conservation of area, so far, all the surfaces used have been in one plane (i.e. flat surfaces) and as a final study we examined the children's responses to conservation of area when areas of a curved surface were examined.

Results: item 10

As a first step children were given a wooden cylinder and asked 'How many surfaces has this shape? Show me as you count.' A high proportion of the children did not regard the curved surface of the cylinder as a surface (Table 35); it appeared that, owing to their limited experience of three-dimensional objects, the word 'surface' was not associated with such curved surfaces.

Two identical cylinders with their surfaces exactly covered by a plastic material were then given to the children, and agreement was reached that both plastic materials covered the same amount of surface. The plastic material with

Table 35   Results for area item 10a (average ability)

Answer	7y 5m	7y 11m	8y 5m	8y 11m	9y 5m	9y 11m
	%	%	%	%	%	%
Counted all 3 surfaces	40	34	47	46	57	60
Did not count curved surface	34	42	40	42	37	33
Incorrect: other	26	24	13	14	6	7
Sample size (= 100%)	75	72	79	78	79	76

a vertical join was then peeled off and compared with the plastic material still on the curved surface of the second cylinder. We wondered whether the spreading out of the material would cause children to focus their attention on this apparent increase in dimension and conclude that the area was no longer conserved.

The correct answers, in the main, match those of items 6b and 7b whilst incorrect answers based on perceptual features are lower than in previous items (Table 36). An obvious step was to stress the visual aspect by peeling off the

Table 36   Results for area item 10b (average ability)

Answer	7y 5m	7y 11m	8y 5m	8y 11m	9y 5m	9y 11m
	%	%	%	%	%	%
Correct	65	53	82	85	89	87
Incorrect: centring	13	15	8	3	5	4
Incorrect: other	21	32	10	11	6	9
Sample size (= 100%)	75	72	79	78	79	76

plastic material covering the second cylinder, which had a diagonal join, and placing this parallelogram-shaped plastic alongside the oblong-shaped plastic from the first cylinder. The children were now in a situation likely to produce conflict in their minds. They could either remember that originally the material covered the surfaces of two identical cylinders and conserve area using the concreto-logical argument of reversibility or that nothing had been added or removed, or else they could judge by appearances alone that the area of one shape was equal to or greater than the other.

Once more there is a significant drop in the number of correct responses whilst incorrect answers based on reasons due to appearances increase (Table 37). As children were asked the question in realistic terms, problems concerning

Table 37   Results for area item 10c (average ability)

Answer	7y 5m	7y 11m	8y 5m	8y 11m	9y 5m	9y 11m
	%	%	%	%	%	%
Correct	47	36	68	58	75	82
Compensatory reason	8	11	4	13	6	7
Incorrect: centring	35	28	18	15	10	7
Incorrect: other	11	25	10	14	9	4
Sample size (= 100%)	75	72	79	78	79	76

understanding of the question do not explain these changes of opinion. One can only conclude that there are many children in this age range who use Piagetian concreto-logical arguments in one practical situation but decide to use arguments based on appearances alone in other situations, *even though they are shown all the observations necessary in order to use the logical argument.*

Summary of test results: conservation of area

1. The general pattern of sequential stages of mental operation as described by Piaget is confirmed in our sample. Conclusions based on the immediately observable dominate the younger child's thinking whereas the older children begin to think more in terms of logical operations. In the concept of area there seems to be a critical stage between the ages of 8 and 8½ but this evidence does not allow a definitive statement on the relationship between stages and ages to be stated.
2. At least 25% of children aged 7½ years demonstrate that they can and consistently do use concreto-logical forms of reasoning, whereas many of the 10 year-olds easily resort to conclusions based on simple perception when the presented situation has dominant perceptual features.
3. The results fluctuate considerably, especially at the lower ages, from test item to item. Although attempts were made to control some of the variables likely to affect the children's responses, probably the most important conclusion emerging from these studies is that a very high proportion of the children of average ability in our sample used alterna-

tive forms of thinking depending on how they perceived the problem. This flitting from one form of reasoning to another emerges strongly in our results (particularly between items 7 and 8). Because of this it is extremely unlikely that any *individual child* will fall neatly into one stage or another in all situations.

It appears that Piaget's process of equilibration is mental perpetual motion and the resulting zigzag development of the child's thinking powers presents the research worker with a situation similar to the atomic physicists' Uncertainty Principle. As soon as the researcher attempts to measure the stage of development reached by a child by using any communication and practical technique he causes the child to grapple with the problem and, in effect, encourages the equilibration process. The children already realize that the world is full of unexpected happenings that are not easily explained, and the lack of consistency in their reasoning does not indicate an absolute measure of poor conceptual development. On the contrary, our results shows that the children tackle every problem, however similar to another it may at first appear, on its own merits and reason out answers for that situation alone; they reflect an approach to learning far removed from those suggested by stimulus-response theories.

4. The importance of communication skill is highlighted in these results. More children give correct responses when the situations are presented less abstractly using more realistic terms. Nevertheless, even in these latter presentations non-conservation and reasons based on perception are common in our children.

5. Piaget has pointed out that compensatory reasons may be taken as evidence of conceptual development. We have already pointed out that reasons of this type, e.g. 'The oblong and triangle have the same amount of surface as the oblong is fatter but the triangle is longer', merely show that the children are grappling with area in terms of two dimensions. They cannot possibly conclude that the areas are indeed similar by such comparisons. In all our tests very few children, in fact, used this form of reasoning, and one doubts whether it is a necessary or important stage in the development of two- and three-dimensional concepts. Pupils seemed to see surfaces as whole planes rather than arising from combinations of linear dimensions. We shall return to this point when we consider the problem of measurement of area.

For the research worker these interpretations seem to support the recent debates on Piagetian research techniques referred to earlier. As soon as one attempts to standardize and purify the research design, then the resulting rigid structure limits the view of the child's thinking powers that may be obtained. Adopting the clinical open-ended approach, on the other hand, introduces the variables of communication ability and different ways of presenting the practical situations. Used in considerable depth, the latter method undoubtedly allows the research worker to explore the limits of *individual* children's thinking powers in any particular situation, but the collection and analysis of data by this method is such a time-consuming and complicated process that it is unlikely to be improved upon further as a method of assessing the conceptual abilities of large groups of children. It would seem that, in order to provide a finer mesh for our measuring instruments, it is necessary to examine further than hitherto:

1. the analysis of the form of communication used in the testing;
2. the design of the practical problems in a sequential form;
3. the need for standardization of procedure, the limitations of which could be compensated for by having a number of practical test situations;
4. the problem of sample size.

All our testing was carried out on a one-to-one basis; the development of satisfactory group tests in this field has hardly been started. As a diagnostic tool, such a development would be welcomed by teachers and research workers.

Our interpretations have many implications for the teacher in the classroom. The place of communication and consistent use of terminology alongside the development of oral skills in general seems to be of paramount importance for concept development. Children need a number of *allied practical* experiences if they are to form sound, generally applicable concepts. Practical experiences of limited examples may allow the children to obtain right answers in these cases, but such experiences are no guarantee that the children can apply the same form of reasoning to other situations involving the same general principles. Structuring of teaching and learning materials seems to be of great importance and, to do this effectively, it is clear that teachers need to observe and communicate with their charges carefully before, during and after each practical activity. It was because of these convictions, together with an awareness of the problems facing the teacher in everyday work, that we felt obliged to write a separate teachers' guide.

MEASUREMENT OF AREA

Piaget maintains that it is after understanding conservation of area that children develop the ability to measure area using appropriate units in practical, concrete form, and the final stage of this development is the realization that areas can be calculated by the multiplication of linear dimensions.

As a number of the children in the present sample had expressed the opinion in earlier items that the reorientation or change of shape of an area altered its area, it was of interest to speculate how the children would cope when they used area units to cover surfaces in order to determine their areas. Piaget's work has also demonstrated that children do not at first realize the need for all the units of measurement to be identical in area; it is only at a higher level of understanding that they understand the notion of a unit, and take the area of the measuring elements into account. It was reasonable to suppose that, as the concept of area measurement is a common topic of study in the modern primary school classroom, this general pattern of concept development would be modified in our sample. As the children came from a wide variety of schools, no particular method of teaching was studied; indeed, it was reasonable to suppose that our sample represented experiences of varied learning situations and could be said to represent a fair overall picture of average children's conceptual ability in the age range and schools involved.

Assessment items 11–13 correspond to *AWV*, Tests 9, 13 and 14 for area.

Item 11: red   **shape and 12 white unit squares**

[NB 10 units cover red shape.]

Place the red shape and the unit squares on the table in front of S. S is allowed to handle the shapes.
> *'Find out how many white squares have the same amount of surface as the red shape.'*

Item 11 (alternative)

Place the red shape and the unit squares on the table in front of S. S is allowed to handle the shapes.
> *'Imagine that I am going to paint the red shape.*
> *Find out how many white squares I would have to paint to use up the same amount of paint.'*

Item 12: 2 yellow irregular shapes of equal area; 2 plastic grids

Place the two shapes on the table in front of S. Pick up a plastic grid.
> *'Have you used one of these before?'*

If S answers '*no*',
> '*It is made of clear plastic and marked off into squares.*'

Place the grids over the shapes aligning them correctly so that their areas can be calculated.

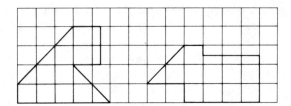

> '*I want you to find out which of these shapes has more surface.*'

If S begins to count squares,
> '*Show me as you count, and count aloud.*'

After S has completed the operation,
> '*What have you found out?*'

Item 12 (alternative)

> '*If I were to paint these shapes, find out which one would need more paint.*'

If S begins to count squares,
> '*Show me as you count, and count aloud.*'

After S has completed the operation,
> '*What have you found out?*'

Item 13: 1 white square X; 1 white rectangle Y; ruler

[NB Area of square = 9 cm^2, of rectangle = 8 cm^2.]

Place the two shapes next to each other on the table.
Give the ruler to S.
> '*Use the ruler to find out which shape has more surface.*

After S has finished measuring,
> '*Which shape has more surface?*'
> '*How did you work that out?*'

Item 13 (alternative)

Place the two shapes next to each other on the table.
Give the ruler to S.
> *'If I were to paint these shapes, use the ruler to find out which one
> would need more paint.'*

After S has finished measuring,
> *'Which shape would need more paint?'*
> *'How did you work that out?'*

Results: item 11

This item simply tests children's ability to use the squares as units of area.
Although the majority of the children carried out this task successfully (Table
38) it is interesting to note that, of those who were unable to carry out the

Table 38   Results for area item 11 (average ability)

Answer	7y 5m	7y 11m	8y 5m	8y 11m	9y 5m	9y 11m
	%	%	%	%	%	%
Correct: placed 10 units over red shape or built identical shape next to red shape	73	76	78	88	90	91
Incorrect: placed units round outside of red shape	11	13	8	5	4	6
Incorrect: other	16	11	14	7	6	3
Sample size (= 100%)	75	72	79	78	79	76

task, a considerable proportion used the units but interpreted the question in
such a fashion that they placed the units round the perimeter of the shape to
be measured, whilst others, possibly with the notion that area must be a
square (associated perhaps with the words 'square centimetres'), answered the
problem by using the units to complete the shape as a square and then counted
the units to do this.

Results: item 12

Children were asked to compare the areas of two irregular shapes after identical grids had been placed over them by the questioner. It was not possible for the children to estimate which had the greater area and they could only arrive at an answer by measuring and counting. The shapes had been so arranged that, to arrive at a correct answer, the children had to display an understanding of half units and realize that similar area units could have different shapes.

This was obviously a more difficult task than the earlier items. Up to the age of nine or even ten relatively few children of average ability were able to carry out this task satisfactorily (Table 39). Of those incorrect, the younger

Table 39   Results for area item 12 (average ability)

Answer	7y 5m	7y 11m	8y 5m	8y 11m	9y 5m	9y 11m
	%	%	%	%	%	%
Correct: counted whole and $\frac{1}{2}$ squares correctly	9	3	25	31	60	49
Incorrect: careless counting	4	11	19	19	22	21
Incorrect: ignored $\frac{1}{2}$ squares or counted them as whole squares	32	32	25	23	11	21
Incorrect: other	54	54	31	27	7	9
Sample size (= 100%)	75	72	79	78	79	76

pupils failed to realize the significance of half-units and merely counted all the shapes as individual units. The older children, on the other hand, took into account the half-units but many failed because they were unable to work out a rational method of counting the units; they often missed out a line of square units or counted some units more than once. A significant point emerged in that all the children counted something and eventually arrived at number answers. There was a strong inclination to have faith in a *number* answer, and the main objective of the children seemed to be simply counting something or other. In other words, for these children the concept of area as such did not appear to be the main feature of the problem.

As the number of correct results for this test is surprisingly low considering the type of work now carried out on the topic of area in primary schools, it is of interest to compare these results with those for the next item, testing for the measurement of a simple rectangular area using a ruler.

Results: item 13

The results were somewhat startling. Very few children could carry out this task successfully. Two significant points emerged from the observations. First, the younger children simply used the ruler to obtain a linear measurement of one side of the rectangles only; having obtained two number answers, they then answered the question relating to the two areas using these figures. Once more it seemed that, as long as a number answer was obtainable, then the children were satisfied that they had arrived at a rational conclusion. It can be seen that answers of this type steadily decrease as the pupils get older but the figure is still high for these children of average ability at ten years of age.

Table 40   Results for area item 13 (average ability)

Answer	7y 5m	7y 11m	8y 5m	8y 11m	9y 5m	9y 11m
	%	%	%	%	%	%
Correct	1	1	6	6	15	14
Incorrect: measured length x breadth but miscalculated	1	1	1	4	4	1
Incorrect: measured perimeter	7	14	19	24	30	25
Incorrect: *added* length + breadth	1	4	9	3	11	8
Incorrect: measured 1 side of shapes only	55	49	38	37	13	18
Incorrect: used ruler as unit square measure	9	2	11	4	9	12
Incorrect: other	26	29	16	22	18	22
Sample size (= 100%)	75	72	79	78	79	76

Secondly, and progressively with age, pupils realized that measurement of area using a ruler is related to both the length and breadth but they did not realize the significance of multiplication. These children simply measured the perimeter or added the length and breadth of the rectangles, i.e. summation of length and breadth was the significant misconception. Answers of this type increased with the age of the pupils. It seemed as if they were familiar with a *technique* of measurement of area using a ruler but, because they had not formed a sound concept of this principle of measurement, they resorted to memory rather than understanding in order to arrive at a solution.

Summary of test results: simple measurement of area

It was surprising to record that Piaget's levels of achievement were borne out strongly in our sample, as classroom experience was expected to have distorted the Piagetian pattern. For teachers it would seem to indicate the need for very carefuly study of classroom practices concerning the measurement of area. Area work using cutout shapes is now so common in primary schools that one is bound to ask whether the children, who are certainly highly motivated by this type of work, merely follow workcard instructions and arrive at number answers without ever being challenged to think about the concept of measurement of area. Once more the results strongly suggest the need for sequential learning and certainly indicate that, throughout work of this type, the teacher should frequently play the role of questioner and observer.

Children obviously need to have a good concept of conservation of area before they can begin to understand the concept of measurement of area; at the other end of the learning sequence, they need to have a wide experience of measurement of areas using practical units of various dimensions before they tackle measurement of areas using a ruler and cutouts, and well before they tackle more abstract *number* problems concerning area. (See *Area, Weight, and Volume* for a further consideration of this aspect of the concept.)

FURTHER MEASUREMENT OF AREA AND THE USE OF SIMPLE LOGIC

If children understood the basic principles of measurement of areas using simple practical units, we wondered to what extent they could apply this technique in working out simple problems. In other words, the simple use of logic was added to the problem of practical measurement, and it was hypothesized that, if the Piagetian theory of sequential development of concepts was correct, such tasks would prove more difficult than the earlier test items.

First of all it was decided that the 'meadows and potato plots' experiment used by Piaget to study conservation of areas and of complementary areas required a more complex form of logic for its solution than had been used in the earlier items concerned with conservation and was a natural preliminary study for this section of the research. The following three items encouraged the children to use practical units in order to solve specific problems comparing two areas but, in order to arrive at a solution, they had to digest and think about the raw data and relate the separate pieces of information in their minds.

Assessment items 14–17 correspond to *AWV*, Tests 16–19 for area.

Item 14: 2 oblongs, each consisting of 2 shapes

Assemble the oblongs on the table in front of S.

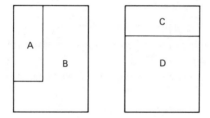

'*Has this oblong* [indicate] *the same amount of surface as that oblong, or does it have a different amount of surface?*'
If S answers '*different*', match the oblongs by placing A and B over C and D and repeat the question. Replace shapes as above. Otherwise proceed.
'*Watch carefully.*'
Place oblongs A and C close to each other on the table in front of S.

'*Does this oblong* [indicate A] *have the same amount of surface as that oblong* [indicate C] *or does it have a different amount of surface?*'
If S answers '*different*', place A over C and repeat the question. Replace A and C as above. Otherwise proceed.

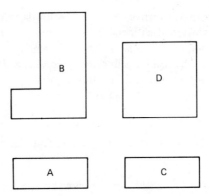

'*Does this shape* [indicate B] *have the same amount of surface as that*
shape [indicate D] *or does it have a different amount of surface?*'
If S answers '*the same*',
     '*Why do you say that?*'
If S answers '*the same because one is longer but the other is fatter*' or similar
compensatory reason,
     '*Is there any other reason why they have the same amount of surface?*'
If S answers '*different*',
     '*Which has more surface?*'
     '*Why do you say that?*'

Item 14 (alternative)

Assemble the oblongs on the table in front of S.

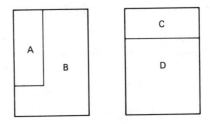

'*If I were to paint this oblong* [indicate] *would I need the same amount*
of paint, or a different amount, to paint that oblong?'
If S answers '*different*', match the oblongs by placing A and B over C and D

and repeat the question. Replace shapes as above. Otherwise proceed.

'Watch carefully.'

Place oblongs A and C close to each other on the table in front of S.

'If I were to paint this oblong [indicate A] *would I need the same amount of paint, or a different amount, to paint that oblong* [indicate C] *?'*

If S answers *'different'*, place A over C and repeat the question. Replace A and C as above. Otherwise proceed.

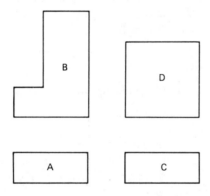

'If I were to paint this shape [indicate B] *would I need the same amount of paint, or a different amount, to paint that shape* [indicate D] *?'*

If S answers *'the same'*,

'Why do you say that?'

If S answers *'the same because one is longer but the other is fatter'* or similar compensatory reason,

'Is there any other reason why they would need the same amount of paint?'

If S answers *'different'*,

'Which would need more paint?'

'Why do you say that?'

Item 15: 1 red square; 6 smaller white squares; 6 small blue squares

[NB 1 red = 4 white = 4 x 4 blue.]

Place the red square and the six white squares on the table in front of S. S is allowed to handle the shapes.

> *'Find out how many white squares would be needed to cover the same amount of surface as the red one.'*

Remove *five* white squares. Place six blue squares on the table by the remaining red and white squares.

> *'How many blue squares would be needed to cover the same amount of surface as the white one?'*

Remove *five* blue squares, leaving one red, one white and one blue square on the table in front of S.

> *'Now, without touching any of the squares, how many blue squares would be needed to cover the same amount of surface as the red one?'*

If S states a number of squares,

> *'How did you work that out?'*

Item 16: 1 yellow square; 1 blue oblong; grey unit shapes

[NB Square = 18 units, oblong = 6.]

Place the materials on the table in front of S.

> *'Use these* [indicate units] *to find out how many blue oblongs have the same amount of surface as the yellow square. You must not put the blue oblong on the square.'*

If necessary repeat the question.

When S has finished experimenting,

> *'How many blue oblongs have the same amount of surface as the yellow square?'*
> *'How did you work that out?'*

Item 16 (alternative)

Place the materials on the table in front of S.

> *'Imagine that I am going to paint the yellow square. Use these* [indicate units] *to find out how many blue oblongs would use the same amount of paint. You must not put the blue oblong on the square.'*

If necessary repeat the question.

When S has finished experimenting,
> 'How many blue oblongs would use up the same amount of paint as
> the yellow square?'
> 'How did you work that out?'

Item 17: 8 yellow triangles

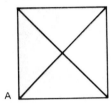 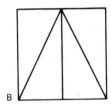

Assemble the triangles to form two squares A and B.
> 'Does this square [indicate A] have the same amount of surface as that
> square [indicate B] or does it have a different amount of surface?'

If S answers 'different', demonstrate equality of area by fitting A over B.
Repeat the question. Otherwise proceed.

Dismantle A as above.
> 'Have these four shapes the same amount of surface as each other, or do
> they have different amounts of surface?'

If S answers 'different', fit the triangles over each other and repeat the
question. Otherwise proceed.

Remove three triangles from square A to one side.
Dismantle square B.

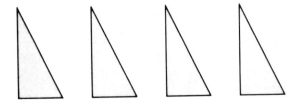

'Have these four shapes the same amount of surface as each other, or do they have different amounts of surface?'
If S answers *'different'*, fit the triangles over each other and repeat the question. Otherwise proceed.

Remove three triangles from square B to one side. Place the remaining triangles close to each other in front of S.

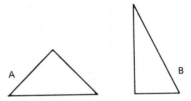

'Does this shape [indicate triangle from square A] *have the same amount of surface as that shape* [indicate triangle from square B] *or does it have a different amount of surface?'*
If S answers *'the same'*,
    'Why do you say that?'
If S answers *'the same because one is longer but the other is fatter'* or similar compensatory reason,
    'Is there any other reason why they have the same amount of surface as each other?'
If S answers *'different'*,
    'Which shape has more surface?'
    'Why do you say that?'

Item 17 (alternative)

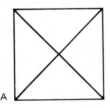 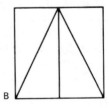

Assemble the triangles to form two squares A and B.
    'If I were to paint this square [indicate A] *would I need the same amount of paint, or a different amount, to paint that square* [indicate B] *?'*

If S answers '*different*', demonstrate equality of area by fitting A over B.
Repeat the question. Otherwise proceed.

Dismantle A as above.

> '*If I were to paint these four shapes would they each need the same
> amount of paint, or would they need different amounts of paint?*'

If S answers '*different*', fit the triangles over each other and repeat the
question. Otherwise proceed.

Remove three triangles from square A to one side.
Dismantle square B.

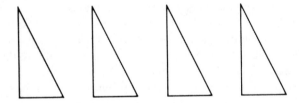

> '*If I were to paint these four shapes would they each need the same
> amount of paint, or would they need different amounts of paint?*'

If S answers '*different*', fit the triangles over each other and repeat the
question. Otherwise proceed.

Remove three triangles from square B to one side. Place the remaining triangles
close to each other in front of S.

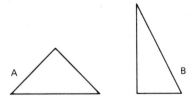

> '*If I were to paint this shape* [indicate triangle from square A] *would I
> need the same amount of paint, or a different amount, to paint that
> shape* [indicate triangle from square B] *?*'

If S answers *'the same'*,
>   *'Why do you say that?'*

If S answers *'the same because one is longer but the other is fatter'* or similar compensatory reason,
>   *'Is there any other reason they would need the same amount of paint as each other?'*

If S answers *'different'*,
>   *'Which shape would need more paint?'*
>   *'Why do you say that?'*

Results: item 14

In the first part the children see and agree that two rectangles have the same area $(A + B) = (C + D)$ and also that part A has the same area as part C. When the question is asked about the similarity or otherwise of areas B and D, the pupil has to choose between two possible arguments. The first is related to appearance alone, and the pupil may select area B as being greater than area D on the basis that 'B is longer than D' or, *vice versa,* because 'D is fatter than B'. The second argument disregards appearances and relies entirely on the logical idea that since area $A + B =$ area $C + D$ and also area $A =$ area C, then it must follow that area $B =$ area D. It should be noted that to minimize the memory factor all the pieces are displayed to the pupil when the final question is asked. Piaget maintains that this type of logical thought process, where two pieces of information based on direct observation can be linked in the mind to produce another piece of information, is only displayed by a person well advanced in conceptualization.

Table 41   Results for area item 14 (average ability)

Answer	7y 5m	7y 11m	8y 5m	8y 11m	9y 5m	9y 11m
	%	%	%	%	%	%
Correct reasoning	33	29	54	50	71	74
Incorrect: compensatory reason only	0	8	9	14	10	1
Incorrect: centring on a linear dimension	37	40	29	28	13	12
Incorrect: other	30	23	8	8	6	13
Sample size (= 100%)	75	72	79	78	79	76

The numbers of correct responses at all ages (Table 41) are indeed lower than those for straightforward tests on conservation with the exception of item 5a (the first of the conservation tests), and the numbers of children focusing their attention on linear dimensions increase to the level of item number 7a for the two lowest age groups and even higher for the $8\frac{1}{2}$ and 9 year-olds. It is clear that some children who originally conserved area in the straightforward examples have reverted to reasons based on perceptual features in this more complicated test. Furthermore, because logic has to be used in order to arrive at the right answer, other children do grapple with the problem in a logical fashion but through faulty reasoning they arrive at the wrong conclusions. Once more the results show that 33% of the $7\frac{1}{2}$ year-old children were capable of using logical reasoning correctly and, conversely, 26% of the 10 year-olds failed to do so. Age within this span provides little guidance on the likely performance of children of average ability in this sample.

Results: item 15

Again this item asks the pupil to link two pieces of information to give an answer based on deduction. It should be noted that this item does not rely on the rote learning of the 4 x 4 multiplication table for a correct answer; rather, it encourages the pupil to think in terms of 'each of four white areas being equal to four blue areas, therefore the total area must be equal to 4 + 4 + 4 + 4 blue areas'.

Table 42   Results for area item 15 (average ability)

Answer	7y 5m	7y 11m	8y 5m	8y 11m	9y 5m	9y 11m
	%	%	%	%	%	%
Correct	12	25	46	55	65	64
Correct reasoning but failed to work out that four 4s = 16	8	3	5	2	4	5
Incorrect	80	72	49	43	31	31
Sample size (= 100%)	75	72	79	78	79	76

The results are again lower than for previous items (Table 42). Many children made no attempt to link up the two pieces of information and tried to answer the question by imagining the direct operation of counting how many blue squares would cover the white squares. Nearly all the children were able to carry out the separate activities of measurement, but the greater majority were baffled when asked to use this information to answer the final question.

Results: item 16

This was added to confirm the general findings of the two previous items. Once more the units are used as intermediary devices for determining the relationship between the area of the blue oblong and the yellow square. The materials are so devised that it is not possible for the child to determine how many blue oblongs are equal in area to the yellow square by simple observation. He has first to find out the areas of the two shapes using the units and then relate these two pieces of information in his mind in order to find the answer.

Table 43   Results for area item 16 (average ability)

Answer	7y 5m	7y 11m	8y 5m	8y 11m	9y 5m	9y 11m
	%	%	%	%	%	%
Correct	16	13	35	35	59	57
Incorrect: placed units on both shapes but unable to form any conclusions	12	7	4	9	12	10
Incorrect: placed units on 1 shape only	27	24	22	22	14	8
Incorrect: other	45	56	39	34	15	25
Sample size (= 100%)	75	72	79	78	79	76

Once more the task proved too difficult for the majority of the children (Table 43). Although the logic required is very similar to the previous item, except that division is called for rather than successive addition or multiplication, it is generally a more difficult task. The essential difference between the two tests is that in item 16 the pupil has to work out the procedure to enable him to make the necessary measurements. In item 15 the questioner directed the pupil on the correct procedure and simply tested for the ability to measure and then to use these measurements in a logical fashion. In the present example a high proportion of the children failed to work out this procedure and only measured the area of one of the shapes using the units. As before, however, it is observed that 16% of the children of average ability at $7\frac{1}{2}$ years of age *were* able to work out the necessary procedures, carry out the measurements and also operate logically in their findings, whilst 43% of the 10 year-olds could not answer the problem.

Results: item 17

The concept of fractions embodies all the features of the previous three items. Fully to understand, say, the idea of three-quarters of a whole, the pupil has to assimilate and interrelate three pieces of information: (*a*) that the whole is cut up into four parts; (*b*) that each part is equal to the others in area; and (*c*) that there are three of these parts in the given fraction. Furthermore, the concept of reversibility must be firmly in the child's mind, as he must realize that the separate fractions are integral parts of the whole and that they can always be brought together to form the whole again. By comparison with the design of the previous three items it would be reasonable to expect the results of this test to equate fairly closely with them. The item is so designed that the child is ultimately placed in a conflict situation; he can choose between an argument based on a good concept of fractions and the use of logic, or he can arrive at an answer based on the visual comparison of the last two shapes presented to him. In order to accentuate this conflict, the linear dimension of one of the triangular shapes is deliberately accentuated.

Only a small proportion of the children were able to give adequate expression of accurate logic behind their choice of answers (Table 44). Those judged to be partially correct gave an answer of the type 'Both triangles have the same amount of surface as they come from squares which have been cut into four parts', and it was impossible to determine whether they realized the significance of four *equal* parts or whether they concluded that they had the same area because the number of parts was the same. A high proportion of the children resorted to answers based on perceptual features and did not use logic at all, e.g. 'Both triangles have the same amount of surface as one is longer but the other is wider' or 'One triangle has more surface as it is longer (wider, looks more)'. Other incorrect answers are also given by a significant proportion of the children. Once more it is seen that children who had earlier used concreto-logical reasons resort to answers based

Table 44   Results for area item 17 (average ability)

Answer	7y 5m	7y 11m	8y 5m	8y 11m	9y 5m	9y 11m
	%	%	%	%	%	%
Absolutely correct	12	4	19	22	34	45
Partially correct	5	4	13	13	19	22
Incorrect: centred on length	44	38	29	27	18	12
Incorrect: compensatory reason	13	22	13	14	14	11
Incorrect: other	26	32	26	24	15	10
Sample size (= 100%)	75	72	79	78	79	76

on appearances in this example, although reasons due to centring on such aspects do decrease with age. This task proved to be more difficult than any of the others involving logic.

Summary of test results: further measurement of area and the use of simple logic

1. All these items are harder to solve than earlier ones and there is strong agreement with Piaget's sequence of conceptual growth by stages.
2. Although the general pattern of performance suggested by Piaget is observed, a considerable proportion of children reverted to answers based on perception in these harder tasks although they had used concreto-logical reasons in earlier items.
3. In tests involving the use of logic it is often difficult to determine whether the child obtaining the right answer has really used the correct logical steps. The questioner relies on the child's communication ability to determine this and such communication ability may not match the child's mental dexterity.
4. A fair proportion of the $7\frac{1}{2}$ year-olds were able to think in concreto-logical fashion.

Most of the replicated research on these fundamental concepts is concerned with the question of conservation and comparatively few studies have been carried out on the ability of young children to think in concreto-logical fashion.

More data are required in this area of concept development, but in general our results confirm the order of appearance of this ability in children.

For the teacher this series of tests indicates the nature of the tasks that could be given to children who have reached this stage of conceptual development. Exercises developing both the concept in question and the ability to think in such logical terms are not normally introduced in such a deliberate fashion in the school classroom. It is for this reason that suggestions for such problems appear at the appropriate point in the companion teachers' guide.

ADDITIONAL ASSESSMENT ITEM: AREA AND PERIMETER

Assessment item 18 corresponds to *AWV*, Test 15 for area.

Item 18: red oblong; red parallelogram; red geoshape

Place the geoshape over the red oblong so that it fits exactly.
 'This shape [indicate geoshape] *fits exactly over the red oblong.'*

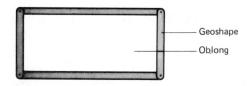

 'Watch carefully.'
Remove the geoshape from the oblong, elongate it and place it over the parallelogram so that it fits exactly.

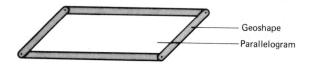

 'The shape [indicate geoshape] *fits over this red cardboard too.'*
Remove the geoshape to one side. Place the oblong and the parallelogram close to each other.

18a   *'Does this oblong have the same amount of surface as that shape*
          [indicate parallelogram] *or does it have a different amount of surface?'*
If S answers *'different'*,
          'Which has more surface?'
          'Why do you say that?'
If S answers *'the same'*,
          'Why do you say that?'
If S answers *'the same because one is longer but the other is fatter'* or similar
compensatory reason,
          'Is there any other reason why they have the same amount of surface?'
If S answers *'the same because they both measure the same round the outside'*,
end item. Otherwise proceed.

18b   *'Does the oblong measure the same round the outside as that shape*
          [indicate parallelogram] *or does it measure a different amount?'*
If S answers *'the same'*,
          'Why do you say that?'
If S answers *'the same because one is longer but the other is fatter'* or similar
compensatory reason,
          'Is there any other reason why they measure the same round the outside?'
If S answers *'different'*,
          'Which shape measures more round the outside?'
          'Why do you say that?'

Item 18 (alternative)

Place the geoshape over the red oblong so that it fits exactly.
          'This shape [indicate geoshape] *fits exactly over the red oblong.'*

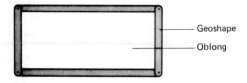

Geoshape

Oblong

'Watch carefully.'
Remove the geoshape from the oblong, elongate it and place it over the
parallelogram so that it fits exactly.

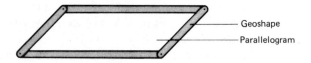

Geoshape
Parallelogram

'The shape [indicate geoshape] *fits over this red cardboard too.'*
Remove the geoshape to one side. Place the oblong and the parallelogram close
to each other.

18a   *'If I were to paint this oblong would I need the same amount of paint,
        or a different amount, to paint that shape* [indicate parallelogram] *?'*
If S answers *'different'*,
        'Which shape would need more paint?'
        'Why do you say that?'
If S answers *'the same'*,
        'Why do you say that?'
If S answers *'the same because one is longer but the other is fatter'* or similar
compensatory reason,
        *'Is there any other reason why they would need the same amount of
        paint as each other?'*
If S answers *'the same because they both measure the same round the outside'*,
end item. Otherwise proceed.

18b   *'Does the oblong measure the same round the outside as that shape*
        [indicate parallelogram] *or does it measure a different amount?'*
If S answers *'the same'*,
        'Why do you say that?'
If S answers *'the same because one is longer but the other is fatter'* or similar
compensatory reason,
        'Is there any other reason why they measure the same round the outside?'

If S answers *'different'*,
> *'Which shape measures more round the outside?'*
> *'Why do you say that?'*

As the child's concept of area develops, it seems clear that he always recognizes that, when a shape is broken up and all the pieces reassembled, the total area always remains the same although a single dimension may be greatly increased. This idea of conservation is considered to be an important step in the reasoning power of the pupil. Piaget stresses this factor and describes many practical situations to illustrate it. However, we cannot rely entirely on a general application of this argument. For example, a shape may be altered in such a fashion that, although its perimeter remains the same, its area is changed. An example of this is seen in the assessment procedure described in item 18.

It is held that reasons based on reversibility of thought are more advanced than reasons based on perception, and if the former type of reasoning is witnessed in typical Piagetian test situations, then the child using this argument is considered to be at a more advanced stage than a child who uses arguments based on perceptual features.

We have argued, so far, that such a sequence is an over-simplification of the conceptual process. From the results it is clear that arguments based on perception do dominate the younger child's thinking but the key to conceptual development seems to be more related to the ability of the child to select correctly between arguments based on appearances and those based on concreto-logical reasons. Earlier items clearly demonstrate that children in our age range do carry out this selection procedure, often incorrectly, and vary their reasons according to the test situation. The consistent use of one form of argument rather than the other does not give a firm indication of the stage of conceptualization reached by the child.

In the present example the child should use the perceptual features in order to arrive at the correct answer. If answers of the reversible type are used, e.g. 'The areas must be the same as we can change it back into its original shape' or answers of the type 'The areas must be the same because nothing has been added or removed', then the child will in fact be wrong.

This particular test item is an important one, as it could be argued that Piagetian test situations are always carefully selected so that conservation based on concreto-logical argument is the right answer. In reality, the idea of conservation cannot be applied generally. The hypothesis is therefore put forward that many of the older children will choose concreto-logical arguments in this test, i.e. they will rely on the wrong argument because they may tend to apply this in all situations involving area, believing area is always conserved. True conceptualization is only witnessed when the child has the ability to work out the correct form of reasoning to use in the given situation.

Results: item 18

Children did seem to focus their attention on conservation reasons progressively with age (Table 45); they appeared to disregard the possibly correct reason

Table 45   Results for area item 18 (average ability)

Answer	7y 5m	7y 11m	8y 5m	8y 11m	9y 5m	9y 11m
	%	%	%	%	%	%
Correct: oblong has greater area	23	22	16	19	14	9
Incorrect: parallelogram has greater area	15	10	4	1	2	0
Incorrect: both have same area	51	56	72	68	80	87
Incorrect: other	12	13	8	12	4	4
Sample size (= 100%)	75	72	79	78	79	76

based on appearances alone. Simply to relate conservation reasons to good conceptualization ability does not seem entirely warranted. It is the ability to decide between the two types of reasoning which is the key factor in conceptualization. On the other hand, it can be seen that a higher proportion of the younger children got the right answer because they used arguments based on appearances. Once more, however, it cannot be concluded in this test item, that these children had a better concept than their older colleagues. It is more probable that they could *only* use this form of argument; they had probably not developed the ability to think in a concreto-logical fashion and therefore the problem of selection of argument did not arise. This is particularly confirmed by the fact that an equal proportion of younger children selected the parallelogram as having the larger area because 'It is longer', i.e. the perceptual reasons vary according to which dimension the seven-year-old child happens to focus upon.

Summarizing, therefore, we conclude that:

1. Piagetian stages of development from perceptual reasoning to concreto-logical reasoning are generally confirmed.
2. The relationship between stages and ages of individual children is by no means clearcut.
3. In addition to this general pattern of thinking individual children, because

they are continually developing, often apply different forms of reasoning in different test situations. This prevents the research worker from ever witnessing pure, sequential stages in any one child.

4. When the child has matured sufficiently to be able to reason in a variety of ways, it is the ability to select the correct argument in a given situation that indicates true conceptualization.

7 The concept of volume

It has often been stated that the concept of volume is not developed by children until late in the primary school and the researches of Piaget and others are quoted to support this general theory. Such statements may have encouraged the idea of 'learning readiness' and, because few children have much practical experience of this concept in the classroom, the prophecy could be self-fulfilling in that lack of experience would result in the children developing this concept later than that of area or weight.

Everyday experience demonstrates that the properties and characteristics of volume are more varied than those of weight and area. Ideas about occupied, interior and displaced volume, together with the realization that different shapes can have similar volumes, do demand a greater degree of mental dexterity than is required for the other two concepts. Whilst the ability to hold on to and combine all the variables involved in the more advanced stages of the concept of volume is obviously beyond younger pupils, it could be hypothesized that there is likely to be little difference between the levels of understanding and misunderstanding in the early stages of this concept and those of weight and area. Before making comparisons of this type in the present study, however, it is necessary both to analyse the results and practices of earlier research on this topic and to explore, in reasonable depth, how far the concept of volume was understood by the children in our sample who had earlier experienced the battery of tests in weight and area.

Studies on the concept of volume were first reported by Piaget and Inhelder in 1941 and from this research it was concluded that children attain conservation of substance at about seven years of age, of weight at about nine years of age and of volume at about twelve. These early studies did not probe deeply the ability of children to understand the concept of volume, and it was not until 1948 (English 1960) that Piaget, Inhelder and Szeminska published in English the result of their further inquiries in this field.

Once more, Piaget interpreted his findings in terms of a sequential growth of understanding of the concept of volume. At first the young child does not conserve volume at all, and if objects of similar volumes but different shapes are compared, the appearances of the shapes themselves dominate the child's reasonings. Attention is again focused on single dimensions and the total three-dimensional concept of volume is ignored. Even when an object made up of blocks is changed in shape in front of this child, so that he sees that nothing has been added or removed, he maintains that there is no conservation of volume because 'It is now taller (longer, wider, etc.)'.

At a more advanced stage, conservation in this particular practical situation is understood but such conservation pertains to the object alone. When such a block is placed inside a larger box and its shape changed, conservation of volume of the block is maintained but there is no resultant conservation of the surrounding volume in the box. That is, the volume 'used up' by the block is conserved but not necessarily that of the remainder of the box — the complementary volume. At a still later stage, children begin to grasp the idea of displaced volume when solid objects are immersed in water. Piaget maintains that it is only at the more advanced stages that children begin to work out the relations between the three dimensions and gradually become capable of measuring volumes of blocks using unit cubes. Of necessity, from this interpretation, the child must have grasped the concept of conservation with change of shape clearly before he can understand the principle of measurement of volume by the use of unit blocks. Even so, such understanding apparently does not lead directly to ability to measure volume in such a fashion. At first children simply equate the volume with a number of unit blocks: it seems that, as long as a number is obtained, comparisons can be made; the manner in which the number is obtained is not analysed. Sometimes the numbers are found by stacking the cubes against one or more faces of the block, at other times by counting the number of cubes taken to surround the block. Even when children carry out this task successfully, they do not at first use the blocks as measures of three dimensions. Multiplication of lengths to give products in terms of cubic units is not understood and the blocks are simply used to replicate exactly the shape of the object of unknown volume. Finally children grasp this idea of volume as a relationship between three dimensions, and from this point on begin to demonstrate a growing ability to view volume in more abstract number and logical terms without necessarily having to see and handle actual three-dimensional objects.

From 1960 onwards a number of researches have repeated these experiments in some form or another and, whilst they all agree with the general outline of Piaget's thesis, they also demonstrate the loose nature of this concept of stages in mental development. Lovell and Ogilvie (1961b) carried out three experiments with some 190 children and examined the concepts of internal volume, occupied volume and displacement volume. The first of these ex-

periments used more or less the same materials as in Piaget's study; cubes
were arranged in a 2 x 3 x 2 block and changed into a different shape (e.g.
2 x 2 x 3) and the children were examined for their understanding of the
conservation of volume. However, their experiment differed in a number of
other respects from Piaget's procedure.

Piaget asked his questions in terms of a concrete problem; he referred to
the original block (3 x 3 x 4 cm) as a house on an island (the base 3 x 3 cm)
and told the children, in effect, that they had to build other houses on
different islands (2 x 2 cm, 2 x 3 cm, etc.) that had 'exactly as much room' as
the first house. These other houses were built up of individual blocks. Lovell
and Ogilvie asked their questions in two parts, in both of which the child was
passive, taking no action at all. In part (i) the two blocks to be compared
were not altered in any way during the test, whereas in part (ii) one of the
blocks was rearranged in front of the child. The questions, too, were in a more
abstract form and another variable — the concept of fitting the blocks into a
space — was also introduced. For example, the question in the part (i) (1961b,
p. 118) was:

Here we have two blocks of bricks. If we made two boxes, one for each block
of bricks, so that there was just enough room in each box to hold the bricks,
would there be as much room in one box as in the other? How do you know?
[or] Why?

It can be seen that the mental imagery required of the child is probably greater
in this test than in Piaget's. However, Lovell and Ogilvie did use Piaget's
clinical approach and added supplementary questions if the child seemed to
be unclear about the questions. It should be noticed that all these tests use
the term 'room' to indicate the concept of volume, and the problems associated
with common understanding of terms between the questioner and questioned
again emerges. As mentioned earlier, 'room' may mean area to the child or he
may think of 'room left to move about in' rather than space occupied, and he
answers according to his mental definition of the phrase used rather than in
terms of 'volume'.

Lovell and Ogilvie also categorized the answers of the children (p. 121) in
the Piagetian terms of reversibility (e.g. 'the 1 x 2 x 6 block could be changed
back to a 2 x 2 x 3 block'); 'plus/minus' ('cubes have been neither added nor
taken away'); 'identical action' (one block could be rearranged as the other);
'quantity' (amount of room in boxes is related to number of cubes, which
remains unchanged); and 'compensatory dimensions' (one box is wider but
the other is longer, etc.). The results are summarized at the end of this section,
but three major points emerge from these changes in test design. First, it is
not clear *how* the children concluded in part (i) that the two blocks had the

same volume. The authors point out that it could not be assumed of those children who conserved that they 'necessarily counted the number of cubes in the block; they appeared to observe general likenesses and concluded that the number must be the same' (p. 121). In other words, it is difficult to determine whether their answers were based on guesswork or rational analysis of the two volumes. If the blocks were not altered in any way, it is difficult to know how the child could be certain that the volumes were *really* the same without actually counting.

Secondly, when the child saw in part (ii) of the test that one block was changed into a different shape, one might reasonably expect the number of correct responses to increase but in fact they fell by a significant amount. A slight change in procedure obviously caused children to change their minds.

Table 46   Numbers correct in Lovell and Ogilvie's test, parts (i) and (ii)

Year [in junior school]	Number of children	Q(i): Box for 2 x 3 x 2 block the same size as box for 2 x 2 x 3 block	Q(ii): Box for 2 x 3 x 2 block the same size as box for 1 x 2 x 6 block
1st	51	44 (*86%*)	33 (*65%*)
2nd	40	35 (*87%*)	27 (*67%*)
3rd	45	44 (*98%*)	41 (*91%*)
4th	55	55 (*100%*)	51 (*93%*)
	191	178	152

Source: Lovell and Ogilvie (1961b, Table 1)

Thirdly, of those who gave correct answers in this second part 103 out of 152 gave reasons based on counting (the numbers of cubes were the same). Of the remaining 49, 5 did not give clear reasons and another 20 gave reasons of the compensatory type. It has been argued earlier that such compensatory reasons do not provide evidence for conservation of volume. It is impossible to be certain that an increase in one dimension exactly compensates for a decrease in another without carrying out measurements. Thus, only 24 out of 152 in this sample provided evidence of the type Piaget maintains is important for the concept of conservation. As Piaget had used a solid block for his first 'house', this criticism cannot be applied to his experiment but, as Lovell and Ogilvie had pointed out in a related study on the concept of substance, such experiments seemed to show the 'particularities of child thinking' (1960, p. 117), i.e. the children answer set problems in terms of each particular situation, and general application of a concept emerges slowly with experience and maturation. Such 'particularity' of response in any *one* test situation obviously hinders the tester from observing the general pattern of fixed stages clearly.

Lovell and Ogilvie's experiments enable us to analyse following researches in a like manner. Elkind's (1961a) study attempted to compare the responses of 175 children between the ages of five and eleven to questions concerned with the conservation of substance (termed 'mass' by Elkind), weight and volume. His results agreed with those of Piaget with regard to the conservation of substance and weight, but only 27% of the eleven-year-olds conserved volume. However, this study suffered from two methodological drawbacks. First, although three concepts were tested, Elkind used the same materials for all three tests (the familiar clay ball and sausage) and only varied the questions. It is difficult to conclude whether the children understood that the questions were really different one from another if the materials used remained the same.

Secondly, the questions became more abstract in the order of the concepts – substance, weight, volume (1961a, p. 221). In the first case the sausage shaped volume was referred to as a 'hot dog' (a realistic, concrete term): 'Is there as much clay in the ball as in the hot dog . . .?' The next question was of the type 'Do they both weigh the same, do they both have the same amount of weight?' and finally (for volume) the abstract terms 'room' and 'space' were used: 'Do they both take up the same amount of space, do they both take up as much room?' One cannot be certain whether the drop in the numbers of correct responses was due to the increasing complexity of the form of communication used or whether it was due solely to the differences in complexity of the three concepts.

As with the Lovell and Ogilvie experiments, the questions seem to have been expressed in a confirmatory style, i.e. 'Do they both take up as much room?'; the alternative addition 'or do they take up a different amount of room?' does not seem to have been asked. In other words, the children were not strictly placed in a position where they had to use their understanding to choose between alternatives. Both researches overcame this problem by asking the children their reasons for their answers.

In the light of these studies, Uzgiris (1964) decided to repeat this type of experiment but also decided to examine the effect of varying the materials used for the tests. Plasticine balls, metal tubes, wire coils and plastic wire were used and the children were asked questions concerning the conservation of substance, weight and volume for each material. Thus the criticism of using different questions for the same material can be made once more but Uzgiris's study is a natural development of the earlier researches in that the same set of questions were asked for each set of materials. She supported Piaget and Inhelder's sequence and age of attainment of substance, weight and volume but also demonstrated that there were significant differences in the responses of the children towards conservation in all three concepts when different materials were used. For example, 20% of the nine-year-olds conserved volume when plasticine balls were used but only 5% of the same sample conserved when metal cubes were used. (Between 0% and 10% of the eight-year-olds conserved volume, whilst 20% to 30% of the twelve-year olds conserved.) This research demonstrated, once more, the 'particularity' of individual children's answers and the researcher's difficulty in arriving at conclusions which are 'generalities'.

Another feature of Uzgiris's research introduces further difficulty in analyses. It appears that in examining for conservation of volume with the materials referred to above, the test involved placing the materials in a container of water and the following questions referred to the amount of water displaced. As the problem now involved displaced volume, it is hardly surprising that the task was found to be harder than those concerning substance and weight. In short, it appears that the concept of volume was examined at a higher level of complexity than the other two, and comparisons of conceptual development across the three concepts are thereby made more difficult.

A number of researches have replicated in some form or another the Piagetian tests on occupied volume and displacement volume. Lovell and Ogilvie, in the previously mentioned study (1961b), in turn placed blocks of similar volume but different shapes in a can and asked questions concerning the amount of water that the can would then hold. The numbers of conservers at all ages fell from those for the straightforward comparison of two blocks (Table 2). Thirty-nine per cent of the first-year junior school pupils (probably between seven and eight years of age) and 56% of the third-year junior pupils (probably between nine and ten) conserved. Vernon (1965), using plasticine, obtained an even more dramatic drop in the number of correct responses in a similar experiment. In a sample of 100 children, 97% of the 10–11 year-old boys had conserved 'amount of plasticine' when one of the similar balls was elongated into a sausage form. When asked: 'Now make your plasticine into a plate. If you put my ball into this jar and you put the plate into yours, will the water in my jar rise more than yours, or less, or the same amount? Why?' (p. 16) only 45 still conserved the occupied volume. Beard (1963) repeated these experiments using plasticine and obtained even lower results. Of the seven-year-olds 33% conserved and of the nine-year-olds 31%. Clearly, occupied volume introduces a more complicated idea of the concept of volume and Piaget's conclusions seem to be borne out.

Inhelder (1962) and Vinh-Bang introduced another variable into this problem by placing the child in a conflict situation. Two cylinders of similar volume but of different weights were shown to the child; after the child had established the difference in weight, the cylinders were immersed in the water and the child asked to explain why the water levels were the same. The sample size used was extremely small; nevertheless, it was demonstrated that only 7% of the eight-year-olds, 15% of the ten-year-olds and 37% of the eleven-year-olds could answer correctly. Beard (1963) repeated this experiment using a table-tennis ball and a ball of plasticine of identical volume. Nineteen per cent of the $7\frac{1}{2}$ year-olds and 9·4% of the 9 year-olds gave the correct answers and reasons. The introduction of a confusing and — in adult terms — irrelevant variable (in this case, weight) obviously disturbs the children's beliefs about occupied and displaced volume. Lovell and Ogilvie (1961b) had found evidence of similar disturbance when they had placed blocks of similar volume (but different shape) in *two cans of differing capacity*, and asked questions concerning the respective volumes of water displaced. Unfortunately, children's understanding of the relationship between weight and volume and displaced water was not explored further in any of these researches, nor indeed was the ability to *use* basic concepts of volume to solve slightly more complicated problems like determining the relative volumes of two containers.

In both the concepts of weight and area it has been suggested that conservation of discontinuous quantities is easier to grasp than conservation of continuous quantities, and this hypothesis also seems to be justified in the case of volume. It has already been suggested that conservation of volume of blocks (solid volume) is gradually arrived at when children have experience of reconstructing a block into different shapes by reorientating the constituent pieces. Piaget and Szeminska (1941) carried out a similar experiment but with equal quantities of liquid. Equal volumes of liquid, as indicated by the levels in similar beakers, were shown to the child and then poured into containers of different shapes so that the levels were no longer equal. Many children failed to conserve in this situation, and were clearly deceived by the heights of the liquid. A similar result emerged when liquids originally in similar beakers and having the same volume were respectively poured one into two containers and the other into two or three containers all at different levels. Children obviously focused their attention on these different levels and were unable to conserve the volume of the liquids. As liquids can be considered to be continuous quantities (the first of the above experiments) or, in effect, discontinuous quantities (the second of the above experiments) it was of interest to speculate how children would compare in their responses to a number of such tests.

A number of conclusions may be inferred if the interpretation given of these researches is a reasonable one. Obviously a single practical test or small number of tests supplies very little evidence of children's conceptual ability in such a complex concept as volume. Lovell and Ogilvie's comment (1961b, p. 125) that

It seems that Piaget et al. are optimistic if they think that the single test, in which they employed 36 unit cubes in a bowl, will enable them to distinguish between those who have developed a complete concept of physical volume from those who have not

seems to be justified. On the other hand Piaget, as in the concept of area, has distinguished levels of achievement in the concept of volume and the present research attempted to explore the children's reactions to problems concerned with internal and solid volume, occupied volume and displaced volume to see, in particular, if such levels of complexity were confirmed.

Furthermore, it was apparent that slight variation in the materials or wording of the question greatly altered the nature of the children's responses in this concept, and an attempt was therefore made to explore the children's understanding of the words used. From the earlier researches no clearcut relationship between levels of achievement and age emerges; indeed, as Fogelman (1970) has noted, the inconsistencies in these results are even greater than they were for conservation of quantity and weight. The present research explored this apparent relationship further.

A NOTE ON THE CONCEPTS OF SUBSTANCE AND VOLUME

Piaget and all following researchers have maintained that the concept of substance or quantity is easier to grasp than that of weight or volume. Analysis of what is indicated by the terms 'substance' or 'quantity' in such tests reveals that two features dominate the practical procedures. The questions are always asked in terms of a real object, and they always use ambiguous words such as 'amount of' (e.g. 'Does this have the same amount of plasticine as this?'). When children respond to such questions, it is impossible to determine what concepts they are thinking about. It is very likely that on many occasions the child is thinking of volume when he answers questions of this realistic form whereas, in the case of the question using the more abstract term 'amount of space' or 'amount of room', the child may be bewildered by the term and simply fails to relate the question to the concept of volume at all. The present writer has not found a satisfactorily rigid definition of 'substance' or 'quantity' in Piagetian research and the conclusion is that when children have conserved in such tests, this simply indicates that they believe a property of the material has remained unchanged but it is impossible to determine what property they have in mind! In the following series of tests, terms involving such real objects as 'amount of chocolate', 'amount of Smarties' are used in some items, as it is argued that such questions in realistic form and in association with the practical materials do encourage children to focus their attention on the total volume of the space or object in question. The responses of the children to such questions are compared with their responses to similar test items using the more abstract 'amount of room'.

SORTING, SETTING AND TERMINOLOGY

These introductory items test the children's ability to look at the volume of an object in terms of the total space occupied by that object. Children at an early stage find difficulty in understanding the terminology used to convey the idea of volume. In the pilot survey children were examined on their under-standing of terms such as 'volume', 'space occupied', 'space taken up', 'amount of room', etc. Needless to say, the word 'volume' conveyed little to them and 'space' was an equally intangible abstract word for most children. The phrase 'amount of room' was commonly used by the children, but even so this did not always have a three-dimensional meaning for them. They often changed the meaning of these phrases at various times; at one point 'amount of room' was taken to indicate area and at another time indicated volume.

It was concluded that abstract words such as 'amount of room' do not always give a mental picture of the volume of an object to the child and, as indicated above, it was decided also to design test items using words or phrases which could be considered to give real impressions of total volume, e.g. 'amount of wood', 'amount of chocolate'. It can be argued that such terms mean more than just volume and, whilst agreeing that this is so for the scien-tist, we believed that in the present study the use of such phrases would help the child to think about total space occupied or enclosed (see also the earlier note on the Piagetian concept of substance, facing). Our pilot survey had also indicated that certain words such as 'size', 'bigger', etc. should be avoided in the questioning procedure, as it was impossible to judge the meaning attached to these words by the children. The following items are of an introductory nature and precede the more detailed study of the concept of conservation of volume.

Assessment items 1—5 correspond to *AWV*, Tests 1—5 for volume.
Assessment item 6 is additional and does not appear in *AWV*.

Item 1: 4 yellow blocks: A, B, C, D

[NB B = C; each dimension of B/C is matched by a dimension of A or D.]

Place the blocks on the table in front of S as shown.

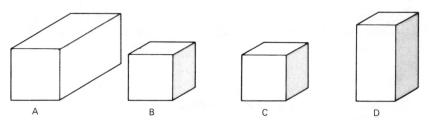

A   B   C   D

1a   *'I want you to imagine that these* [indicate blocks] *are blocks of chocolate. Can you find out which blocks have the same amount of chocolate as each other? You can move the blocks around.'*

If necessary repeat the question.

When S makes a choice,

  'Why have they the same amount of chocolate as each other?'

If S answers (i) *'because they are the same size, shape, etc.'*

  'What do you mean by the same shape/size? Can you show me?'

If S answers (ii) *'because they have the same height/width/thickness/base, etc.'*

Point to another block which has the same measurement for the dimension referred to,

  'This also has the same height/width, etc. Does it also have the same amount of chocolate?'

  'Why do you say that?'

Item 1 (cont): 4 yellow blocks: C, D, E, F

[NB D, E and F are of equal volume.]

Place the blocks on the table in front of S as shown.

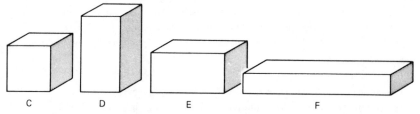

C   D   E   F

1b   *'How many of these blocks have the same amount of chocolate as each other? You can move the blocks around.'*

If necessary repeat the question.

  'Show me which blocks have the same amount of chocolate.'

If S chooses any pair without moving or turning the blocks for 'matching' purposes,

*   '*Show me why the blocks have the same amount of chocolate as each other.*'

Positions in which D and E can be matched by pupil

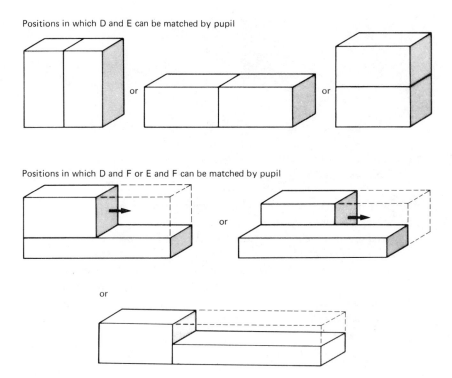

Positions in which D and F or E and F can be matched by pupil

If S chooses two out of the three blocks (D, E & F) replace the blocks in their original positions.

> '*Are there any more blocks which have the same amount of chocolate as each other?*'

If S chooses the second pair without 'matching' the blocks, repeat the question marked *.

Item 2: 4 boxes with lids: red, blue, yellow, orange

[Blue = yellow; each dimension of blue/yellow is matched by a dimension of red or orange.]

Place the boxes on the table in front of S in the following order: red, blue, yellow (on its side) and orange.

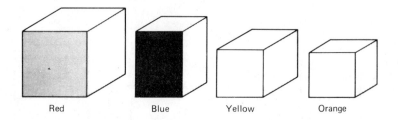

Red   Blue   Yellow   Orange

'Can you find out which two boxes take up the same amount of room as each other? You can move the boxes around.'
If necessary repeat the question.
When S makes a choice,
'Why have you chosen those two?'
If S makes an incorrect choice, end item and proceed to No. 3.
If S answers *'because they are the same size/shape, etc.'*
'What do you mean by the same size/shape? Can you show me?'
If S cannot explain, end item and proceed to No. 3. Otherwise proceed.
If S chooses the blue and yellow boxes and mentions one dimension only, e.g. height, point to either the red or the orange box which has a matching dimension to answer given by S.
'This also has the same height/width, etc. Does it also take up the same amount of room?'
'Why do you say that?'

Item 3: pale orange box without lid; 2 blocks

[NB The 2 blocks together fill the box.]

Show the interior of the box to S.
'Is there room inside this box?'
Place one block in the box.
'Is there any room left over inside the box now?'
Place the second block in the box with the first.
'Is there any room left over inside the box now?'

Item 4: red box; blue box from item 2

[NB Remove lids. Red has smaller internal volume.]

4a Place the red and blue boxes close to each other on the table in front of S.

'Stand up and look at the boxes carefully. If I poured Smarties into each of these boxes and filled them to the top, would the red box hold the same amount of Smarties as the blue box, or would it hold a different amount?'

If S answers *'the same'*,

'Why do you say that?'

If S answers *'different'*,

'Which would hold more?'

'Why do you say that?'

Item 4 (cont): red box; yellow box from item 2

[NB Remove lids. Red has smaller internal volume.]

4b Place the red and yellow boxes close to each other on the table in front of S.

'Stand up and look inside these boxes carefully. Does the red box have the same amount of room inside as the yellow box, or does it have a different amount of room?'

If S answers *'the same'*,

'Why do you say that?'

If S answers *'different'*,

'Which box has more room inside?'

'Why do you say that?'

Item 4 (cont): yellow box from item 2; green box

[NB Remove lids. Green has smaller internal volume.]

4c Place the green box close to the yellow one on the table in front of S.

'Look inside these boxes carefully. Does the yellow box have the same amount of room inside as the green box, or does it have a different amount of room?'

If S answers *'the same'*,

'Why do you say that?'

If S answers *'different'*,

'Which box has more room inside?'

'Why do you say that?'

Item 5: 2 green blocks: 1 in 2 halves

Place the green blocks on the table in front of S as shown.

> *'Does this block* [indicate single block] *take up the same amount of room as those blocks together, or does it take up a different amount of room? You can pick up the blocks.'*

If S answers *'the same'*,

> *'Why do you say that?'*

If S answers *'one is longer but the other is wider'* or similar compensatory reason,

> *'Is there any other reason why it takes up the same amount of room?'*

If S answers *'different'*,

> *'Which block takes up more room?'*
> *'Why do you say that?'*

Item 6: 2 Perspex boxes; 2 wooden blocks

> *'Watch carefully.'*

Demonstrate to S that the two wooden blocks have similar dimensions as shown.

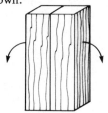

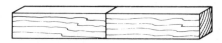

Place the blocks inside the two Perspex boxes and turn the boxes so that their openings face S, as shown.

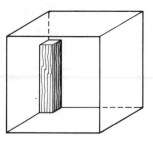

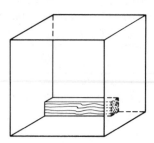

6a   *'Does this block take up the same amount of room as that block, or does it take up a different amount of room?'*
If S answers *'the same'*,
   'Why do you say that?'
If S answers *'different'*,
   'Which block takes up more room?'
   'Why do you say that?'

Item 6 (cont): 2 Perspex boxes; 2 yellow blocks

Match the dimensions of the yellow blocks as shown.

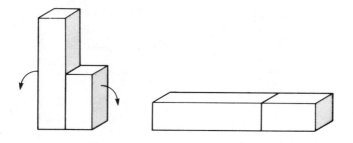

Place the blocks inside the Perspex boxes and turn the boxes so that their openings face S, as shown.

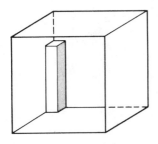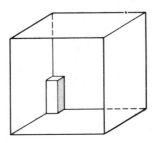

6b   *'Does this block take up the same amount of room as that block or does it take up a different amount of room?'*
If S answers *'the same'*,
   'Why do you say that?'
If S answers *'different'*,
   'Which block takes up more room?'
   'Why do you say that?'

Item 6 (cont): 2 Perspex boxes: 2 orange blocks

Match the dimensions of the orange blocks as shown.

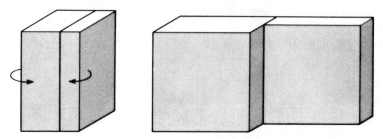

Place the orange blocks inside the Perspex boxes and turn the boxes so that their openings face S, as shown.

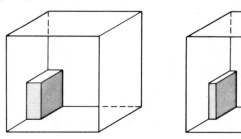

6c   *'Does this block take up the same amount of room as that block, or does it take up a different amount of room?'*
If S answers *'the same'*,
   'Why do you say that?'
If S answers *'different'*,
   'Which block takes up more room?'
   'Why do you say that?'

Results: item 1

In the first part the children simply pick out objects of similar volumes and shapes. The objects to be matched are cubes and the matching is thus of the simplest kind. In the second part two matchings are possible. First one block has to be turned on to a different face (actually or in the pupil's mind) for exact matching (blocks D and E) and, secondly, one block (F) has mentally to be cut in half and the two halves stacked on top of one another for exact matching with the volume of the other block (D or E) to be possible. Throughout the item the idea of volume is conveyed by a realistic term ('blocks of chocolate').

Over 90% of the-seven-year-old children and nearly all the older children picked out the two cubes in the first part of the question. There were no dissimilar dimensions and similarity of shape also represented equality of volume. The second part of the item proved more difficult (Table 47). Most

Table 47   Results for volume item 1b

Answer	7y 5m	7y 11m	8y 5m	8y 11m	9y 5m	9y 11m
	%	%	%	%	%	%
Correct: selects blocks D and E	85	87	89	89	89	93
Correct: selects blocks D and F or E and F	12	17	14	20	21	29
Sample size, N (= 100%)	146	150	150	155	155	149

of the children selected the blocks D and E and were capable of doing this by turning one block around. The fact that the children were seen to do this demonstrates that they were thinking of blocks of chocolate in terms of volume. However, of the $7\frac{1}{2}$ year-old children who selected the correct blocks, a quarter were unable to explain their reasons in words although they had clearly demonstrated that they were using the correct conceptual process (a sixth of the corresponding 9 year-olds were unable to explain their choices in words).

The picking out of the shape which is twice the length but only half the height of the other block is a more difficult task. The figures are much lower and even the older children who demonstrated in later items that they had quite a good concept of solid volume showed low scores in this item. For many children the different dimensions of the blocks are confusing, and they are obviously incapable of visualizing volume relationships between block F and block D or E. It would seem that for these children different shapes have different volumes. It is surprising that so many of the older children failed to match the blocks, especially as they were encouraged to handle them. In the light of their later responses, one might conclude that in these early items a lack of confidence masked the true ability of those children. The importance of a number of tests rather than single items is indicated once more. In this item children display their conceptual abilities through action rather than by the use of words.

Results: item 2

This repeats the first part of the previous item but larger objects (coloured boxes) are used and the question uses the more abstract term 'amount of room'. The numbers of absolutely correct answers (Table 48) fall dramatically

Table 48   Results for volume item 2

Answer	7y 5m	7y 11m	8y 5m	8y 11m	9y 5m	9y 11m
	%	%	%	%	%	%
Correct: selects correct boxes and gives correct verbal explanation	27	14	26	28	37	36
Correct: selects correct boxes but cannot give correct verbal explan.	25	40	45	52	35	33
Incorrect: selects wrong boxes by matching one or two dimensions only	17	15	6	5	10	6
Incorrect: other	31	31	23	15	18	25
Sample size, N (= 100%)	146	150	150	155	155	149

(ranging from 27% to 37%) although there is a trend of improvement with age. A considerable proportion of the children (ranging from 25% at $7\frac{1}{2}$ years to 52% at 9 years) selected the correct boxes but were either unable to express a reason for their choices or else based their reasons on the matching of one or two dimensions only. E.g. 'They take up the same amount of room because they have the same height'. From the responses it is impossible to determine whether these children had a poor concept of volume or whether they misinterpreted the phrase 'amount of room'. The remainder of the children clearly did not use the term 'amount of room' to indicate volume and for them communication in such terms had no meaning.

Understanding of the rudimentary stages of the concept of occupied (solid) volume already seems to be related not only to a necessary three-dimensional view but also to terminology, and the children were next tested on their understanding of the phrase 'room inside the box'. This was a necessary preliminary test so that the phrase could be used to explore the children's early concept of enclosed volume.

Results: item 3

Ninety-four per cent of the $7\frac{1}{2}$ year-olds and 99% of the 10 year-olds clearly understood the term in terms of interior volume or space and it is therefore used in the following item.

Results: item 4

In the first part the red and blue boxes have interiors of similar width and breadth but the blue box is deeper. The red box (of smaller internal volume) has thicker walls. The question is asked in realistic terms as 'amount of Smarties' to fill the boxes.

Table 49   Results for volume item 4a (average ability)

Answer	7y 5m	7y 11m	8y 5m	8y 11m	9y 5m	9y 11m
	%	%	%	%	%	%
Correct: correct reasoning	43	47	52	59	51	55
Incorrect: matched cross-section of space only	12	22	25	15	25	25
Incorrect: other	45	31	23	27	24	20
Sample size (= 100%)	75	72	79	78	79	76

Many of the children failed to examine the depth of the box or could not detect that the depth of one box was greater than the other, even though the degree of perception required was relatively simple. Others were clearly confused by the different thickness of the walls, whilst a considerable proportion arrived at an answer by simply matching the size of the hole, i.e. the cross-sectional area of the space (Table 49). Piaget's view that young children are easily influenced by appearances is confirmed, although it is surprising to note that the abilities of even the older children to compare volumes on a perceptual matching basis appears to be poorly developed. This conclusion has obvious implications when reasons based on compensatory dimensions are given as a basis for conservation of volume in later items.

Table 50 Results for volume item 4b (average ability)

Answer	7y 5m	7y 11m	8y 5m	8y 11m	9y 5m	9y 11m
	%	%	%	%	%	%
Correct: correct reasons	56	57	56	64	67	66
Incorrect: matched cross-section of space only	8	11	18	12	14	14
Incorrect: other	36	22	26	24	17	20
Sample size (= 100%)	75	72	79	78	79	76

This item was repeated (4b) substituting a box of identical dimensions but of different colour (yellow) to the blue box and substituting the term 'amount of room inside' for the 'Smarties' phrase. This slight variation causes the number of correct responses to increase at all ages (Table 50). Either a proportion of the children were learning as they proceeded with the tests, or else they had a better understanding of the question. Again, however, the proportion of older children failing to examine the depth of the box is rather surprising; the more obvious area of the hole or the thickness of the walls seem to have dominated the thinking of many of the children.

Finally (4c), the red box was replaced by a green box which had identical exterior dimensions to the yellow box and a similar interior depth. The width of the hole, i.e. its cross-sectional interior area was, however, less than that of the yellow box. In other words, there were fewer distracting features (i.e. there was only one variable and that was visually obvious). Results are given in Table 51.

Table 51 Results for volume item 4c (average ability)

Answer	7y 5m	7y 11m	8y 5m	8y 11m	9y 5m	9y 11m
	%	%	%	%	%	%
Correct	69	85	82	91	94	99
Incorrect	31	15	18	9	6	1
Sample size (= 100%)	75	72	79	78	79	76

Results: item 5

This test corresponds to item 1b in that it examines the ability of the pupil to compensate one dimension with another. The phrase 'take up the same amount of room' is used to indicate volume.

Table 52   Results for volume item 5 (average ability)

Answer	7y 5m	7y 11m	8y 5m	8y 11m	9y 5m	9y 11m
	%	%	%	%	%	%
Correct choice and reasoning	60	63	73	86	84	84
Compensatory reason	3	1	0	3	2	3
Incorrect: centring	29	24	24	11	6	10
Incorrect: other	8	13	3	0	8	3
Sample size (= 100%)	75	72	79	78	79	76

The number of correct answers shows a steady improvement with age. It seems that the fact that one block is already cut into halves encouraged many children to reconstruct this block so that it had the same shape as the other. If this is so, then this agrees with the conclusion of earlier researches that the idea of conservation of discontinuous objects is easier to grasp than the idea of conservation of continuous objects (blocks D or E and F in item 1). Compensatory reasons were rarely given by the children in this sample but, of those who failed, the majority did give reasons based on appearances; they concluded that one block took up more room because it was 'longer (larger, bigger, etc.)'. It is impossible to determine whether they really believed the volume of one block was greater than the other or whether they thought the phrase 'amount of room' meant 'length' and answered accordingly. In either case, however, we can argue that they had a poorly developed concept of volume as, at best, they did not understand what was meant by the common phrase used to indicate volume.

Results: item 6

As these children had clearly understood the term 'amount of room inside a box', it was therefore decided first to compare blocks side by side and then to place them in different positions inside two identical transparent boxes and, in effect, link up the phrase 'take up the same amount (or different amount) of room' with the visual realization of room inside a box.

In item 6a the two wooden blocks are first seen to have identical dimensions but one is placed in the box in an upright position and the other on its side.

Table 53 Results for volume item 6a (average ability)

Answer	7y 5m	7y 11m	8y 5m	8y 11m	9y 5m	9y 11m
	%	%	%	%	%	%
Correct: both take up same amount of room	47	56	61	60	75	76
Incorrect: 'taller' block takes up more room	28	24	18	21	6	12
Incorrect: other	25	20	21	19	19	12
Sample size (= 100%)	75	72	79	78	79	76

The numbers of correct responses (Table 53) fall, although again there is a steady increase with age. This result accords well with Piaget's theory that children first examine volume in terms of the object alone (item 5) and later develop the idea of occupied volume (item 6).

Of those who were incorrect, the majority focused their attention on the greater height of one block and concluded that it 'took up more room'. We can infer either that they used the phrase 'amount of room' to indicate volume but had a poor concept of volume, or else that the phrase now meant 'height', that is, they had altered the meaning of the words in their minds in order to give an answer. In contrast to the answers in the previous item, relatively few children focused their attention on the greater 'length' of the other block. Once more we conclude that these children tend to rely on immediate appearances and do not use terminology in a consistent fashion.

Items 6b and 6c, at first sight, merely check the above results but on closer inspection the results raise questions concerning test design. In 6b the blocks are matched and placed in the boxes in such a way that their cross-sectional areas are the same but their heights are different (that is, their volumes are also different). In 6c their volumes can be seen to be different because their cross-sectional areas are different (their heights are the same).

Table 54   Results for volume item 6b (average ability)

Answer	7y 5m	7y 11m	8y 5m	8y 11m	9y 5m	9y 11m
	%	%	%	%	%	%
Correct	77	78	80	83	82	84
Incorrect: volumes the same because cross-sectional areas the same	15	11	9	9	8	7
Incorrect: other	8	11	11	8	10	9
Sample size (= 100%)	75	72	79	78	79	76

Table 55   Results for volume item 6c (average ability)

Answer	7y 5m	7y 11m	8y 5m	8y 11m	9y 5m	9y 11m
	%	%	%	%	%	%
Correct	86	85	93	94	95	95
Incorrect: volumes the same because heights the same	8	6	1	1	3	3
Incorrect: other	6	9	6	5	2	2
Sample size (= 100%)	75	72	79	78	79	76

The results (Tables 54, 55) show a dramatic improvement and, at first sight, the children seem to have suddenly grasped the concept of occupied volume. On closer inspection, however, this part of the test tells us little about the conceptual development of the children. In both cases children can give the 'correct' answer but not necessarily use the correct conceptual argument. In 6b, if they focus their attention on the heights of the blocks, they will give the correct answer but they may not have looked at the total volumes of the blocks at all; they may have only considered one dimension. In a similar fashion in 6c, they may only examine the differences in cross-sectional area and, again, give the 'correct' answer. Unless the children explain their answers completely by saying 'They take up different amounts of room because one is taller than the other *although they both have the same cross-sectional area*' (this answer was never given), it is impossible to arrive at any firm conclusions from the results. At best, it can be said that children prefer to base their answers on differences rather than similarities.

The test brings out the difficulties of designing materials in this type of study and stresses the importance of rigid examination of the actual tests used in other researches before accepting the interpretations of the responses to such tests.

Summary of test results: sorting of volumes and terminology

All the tests show that children's ability to estimate volume in terms of three dimensions increases with age. The tests given in this section were relatively simple, and called upon the child to make simple comparisons of solid and enclosed volume. It was surprising to find that children of average ability up to the ages of nine had considerable difficulty in all these tasks. A substantial proportion of the older children also failed in some of the tests. When blocks of the same shape were reorientated, equal volumes could not be recognized and, in the case of enclosed volumes, children often did not realize that it was necessary to examine all three dimensions before making deductions about the volumes. When solids of similar volume but different dimensions were presented to the children, their inability to deduce this similarity became even more marked. This was true even when the increase in one dimension was easily seen to be compensated by a decrease in the other. It appears that the ability of children in this age range to compensate one dimension by another is very poorly developed for the three-dimensional concept of volume. Indeed, it can be reasonably supposed that such tasks would prove to be difficult for most adults. In the light of this finding, it is therefore extremely unlikely that, when such reasons are given in typical Piagetian tests on conservation of solid or liquid volume (see next section), the children are really *able to conclude* that there is conservation of volume. In other words, such reasons alone cannot be considered as evidence for conservation. In most researches to date, however, these reasons are used as positive evidence for conservation.

When visual features encouraged children to think in terms of cutting up and reconstructing one block to be the same shape as another, the number of correct selections of equal volumes increased. These children seemed to consider the volumes as wholes and not as separate dimensions. Nearly all the children who were incorrect, on the other hand, seemed to focus their attention on one dimension at a time.

Misunderstanding of terminology proved to be an even greater barrier in these tasks than in the concepts of area and weight. Even when concrete terms such as 'amount of wood' or 'amount of chocolate' was used to convey volume, children often found difficulty in expressing reasons for their choices. Abstract terms such as 'amount of room' proved to be still more difficult to understand. There were indications that children often changed the meaning that they attached to such terms from one test to another.

For the research worker these relatively simple tests demonstrate the wide variation of responses that can be expected as the materials are changed from test to test. The more varied are the manifestations of a particular concept in the everyday life of the child, the more likely it is that a considerable number of test items will be needed to examine the level of the child's understanding.

For the teacher designing tasks for the children, these results imply that a wide variety of carefully selected materials should be presented to the pupils. It is suspected that, for reasons stated earlier (p. 135), that such relatively simple matching and comparison tasks are not often given to younger children and that, when the concept of volume is introduced to older pupils, the level and nature of the tasks given to them (e.g. calculations on volumes) are too advanced for their experience. This argument for early introduction of the concept of volume is developed further in the next chapter.

Once more, too, the problem of communication is brought out in the results and this has an obvious implication for the teacher.

CONSERVATION OF VOLUME

So far the children had not had any tests of conservation of the typical Piagetian pattern, where two volumes originally seen to be the same are changed in shape so that one dimension is deliberately elongated. In such tests the children are placed in a dilemma. It is argued that poor conservers will rely on answers based on visual appearances only whereas strong conservers will rely on more logical reasons. The following series of tests examines the responses of the children to such situations.

Assessment items 7–10 correspond to *AWV*, Tests 6–8 and 14 for volume.

Item 7: 2 tall red boxes: 1 in 2 halves

Place the two boxes close to each other on the table in front of S.

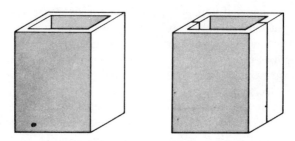

'Stand up and look inside these boxes. If I poured Smarties into each of these boxes and filled them to the top, would this box hold the same amount as that box or would it hold a different amount?'
If S answers *'different'*,
Match the external dimensions and use a ruler to measure the internal depth.
Then repeat the question.
If S still answers *'different'*, end item and proceed to No. 8.
If S answers *'the same'*, proceed.
'Watch carefully.'

Reassemble the second box and place it close to the first.

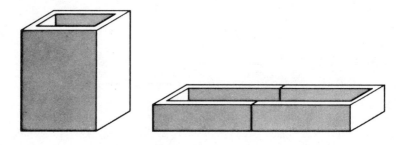

'If I poured Smarties into each of these boxes and filled them to the top, would this box hold the same amount as that box or would it hold a different amount?'
If S answers *'the same'*,
'Why do you say that?'
If S answers *'the same because one is longer but the other is wider'* or similar compensatory reason,
'Is there any other reason why it holds the same amount?'

If S answers *'different'*,
>*'Which box would hold more?'*
>*'Why do you say that?'*

Item 8: 2 flat dishes; 1 tall container; 1 beaker; jug of water

Place the two flat dishes in front of S.
>*'I am going to pour the same amount of water into each dish.'*

Fill them to the same level with water.
>*'Is there the same amount of water in each of these?'*

If necessary, adjust water levels until S is satisfied.
>*'Watch carefully.'*

Pour the water from one flat dish into the tall container.
Pour the water from the other flat dish into the beaker and arrange the containers as shown.

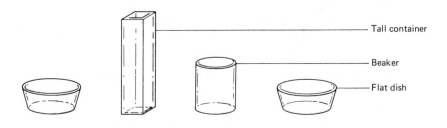

Tall container

Beaker

Flat dish

8a   *'Does this* [indicate tall container] *have the same amount of water in it as that* [indicate beaker] *, or does it have a different amount of water?'*
If S answers *'the same'*,
>*'Why do you say that?'*
If S answers *'the same in both because one is taller and the other wider'* or similar compensatory reason,
>*'Is there any other reason why they each have the same amount of water?'*
If S answers *'different'*,
>*'Which has more water?'*
>*'Why do you say that?'*

Pour the water back into the jug.

Item 8 (cont): 2 plastic beakers; 9 small cylinders (4 squat, 5 tall, thin); jug of water

Set out all the beakers in front of S.

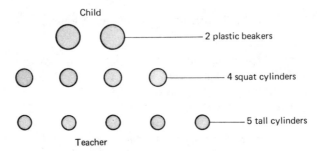

Half fill the two large beakers.
> *'Is there the same amount of water in each of these?'*
If necessary, adjust water levels until S is satisfied.
> *'Watch carefully.'*
Pour all the water from one large beaker into four squat cylinders so that the levels of water are different in each.
Pour all the water from the second large beaker into the other five taller cylinders so that the levels of water are different in each.
Place the two large beakers one at each end of the rows of smaller cylinders.

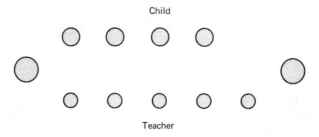

8b *'If you have all of those* [indicate 4 squat beakers] *and I have all of these* [indicate 5 taller cylinders] *will you have more water than me, less water or the same amount?'*
'Why do you say that?'

Item 9: 1 yellow solid block; 1 red extendable block A (of equal volume)

Place the yellow solid block and the extendable block A (closed up) on the table in front of S.

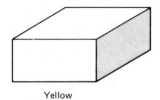
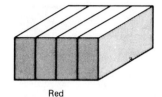

Yellow   Red

> *'Does the red block take up the same amount of room as the yellow
> block, or does it take up a different amount of room?'*

If necessary demonstrate, by picking up the solid block, that the length,
breadth and cross-sectional area of both blocks are identical, and repeat the
above question.

If S answers *'no'*, proceed to *.

If S answers *'yes'*, proceed.

9a Pull out extendable block A to its maximum length.

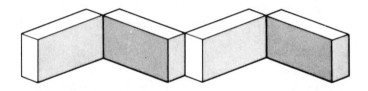

> *'Does the red shape take up the same amount of room as the yellow
> block, or does it take up a different amount of room?'*

If S answers *'the same'*,

> *'Why do you say that?'*

If S answers *'one is longer but the other is wider'* or similar compensatory
reason,

> *'Is there any other reason why it takes up the same amount of room?'*

If S answers *'different'*,

> *'Which takes up more room?'*
> *'Why do you say that?'*

* Remove red block A.

**Item 9 (cont): 1 yellow solid block; 1 orange extendable block B (of equal
volume)**

Place the yellow solid block and the orange extendable block B (closed up)
on the table in front of S.

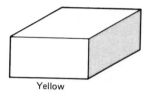

Yellow

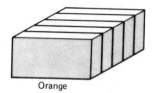

Orange

*'If these two blocks were made of chocolate, would the orange block
have the same amount of chocolate as the yellow block, or would it
have a different amount of chocolate?'*

If necessary demonstrate, by matching dimensions, that both blocks have
identical dimensions, and repeat the above question.

If S answers '*no*', end item and proceed to No. 10.

If S answers '*yes*', proceed.

9b Pull out extendable block B to its maximum length.

*'Does the orange shape have the same amount of chocolate as the yellow
block, or does it have a different amount of chocolate?'*

If S answers '*the same*',

'Why do you say that?'

If S answers '*one is longer but the other is wider*' or similar compensatory
reason,

'Is there any other reason why they have the same amount of chocolate?'

If S answers '*different*',

'Which has more chocolate?'

'Why do you say that?'

**Item 10: 1 set of 5 wooden blocks painted blue; another set of 4 wooden
blocks painted red**

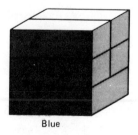

Blue

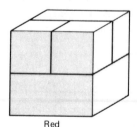

Red

Construct two cubes of identical dimensions, one of blue blocks, the other of red. Place the cubes next to each other in front of S.

>*'Does the blue block* [indicate cubes] *take up the same amount of room as the red block, or does it take up a different amount of room?'*

If S answers *'no'*, match the dimensions and repeat the question.

>*'Watch carefully.'*

10a Dismantle the blue cube and construct a new shape.

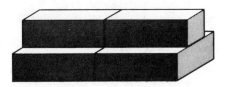

Dismantle the red cube and give the pieces to S.

>*'Make any shape with the red blocks that takes up the same amount of room as this* [indicate blue shape] *.'*

If necessary repeat the instructions.

If S is unable to operate, proceed to *.

Otherwise, after S has completed the red shape:

>*'Does your red shape take up the same amount of room as my blue shape?'*

If S answers *'different'*, proceed to *.

If S answers *'the same'*,

>*'Why do you say that?'*

If S makes any shape and gives a logical answer, end item. Otherwise proceed to *.

*10b Reconstruct the blue cube and the red cube, and place them next to each other in front of S.

>*'I want you to imagine that these blocks are made of chocolate. Does the blue block have the same amount of chocolate as the red block, or does it have a different amount of chocolate?'*

If S answers *'different'*, match the dimensions and repeat the question.

>*'Watch carefully.'*

Dismantle the blue cube and construct a new shape.

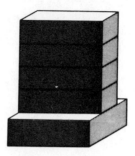

Dismantle the red cube and give the pieces to S.
> '*Make any shape with the red blocks that will have the same amount of chocolate as this* [indicate blue] .'

If necessary repeat the instructions.

If S is unable to operate, end item. Otherwise proceed.
> '*Does your red shape have the same amount of chocolate as my blue shape?*'

If S answers '*different*', end item.

If S answers '*the same*',
> '*Why do you say that?*'

Results: item 7

The child first sees that two boxes are identical in shape and that their internal volumes are the same and match one another exactly. One box is then re-assembled so that it becomes a long box. The child now has to cope with this changed appearance and is examined on his ideas of conservation. The term 'amount of Smarties' is used to convey the idea of internal volume.

Table 56   Results for volume item 7 (average ability)

Answer	7y 5m	7y 11m	8y 5m	8y 11m	9y 5m	9y 11m
	%	%	%	%	%	%
Correct	44	56	66	72	82	79
Compensatory reason	5	7	5	4	2	3
Incorrect: centring	48	36	29	24	16	18
Incorrect: other	3	1	0	0	0	0
Sample size (= 100%)	75	72	79	78	79	76

The results (Table 56) confirm Piaget's categories of answer. The main reason given for maintaining equality of volume was that of reversibility, e.g.

'They both still hold the same amount of Smarties as they were the same at the beginning', etc. A much smaller proportion (on average 5%) maintained equality on the basis that nothing had been added or removed. Once more it can be seen that very few children gave compensatory reasons. Of the children who concluded that volume had changed, nearly all centred their attention on the increased length and concluded that for this box the volume had increased. The numbers of correct responses quite closely matched those of item number 6 (where the blocks were not altered in any way but one was reorientated), but the number of children focusing their attention on the increased length was greater in this item. It appears that the attention and resulting reasoning of many children is easily influenced by visual changes. Once more, other than marking gradual improvement in performance, age gives little guidance on the conceptual understanding of individual children. Over 40% of the $7\frac{1}{2}$ year-old children answered correctly whereas over 20% of the 10 year-olds of average ability were still deceived by the visual changes.

Results: item 8

The previous item examined the understanding of conservation of volume of space in a box. It was wondered to what extent the children would maintain this level of understanding when they faced similar tasks on volumes of solid objects and volumes of liquids. Variation of materials obviously altered the pattern of responses, but if the additional tasks were carefully designed so that, as nearly as possible, they matched one another in complexity, it was probable that evidence would emerge on the general conceptual ability of children to conserve volume when faced with apparently conflicting visual evidence. Alternatively, evidence would emerge on the relative difficulties of conservation of volume in the examples of 'contained space' volume, solid volume and liquid volume.

This item provides the same type of problem as the previous one but uses liquids. However, two variations of the problem are given to the child. In the first part the liquids are eventually poured into two vessels of differing shape, whilst in the second part they are poured into a number of separate cylinders. In the first case, therefore, the liquid from any one container is never divided into smaller volumes, i.e. it remains in a 'continuous' form, whereas in the second part the liquid from any one container is divided up, i.e. it can be considered to be made into a 'discontinuous' form. From previous research it might be hypothesized that the latter presentation would encourage the children to reverse the operation and mentally visualize the liquid made up into its original total volume, so that the discontinuous form of the test would be expected to produce a higher number of correct responses at all ages than the 'continuous' form.

In item 8a the distracting visual elements are the shapes of the two vessels and the resulting different levels of liquid in them. In item 8b the distracting elements are the different numbers of small beakers used (5 for one pouring and 4 for the other), the two different types of beaker used for each pouring (the 5 beaker set are of narrow diameter, the 4 beaker set have a wider diameter) and the different levels of liquid in each beaker. Because of the greater number of distracting visual aspects, and also because the test procedure probably relies more on memory factors than item number 7 (Table 56), it would be reasonable to expect that the number of correct responses to be lower.

Table 57   Results for volume item 8a: 'continuous' form of presentation

Answer	7y 5m	7y 11m	8y 5m	8y 11m	9y 5m	9y 11m
	%	%	%	%	%	%
Correct	43	44	62	62	81	82
Compensatory reason	19	17	19	24	9	14
Incorrect: centring	37	38	16	13	9	4
Incorrect: other	1	1	3	1	1	0
Sample size (= 100%)	75	72	79	78	79	76

Table 58   Results for volume item 8b: 'discontinuous' form of presentation

Answer	7y 5m	7y 11m	8y 5m	8y 11m	9y 5m	9y 11m
	%	%	%	%	%	%
Correct	35	46	56	67	75	78
Compensatory reason	19	14	13	13	9	8
Incorrect: centring	37	26	23	12	11	13
Incorrect: other	9	14	8	8	5	1
Sample size (= 100%)	75	72	79	78	79	76

The results (Tables 57–8) do vary somewhat in the two parts of the test, and also vary from those of the previous item, but all the results at each age tend to display a similar overall pattern. Certainly no clear distinguishing performance levels emerge. The children do seem to use one of two arguments, based either on concreto-logical reasoning or on simple appearances. Furthermore, they tend to use the same arguments when presented with similar problems on enclosed volume and liquid volume, although there is some variation from test to test. Here there is no obvious distinction between the 'continuous' and 'discontinuous' form of the test. In the first part the children giving incorrect answers centred or focused their attention on the different levels of liquid; in the second part there was more variation in the reasons given for the incorrect choices (the number of conflicting visual possibilities is, in any case, greater), but the majority of these children focused their attention on the numbers of beakers, e.g. 'There is more liquid here because there are more beakers'. Once more, too, it is observed that over 40% of the $7\frac{1}{2}$ year-old children of average ability reasoned correctly whilst 20% of their 10 year-old counterparts failed to explain their reasons correctly.

Results: item 9

This is a variation of the previous item but examines conservation in relation to solid volume. The test is presented in a 'continuous' form, in that the pieces of each block are always joined together. Further, the test uses both abstract (9a) and concrete (9b) forms of wording in the questions. Because the degree of manipulation carried out by the tester is more straightforward than in the previous items, it could be hypothesized that the numbers of correct results might be greater than before.

The numbers of correct responses (Table 59), especially at the younger age

Table 59   Results for volume item 9 (average ability)

Answer	7y 5m	7y 11m	8y 5m	8y 11m	9y 5m	9y 11m
	%	%	%	%	%	%
9a (using term 'amount of room')						
Correct	55	51	71	68	80	74
Compensatory reason	4	4	4	2	2	4
Incorrect: centring	40	41	24	28	16	22
Incorrect: other	1	4	1	2	2	0
9b (using term 'amount of chocolate')						
Correct	56	53	73	76	87	79
Compensatory reason	3	5	4	1	3	6
Incorrect: centring	40	36	20	23	9	15
Incorrect: other	1	6	3	0	1	0
Sample size (= 100%)	75	72	79	78	79	76

levels, did improve and answers based on logical reasoning were given. Nearly all the incorrect answers, on the other hand, were based on reasons governed by the increased length. It was assumed that some children would associate 'amount of room' with length and give different responses when the concrete term 'amount of chocolate' was used. This tendency, which had emerged in earlier items, was not evident in the responses of the children of average ability, although it was noticed in the responses of the group of low ability children. (Figures for this latter group have not been given here — see following chapters.)

Results: item 10

In all the previous tests the children remain in a passive situation, without manipulating any of the materials themselves. Examination of other researches seems to show that, if the children have to manipulate the materials in the tests, their responses often differ considerably from their answers in the passive type of test. Item 10 corresponds to the Piagetian 'houses on an island base' problem, in that the children first see that two blocks have the same shape and same volume. The blocks are then dismantled and one is built into a different shape by the tester and the child is asked to build, in effect, any shape that has the same volume as the other. The item is so constructed that the pupil cannot deduce equality by simply counting the numbers of pieces — thereby probably equating number rather than volume — because the number of pieces is different in each block. Nor can he match the two shapes exactly, although he can make a very similar shape that has a different width or height.

By this design it was hoped that evidence would be forthcoming on the degree to which the children conserved volume and used logical reasoning (based on reversibility or non-removal/addition of pieces), or failed to conserve and, centring their attention on the visual aspects, attempted to match shapes or to equate the numbers of blocks. Once more the test was repeated so that item 10a used the term 'amount of room' and 10b used the term 'amount of chocolate'.

The results (Table 60) improve when the more realistic form of questioning is used, and once more indicate that some children did not attach the meaning of 'volume' to the term 'amount of room'. Nevertheless the general pattern of the results agrees quite well with those of the earlier items in this section. Conservation of volume did not seem to be recognized by a considerable proportion of pupils of average ability in our sample. The majority of the incorrect responses show that these pupils concentrated on the immediately visible changes and based their reasoning for volume changes on these irrelevant distractions.

Table 60   Results for volume item 10 (average ability)

Answer	7y 5m	7y 11m	8y 5m	8y 11m	9y 5m	9y 11m
	%	%	%	%	%	%
10a (using term 'amount of room')						
Correct	48	43	44	51	58	63
Incorrect: attempted to make a similar shape	52	57	56	49	42	37
10b (using term 'amount of chocolate')						
Correct	53	50	49	60	70	78
Incorrect: attempted to make a similar shape	47	50	51	40	30	22
Sample size (= 100%)	75	72	79	78	79	76

Summary of test results: conservation of volume

The results of this series of tests agree with one another on the whole, and all clearly show that reasons based on perception are more commonly given by younger ($7\frac{1}{2}$ years of age) than older children (10 years). Reasons based on the idea of reversibility, on the other hand, are more commonly given by the older children. The pattern of these results agrees closely with the findings of Piaget and others although there are generally greater numbers of correct responses at all ages than in many of the researches referred to earlier.

All the tests were designed to match one another as closely as possible in terms of practical procedure and of the questions. Nevertheless, there is some variation in the numbers of correct responses, especially at the younger ages, and also in the number of occasions when incorrect reasons based on visual perception are given. Solid volume seems to present fewer problems than liquid volume or 'contained space' volume, but such a general interpretation may not reflect a true measure of concept development. It may be that correlations of this type are simply indicators of how well the different tests in question match one another in terms of complexity. In these examples the tests were especially designed in an attempt to overcome the matching problem, and the differences in responses are likely to be due to the pupil's conceptual ability. This interpretation is of importance when we consider other researches which maintain that one form of manifestation of volume (e.g. 'occupied space' volume) is harder (say) to grasp than another form (e.g. solid volume). Such conclusions may not be justified if the two tests used to examine these different forms have not been carefully matched in practical design and in the nature of the questions.

Although there is strong evidence of development with age, the proportions of correct and incorrect responses at all ages demonstrate once more the doubtful value of relating knowledge and understanding of conservation of volume to age. This has obvious implications for the teacher in the classroom.

For the teacher the results of this series of tests have considerable bearing on the form of learning sequence that would best promote understanding of the concept of volume. If children cannot conserve volume when changes of dimension occur, they will obviously experience considerable difficulty when attempting to equate volumes at a later stage. Estimation or compensatory reasoning does not allow these children to grasp the idea of conservation, and it can be argued that the only way they can grasp that the long box in item 7, for example, still has the same internal volume as the other box is by measurement using units of volume.

Earlier it was shown that the majority of children were able to pick out equal volume shapes if these shapes were identical (the cubes in item 1 for example, were selected by all the pupils). It is through the use of such cubes as units of volume that children could check for conservation of volume. In a similar way, a unit of liquid volume (a small rectangular container) could be used for liquid measurements. Materials of this type — different shaped boxes, containers of similar shape but with different sides removed for filling purposes, containers of different shapes but similar volumes for liquid pouring experiments — should feature in sequential learning tasks for the children in the 7–9 year-old range (and, as is evident, for a considerable proportion of the older children). Careful selection of such materials by the teacher is by no means an easy task and it is for this reason that we have made further suggestions in the companion teachers' guide.

DISPLACED VOLUME

Tests examining the children's understanding of displaced volume have nearly all involved the placing of objects in containers of water and the asking of questions related to the degree of rise or fall of the level of water in the container. All these researches agree that the concept of displaced volume is more complex than simple conservation of volume. It has been pointed out that the degree of logic required to conclude that, when two objects of similar volume but different shape are placed in turn in a container of water, the volume of water displaced is also the same, is more complicated than that required for concluding that when one volume is transformed in shape the volume is conserved. The complexity of the logic involved in displacement may be illustrated in a simplified Piagetian form as follows. If A is the volume of water in the container and the volumes of the two different shaped objects are B and C, then if the two objects were placed in turn in the water, the apparent increase in volume of the water would be X and Y where $A - B = X$ and $A - C = Y$. But if the child realized that $B = C$ in volume, i.e. he conserved solid volume even though the two shapes were different, he would not be able to conclude that $X = Y$ in volume unless he had the mental ability *logically* to work out that, since $A - B = X$ and $A - C = Y$, since $B = C$ and since A has not changed therefore *X must be equal to Y*.

The only other way the child could conclude that the two displaced volumes were the same was by imagining or realizing in concrete terms that each block would 'push aside' its own volume of water and that this volume of water pushed aside would always be conserved even though it was in imagination pushed aside by the block at the bottom of the container and appeared as an increase in level of the water near the top of the container. To hinder the children's understanding of this idea further, the rise in levels of the water is affected by the surface area of the water in the container, i.e. the increase in height will not necessarily match the height of the displacing blocks. It is extremely difficult to design tests which examine the children's understanding of displaced volume, as one can never be certain that they understand the purpose of the question; the many distracting visual aspects of the test situation may confuse pupils so that they fail to grasp the question at all. In an attempt to isolate fundamental misconceptions, the following materials are designed in a different way from the typical Piagetian tests examining the concept of displaced volume.

Assessment items 11–13 correspond to *AWV*, Tests 10 (item 12 does not appear in *AWV*) and 11.

Item 11: Perspex container and metal block; displacement bucket; shorter glass cylinder; fibre pen; jug of water; red box from item 1

Place the displacement bucket on the box with the glass cylinder under the spout.

>   *'Watch carefully.'*

Fill the displacement bucket to the spout with water, allowing the water to

overflow into the cylinder, and wait until the water overflow stops.
Meanwhile show S the metal block and Perspex container and gently push the
block to the bottom of the container.

'*Look, this block just fits into the box like this.*'

Remove the block from the container and replace the cylinder by the plastic
box (under the spout of the displacement bucket). Hold the block above the
bucket.

'*Look into the bucket. If I put the block into the bucket so that it was
completely under the water, what would happen to the water?*'

If S does not refer to outflow of water through the spout,

'*What else would happen to the water?*'

If S still does not refer to outflow through the spout, end item and proceed to
No. 12. Otherwise proceed.

11a Place the block on the table near to the container so that its base is of
equal area to the base of the container and is similarly orientated.

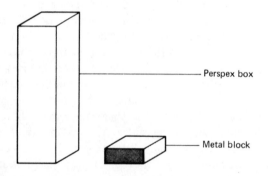

'*If I put the block into the bucket so that it was completely under the
water, can you mark with this pen where the top of the water would
come to in the box?*'

If S marks the container at the correct level,

'*Why do you think that amount of water would come out?*'

11b Hold the block above the can orientated with its longest dimension as its
height.

'*Look, I've turned the block round. If I lowered the block into the
bucket so that it was completely under the water, can you mark where
the top of the water would come to in the box?*'

Immediately and without altering the orientation of the block, place it on the
table close to the Perspex container.

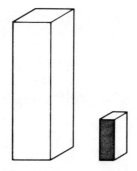

'Why do you think that amount of water would come out?'

Item 12: 2 bar and 1 C magnet; displacement bucket; jug of water; shorter glass cylinder; fibre pen; red box from item 1

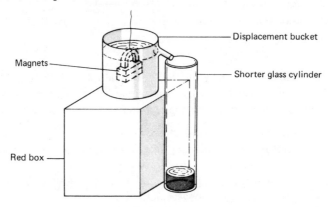

Using the displacement bucket filled to the overflow level (if proceeding from item 11, this has already been achieved), place the empty cylinder under the spout.

'Watch carefully.'

12a Hold the magnets above the bucket and lower them until they are just immersed; wait until the overflow stops. Give the pen to S.

'Look, the object is completely under the water. Mark where the top of the water has come to in the jar.'

'Now, what would happen if I lowered the object to the bottom of the can?'

'Why do you say that?'

Remove the magnets from the bucket.

12b Pour the water from the glass cylinder into the displacement bucket without erasing the ink line. Change the shape of the object to an elongated form.

Hold the magnets above the can.

> '*If I lowered the object so that it was* <u>completely</u> *under the water, mark where the top of the water would come to in the jar* [indicate glass cylinder].'
>
> '*Why have you marked it there?*'

Item 13: 3 cubes: A, B and C (A and B of equal volume, C of greater volume; A and C of equal weight, B heavier than A and C); displacement bucket; shorter glass cylinder; fibre pen; jug of water; red box from item 2; balance

Place cubes A and B on the table in front of S.

> '*Does this block* [indicate A] *take up the same amount of room as that block* [indicate B]*?*'

If necessary demonstrate, by picking up the cubes, that they have matching dimensions, then repeat the above question.

> '*Watch carefully, I am going to weigh them.*'

Place A and B on separate balance pans.

> '*Which block is heavier? Which weighs more?*'

If S does not understand how to use the balance, repeat this item after S has completed the Weight Test [see p. 47]. Otherwise proceed.

> '*That's right, A takes up the same amount of room as B, but B is heavier than A.*'

Fill up the displacement bucket to overflowing, as previously, then place the empty glass cylinder under the spout.

> '*Watch carefully.*'

13a Lower A gently into the displacement bucket. Collect the displaced water in the cylinder and mark the water level with the fibre pen. Remove A from the bucket. Pour the water from the cylinder back into the bucket. Replace the cylinder under the spout.

> *'Do you remember, A takes up the same amount of room as B, but B is heavier than A?*
>
> *'When I put A into the bucket this amount of water came out* [indicate mark on cylinder]. *If I had put B into the bucket instead would more water have come out, less water or the same amount?'*
>
> *'Why do you say that?'*

Place A and C in front of S.

> *'Which block takes up more room?'*
>
> *'Watch carefully, I am going to weigh them.'*

Place A and C on separate balance pans.

> *'Do they both weigh the same?'*
>
> *'That's right, C takes up more room than A, but A weighs the same as C.'*

13b *'When we put this block* [indicate A] *into the bucket, this amount of water came out* [indicate mark on cylinder]. *If we had put this block* [indicate C] *into the bucket instead would more water have come out, less water or the same amount?'*
'Why do you say that?'

Results: item 11

In order to eliminate some of the confusing variables referred to earlier and to guide the children to think in terms of the block pushing aside its own volume of water, this test uses a displacement bucket fitted with an overflow spout. Furthermore the child first sees (11a) that a block fits exactly into a rectangular container, i.e. the cross-sectional area of the block and container are the same. The block is removed, the displacement bucket filled to overflowing with water and the container placed under the spout. The pupil does not actually see what would happen if the object is placed under the water. He is simply asked to express his beliefs and to predict what would happen. To help him, the block is placed alongside the container so that it corresponds to its orientation when in the container. In this item the pupil's understanding is indicated by the marks which he makes on the container in addition to his verbal answers.

The numbers of correct responses (Table 61) are consistently lower at all ages than in previous tests, although once more there is a steady increase with age. Again some 20% of the $7\frac{1}{2}$ year-olds of average ability were able to give the correct answer and correct reasoning whilst 40% of the 10 year-olds could not. All the children realized water was displaced, but many children marked the container at arbitrary heights. A small proportion of children did mark the

Table 61 Results for volume item 11a (average ability)

Answer	7y 5m	7y 11m	8y 5m	8y 11m	9y 5m	9y 11m
	%	%	%	%	%	%
Marks container at correct height and gives correct explanation	20	36	32	46	54	61
Marks container at correct height but cannot give explanation	9	13	8	6	18	7
Marks container at incorrect height	71	51	61	47	28	33
Sample size (= 100%)	75	72	79	78	79	76

container at the correct height but were unable to explain the reason for their choice. These particular children are of interest as they provide some evidence that they may have the concept of displacement in their minds although quite unable to analyse and express their reasons in words.

In order to examine this concept further, the block was then reorientated (11b) so that its longer side was in an upright position and the previous question repeated. Following earlier results, it was anticipated that a proportion of the pupils who were previously correct would now change their minds, focus their attention on the increased dimension and mark the displaced water level higher up the box.

The majority of children did predict that the level of water would be higher in the container as a result of reorientating the block (Table 62). A few of the children who had marked the correct height in the first part also believed that more water would now be displaced and used the new height of the box to mark this predicted level. Their ability to think of volume in terms of three dimensions was limited.

Perhaps the most interesting findings, however, was that a small number of children (shown, in particular, by the increase in correct responses from 20% to 27% at the $7\frac{1}{2}$ year-old level) who had earlier marked the predicted level of water at the obviously incorrect height nevertheless maintained that the same level would be observed when the block was turned round, i.e. they did not relate the actual volume of displaced water to the volume of the block but nevertheless agreed to conservation of the displaced volume when the block

Table 62   Results for volume item 11b (average ability)

Answer	7y 5m	7y 11m	8y 5m	8y 11m	9y 5m	9y 11m
	%	%	%	%	%	%
Correct reasoning: same amount of water would go into box	27	22	38	40	49	54
Correct marking: same amount of water would go into box as block still weighs the same	3	1	4	6	8	4
Incorrect: centring (more water would go into box)	35	50	33	35	32	35
Incorrect: other	35	18	25	19	11	7
Sample size (= 100%)	75	72	79	78	79	76

was reorientated. This finding seems to imply that knowledge of conservation of displaced volume does not necessarily mean that equality of displaced volume with the volume of the displacing block is recognised.

A small proportion of the children equated displaced volume with the weight of the block. As this notion had been witnessed by other researchers (see p. 141), this was explored further in item 13.

Results: item 12

The solid object used in this item consists of three magnets which are first arranged in a compact form and immersed so that they are just under the surface of the water. In the first part the children are asked to predict what would happen if the object was lowered to the bottom of the displacement bucket. Having marked the level of displaced water in the cylinder under the spout, the child is asked in the second part for his views about the volume of displaced water when the solid is rearranged into an elongated form. Once more the visual aspect of an increased dimension is introduced, so that the child has two conflicting viewpoints, one based on logic and conservation of volume and the other on simple appearances.

The introduction of the problem of depth immersed and its likely effect on the displaced water immediately affected the pupils' answers on displaced volume. Very few children of average ability in the age range $7\frac{1}{2}$–10 years in our sample still conserved displaced volume in item 12a (Table 63). The majority of children believed that if objects sank deeper then more water would be displaced, i.e. they associated an increase in something (in this case, depth) with an increase in displaced volume. Some of these children tried to explain their reasoning further; of these, an identifiable proportion talked about the magnets pressing down more or water pressing up more as the magnets went deeper. The children had, in fact, put forward a reasonable hypothesis which could only be checked by measurement.

Table 63   Results for volume item 12a (average ability)

Answer	7y 5m	7y 11m	8y 5m	8y 11m	9y 5m	9y 11m
	%	%	%	%	%	%
Correct: no more water would be displaced	7	4	10	6	15	16
Incorrect: magnets heavier	20	14	19	19	19	7
Incorrect: magnets pressing down more	17	22	20	22	30	24
Incorrect: magnets gone deeper	40	40	35	31	24	32
Incorrect: other	16	20	16	22	12	21
Sample size (= 100%)	75	72	79	78	79	76

The results of these items are of considerable importance, as they raise two issues in relation to previous Piagetian research. First, it has been shown that many children do conserve displaced volume in fairly straightforward examples but, when the problem of depth immersed has also to be considered, they have to rely on hypothesis only. In the Piagetian test using unit blocks and a single container (repeated by Lovell and Ogilvie, 1961b) the blocks are seen to be at the bottom of the container whereas the water is seen to be displaced 'at the top' (i.e. the level of the water changes). When the block is rearranged it is seen, in effect, to be at a different depth and, following their theory, the children are bound to conclude that the volume of water displaced at the top will alter. Obviously this is evidence of a poorly developed concept of volume but the point at issue is that if children believe that increased depth will mean increased displacement then conservation of volume of the original block does not affect their belief about displaced volume. As the results clearly show that this belief is commonly held, the simple explanation of the concept of displaced volume in terms of conservation of volume of the displacing block given in earlier researches is not entirely satisfactory.

Secondly, in giving this answer, especially in terms of further explanations using the idea of 'pressing up' or 'pressing down', the children are, in effect, hypothesizing and displaying a form of reasoning close to the level of formal operations. However, it is unlikely that these children could display further intellectual ability and be able to work out procedures which would verify their hypothesis; it is such ability that distinguishes the child who has reached the advanced stage of formal operations from his less able colleagues. This point is explored further in item 17.

Once more a considerable proportion of the pupils related the volume of displaced water to the weight of the displaced object and, curiously, expressed the belief that the object became heavier as it sank deeper into the water. This idea can be explained if it is assumed that the children have experience of trying to push objects which float (say, blocks of wood or toy boats) under the water; they may have felt an apparent increase of upthrust as they pushed (an apparent real life experience) and concluded that the blocks were 'heavier' without relating the concept of 'heaviness' to a downward force.

Table 64   Results for volume item 12b (average ability)

Answer	7y 5m	7y 11m	8y 5m	8y 11m	9y 5m	9y 11m
	%	%	%	%	%	%
Correct: elongation of magnets has no effect on displaced volume	21	33	51	45	56	62
Incorrect: centred on change in dimensions	19	23	15	7	3	13
Incorrect: magnets heavier	16	11	9	13	14	8
Incorrect: other	44	33	25	35	27	17
Sample size (= 100%)	75	72	79	78	79	76

The numbers of correct responses for item 12b (Table 64) may be compared with those of item 11b. For some children a degree of learning seems to have taken place as there are slightly more correct responses at each age level, i.e. more conserved displaced volume with change of orientation of the displacing block.

Change in dimension and beliefs relating the weight of the block to displaced volume also affected the children's responses. Of interest, however, are the large number of incorrect responses where the reasons given do not fit into well-defined patterns of misconceived ideas. The reasons given are often imaginative and, at best, show that the children have poorly developed ideas on displaced volume.

The final test item explored the misconception of the relationship between the weight of the immersed object and the displaced volume.

Results: item 13

In the previous items it cannot be concluded that those children who maintained that the volume of water displaced would remain unchanged had a sound concept, as their reasons were very often of the form 'It is still the same block, nothing has been added or taken away'. One cannot tell, for example, whether the children thought that the weight of the block or its volume is the important unchanged factor. In the first part of the test item the two blocks have the same volume but are different in weight. In the second part the two blocks have the same weight but different volumes. Earlier research used practical objects of the first type, and it was wondered whether the children centred their attention on the weight factor simply because it was the only difference that was displayed and accentuated. If this hypotheses was true, it would follow that in the second item, where the weight factor was kept

Table 65   Results for volume item 13a (average ability)

Answer	7y 5m	7y 11m	8y 5m	8y 11m	9y 5m	9y 11m
	%	%	%	%	%	%
Correct: displaced volume the same	15	11	19	9	22	26
Incorrect: centred on weight	76	79	78	83	73	71
Incorrect: other	9	10	3	8	5	3
Sample size (= 100%)	75	72	79	78	79	76

Table 66   Results for volume item 13b (average ability)

Answer	7y 5m	7y 11m	8y 5m	8y 11m	9y 5m	9y 11m
	%	%	%	%	%	%
Correct: displaced volume different	31	42	27	24	32	34
Incorrect: centred on weight	60	44	70	69	63	64
Incorrect: other	9	14	3	7	5	2
Sample size (= 100%)	75	72	79	78	79	76

constant but the volumes were clearly seen to be different, the children would change their minds and give reasons based on the visual difference in volume. If children really believed that weight was the important factor affecting displacement then they would be expected to conclude that the displaced volumes would be the same in the second part because 'the weight of the two objects is the same'.

The two sets of results, taken together (Tables 65–6), confirm Piaget's finding that thinking of the children in our age range is easily dominated by immediate appearances. Many children who relied on reasons based on weight differences changed their minds when volume differences dominated in the test situation. This point stresses once more the importance of test design. If our information and interpretation of children's conceptual ability relied on the results of item 13b, for example, the number of correct responses would be an over-estimation.

Although a significant proportion of children did change their minds from one item to the other, it is evident that the majority did believe the weight of the object to be the property affecting the volume displaced. This clear result is rather surprising, especially when older children are considered, as the volumes of the two objects in the second part of the test were clearly very different.

Summary of test results: displaced volume

1. The concept of displaced volume introduces many distracting and often irrelevant factors into the test situation and this makes interpretation of children's responses a very difficult task. Earlier research, relying on one or two practical tests, has probably oversimplified the analysis of concept development in this topic.

2. The concept of displaced volume is harder for the children in the 7–10 year age range to understand than the concepts of solid or occupied volume. Nevertheless, a fifth of the younger children of average ability did display a good understanding of displaced volume, and it is clearly impossible to generalize that such conceptual ideas are beyond the mental ability of children in any of the age groups examined.

3. The majority of the children related displaced volume to the weight of the displacing object and many also concluded that increased depth of immersion would mean an increase in the volume of water displaced.

4. Many children put forward intelligent explanations for their answers even though they were wrong and could, therefore, be ranked as poor conservers. The giving of wrong answers may display misconception but very often fails to indicate the way the children are grappling with the problem. In these concept tests some children were immediately deceived by appearances alone and fitted neatly into the Piagetian pattern. Others, on the other hand, displayed elementary logic and attempted to explain their answers in a reasoned form even though, to adults, their conclusions were incorrect.

The research worker once more beholds the problem of test design and interpretation. There is room for further development in this field and more detailed sequences of tests, carefully analysed and structured, are called for before firm conclusions on the nature of Piagetian stages can be reached. The present study attempted to eliminate many of the variable factors inherent in the more clinical test situations; although the results of this particular section have isolated key misconceptions held by children, there are considerable uncertainties in interpreting the possible reasons for these misconceptions. These uncertainties can only be resolved by more detailed and structured tests. The particularity of individual responses is observed once more and the wide range of performance with age prevents accurate prediction of performance at any given age level.

For the teacher the results and interpretation call for this topic to be introduced with caution. If the apparatus and questioning procedure are not carefully structured and arranged in sequence, it is very likely that the children will merely become more confused in their ideas. On the other hand, the numbers of lower responses do not suggest, as is often stated, that this topic should not be introduced at all in the primary school stage. Indeed, one felt that, as many of the children giving incorrect answers displayed an ability mentally to grapple with the problem of displaced volume, they were ready to explore this concept through meaningful practical experiences. Unfortunately, it is doubtful whether many of the children in the 9–11 year age range have such experiences. Again, too, the importance of discussion is brought out in these findings. It is only through such discussion that the teacher can discover the conceptual ability of the child: merely answering set exercises of a written form does not supply such evidence.

MEASUREMENT OF VOLUME AND THE USE OF LOGIC

Piaget has maintained that logical reasoning can be demonstrated at the concrete stage of operations but the logic displayed is of a limited nature. The nature of this logic is discussed in the introductory chapters. Three test items (14, 15 and 17) examine this growing ability in the children in our sample.

Fundamental to the further understanding of the concept of volume is the ability to measure volume and, as Piaget maintains that this is developed at a later stage than the idea of conservation of volume, item 16, examining this ability, is included in this section.

Assessment items 14–17 correspond to *AWV*, Tests 12, 15, 9 and 13 for volume.

Item 14: 2 T-shaped objects, 1 made up of 2 blocks, the other of 4 blocks; 2 blue boxes (1 and 2) to hold T-shapes

[NB The internal volumes of the boxes are the same.]

Place the T-shapes in front of S as shown in the diagram.

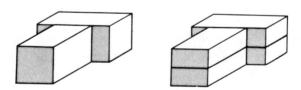

'*Does this T-shape* [indicate] *take up the same amount of room as that T-shape, or does it take up a different amount of room?*'
If S answers '*no*', show that the two T-shapes have matching dimensions and repeat the question.

Match cross-sections

Match heights

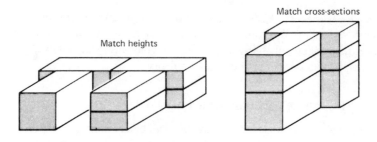

If S still answers '*no*',
    '*Why do you say that?*'
End item. Otherwise proceed.

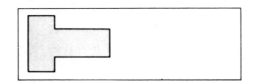

Place box 1 on the table in front of S as shown in the diagram.
Put the solid T-shape into the box.
    '*Look, this shape just fits inside this box and there is no room left over.*'
Take the shape out of the box and place it close to the box on the table in
front of S. Pointing to the *other* T-shape,
    '*Would this fit into the box?*'
S is not allowed to handle the shapes.
If S answers '*no*' or '*I don't know*', end item.
If S answers '*yes*', proceed.
    '*Will there by any room left over in the box?*'
    '*Now, watch carefully.*'
Change the shape of the second T-shape to an elongated form.

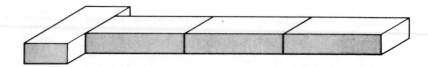

Place box 2 in front of S.

> *'Look, this shape just fits inside this box so that there is no room left over.'*

Demonstrate.

Push the T-shapes to one side and place the boxes close to each other in front of S.

> *'Does this box have the same amount of room inside it as that one, or does it have a different amount of room inside it?'*

If S answers *'the same'*,

> *'Why do you say that?'*

If S answers *'one is longer but the other is deeper'* or similar compensatory reason,

> *'Is there any other reason why it has the same amount of room inside?'*

If S answers *'different'*,

> *'Which has more room inside?'*
> *'Why do you say that?'*

Item 15: 2 wooden cubes A and B, each constructed of 4 equal parts

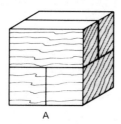 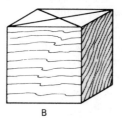

A   B

Place the two cubes in front of S, assembled as in the diagram.

> *'Does this* [indicate one cube] *take up the same amount of room as that* [indicate second cube] *or does it take up a different amount of room?'*

If necessary demonstrate by matching the dimensions, and repeat the question.

Separate the parts of A (rectangular shapes) of one cube.

'Do these blocks take up the same amount of room as each other or different amounts of room?'

If necessary match the dimensions and repeat the question.

Separate the parts of B (triangular shapes) of the other cube.

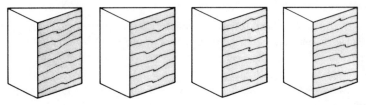

'Do these blocks take up the same amount of room as each other or different amounts of room?'

If necessary match the dimensions and repeat the question.

15a Place one of the rectangular pieces and one of the triangular pieces side by side in front of S. Removing the remaining parts to one side.

'Does this [indicate rectangular shape] *take up the same amount of room as that* [indicate triangular shape] *or does it take up a different amount of room?'*

If S answers *'the same'*,

'Why do you say that?'

If S answers *'different'*,

'Which takes up more room?'

'Why do you say that?'

Remove cube B.

Item 15 (cont): 2 cubes A and C, each constructed of 4 equal parts

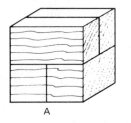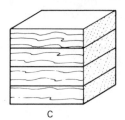

| A | C |

Construct two cubes A and C.

'I want you to imagine that these are made of chocolate. Does this block [indicate A] *have the same amount of chocolate as that block*

[indicate C] *or does it have a different amount of chocolate?'*
If necessary demonstrate by matching the dimensions, and repeat the question.

Separate the parts (rectangular shapes) of one cube A.
   'Do these have the same amount of chocolate as each other, or do they
   have different amounts of chocolate?'
If S answers *'different'*, match the dimensions and repeat the question.

Separate the parts of C.

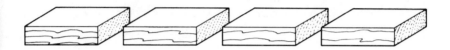

   'Do these have the same amount of chocolate as each other, or do they
   have different amounts of chocolate?'
If S answers *'no'*, match the dimensions and repeat the question.

15b Place one rectangular piece and one square piece side by side in front of S.
Remove the remaining pieces to one side.

 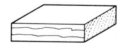

   'Does this [indicate rectangular shape] *have the same amount of*
   chocolate as that [indicate square shape] *or does it have a different*
   amount of chocolate?'
If S answers *'the same'*,
   'Why do you say that?'
If S answers *'different'*,
   'Which has more chocolate?'
   'Why do you say that?'

Item 16: 2 wooden blocks, X and Y; 24 unit blocks

[NB X uses 11 blocks, Y uses 12.]

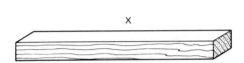

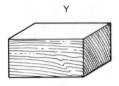

Place the two blocks, X and Y, and the unit blocks on the table in front of S.
  'Find out which of these two blocks takes up more room. Which has
  more wood? I want you to use these blocks [indicate units].'
Repeat the question if S is hesitant.
  'Which one takes up more room? Which one has more wood?'
  'Why do you say that?'

**Item 17: 3 Perspex containers: 1 rectangular-based, A, 1 a cube, B and 1
triangular-based, C. bucket of water; jug; funnel; plastic bowl; 2 glass cylinders;
fibre pen**

[NB Internal volumes, in descending order: A, B, C. The glass cylinders are of
different heights.]

Place a jug of water, taller cylinder, pen, bowl and funnel on the table in front
of S. Show S the rectangular-based container A and cube B.
  'Try to find out which of these two [indicate containers] *has more*
  room inside it. You may use any of these if you wish [indicate
  apparatus].'
If S hesitates repeat the question.
If S is still unable to operate,
  'Which do you think has more room inside it?'
End item. Otherwise proceed.

After S has finished experimenting,
  'Which has more room inside it?'
  'Why have you chosen that one?'
If S answers incorrectly or fails to operate successfully, end item. Otherwise
proceed.

Empty containers A and B. Replace the rectangular-based A with the triangular-
based container C, and the tall glass cylinder with the shorter one.
  'Try to find out which of these two [indicate containers B and C] *has*
  more room inside it. You may use any of these if you wish [indicate
  apparatus].'

If S answers incorrectly, end item. Otherwise proceed.

Empty the Perspex containers and place them on the table in front of S with the cube in the middle. Point to the cube B and the rectangular-based container A.
> *'Do you remember, which of these two has more room inside?'*

If S answers incorrectly, end item. Otherwise proceed.
Point to the cube B and triangular-based container C.
> *'Do you remember, which of these two has more room inside?'*

If S answers incorrectly, end item. Otherwise proceed.

Finally, point to the rectangular- and triangular-based containers A and C.
> *'Which of these two has more room inside?'*
> *'Why do you say that?'*

Results: item 14

In this item the pupil first sees that the two T-shaped blocks have equal volumes and that they both fit into the two boxes. The final question asks him, in effect, to base his answers on one of two ways of thinking. The pupil at the concrete operational level will be unable to work out that the two boxes must have the same volume (because the blocks were originally seen to have the same volume) and he prefers, or can rely on, a conclusion based on direct comparison or observation and usually gives an answer of the type 'There is more room in that box because it is longer'. The pupil at the logical operational stage, however, disregards appearances and relies on deduction alone and gives answers of the type 'They *must* have the same amount of room

Table 67   Results for volume item 14 (average ability)

Answer	7y 5m	7y 11m	8y 5m	8y 11m	9y 5m	9y 11m
	%	%	%	%	%	%
Correct	12	18	22	28	29	42
Compensatory reason	7	18	13	24	24	20
Incorrect: centring on length	72	46	58	43	42	32
Incorrect: other	9	18	7	5	6	6
Sample size (= 100%)	75	72	79	78	79	76

inside as each other because the blocks had the same volume at first'.

This item is more complex than the earlier straightforward conservation of volume tests. Not only does the child have to retain a larger proportion of information in his mind in order to arrive at the correct logical conclusion, but he also has to understand clearly the relationship between solid and occupied (space) volume. As in the case of earlier items the child is once more placed in a situation where the visual aspect is deliberately accentuated in the final step.

The numbers of correct results (Table 67) are consistently lower than in the case of the series on simple conservation of volume. Furthermore, the number of responses based on centring on the increased length, i.e. on immediate appearances, is considerably increased.

Children who had earlier given correct forms of reasoning (reversibility, etc.) now reverted to reasons based on simple appearances. The increased complexity of the test itself is obviously the cause of this and shows that it is impossible to conclude that if a child has used one form of argument in a particular situation he will use it in all similar situations. Compensatory reasons were given once more and, although this leads to the correct answer, earlier tests showed that the children could not possibly be certain that the greater length of one box exactly compensated for the greater depth of the other.

Results: item 15

This tests the children's understanding of fractions of volumes. As in the concept of area, the child who has a clear understanding of fractions could be expected to answer the final question by deduction alone. On the other hand, children who could not relate the earlier observations to one another and had a poor understanding of fractions would be expected to answer the final question on the basis of guesswork or direct observation. This items calls on the child to retain a number of pieces of information and to analyse their relationships before he can make the final deduction. The correct answer would be of the form 'Both cubes took up the same amount of room (or equal volume) and each was cut into four equal volume parts'.

The nature of the task has features which are similar to the previous test in that the retention of information is a key ingredient. The results can be equated, and one can infer that the nature of the deductive process required represents a more advanced conceptual stage than in the earlier items. Although many of the incorrect responses (Table 68) showed that children once more favoured answers based on immediate appearances, e.g. 'This block is bigger (takes up more room) because that side is longer (etc.)', an equal number

Table 68   Results for volume item 15 (average ability)

Answer	7y 5m	7y 11m	8y 5m	8y 11m	9y 5m	9y 11m
	%	%	%	%	%	%
15a (using term 'amount of chocolate')						
Correct: with explanation	19	18	30	22	42	47
Correct: without explanation	5	3	8	6	12	11
Incorrect: centred on dimensions	41	49	28	32	27	16
Incorrect: other	35	30	34	40	19	26
15b (using term 'amount of room')						
Correct: with explanation	17	14	27	23	43	47
Correct: without explanation	4	6	6	6	14	14
Incorrect: centred on dimensions	37	44	28	40	24	18
Incorrect: other	42	36	39	31	19	21
Sample size (= 100%)	75	72	79	78	79	76

resorted to answers and reasons which did not fit any of the Piagetian categories of typical answers. Many of these children — like their counterparts who gave the correct answer — could not explain their choices at all. They resorted to answers such as 'Because I think so' and gave no further clue about their thinking.

One suspects that, when tests exploring more complex stages of conceptual development are given to children, it becomes more difficult for them to explain in verbal terms the reasons for their answers and the problem of interpretation of responses becomes increasingly more difficult.

Results: item 16

In his experiments Piaget found that the concept of measurement of volume was not grasped by children until they had reached a fairly advanced stage of understanding of the properties of volume. He argued that children would only have the mental ability to cope with three-dimensional measurements using unit volume blocks if they had already firmly grasped the concept of conservation of volume with change of shape and also understood the mental operation of reversibility. On the other hand, it can be argued that children will only be able firmly to grasp the concept of conservation of volume if they have considerable practical experience of measurement of the volume of a shape or box interior before and after dimensional changes are made to the objects in question. Although this type of activity is not as common in the primary school classroom as the corresponding activity in the concept of area, it was assumed that children in this particular sample would have some experience of such activities in the modern classroom. For this reason it was expected that Piaget's finding, relating ability to measure volume using unit blocks to later stages of the development of the concept of volume, would not be so clearly witnessed in our research.

Piaget had also demonstrated that the ability to measure volumes first developed using real, solid, unit volume blocks; the ability to measure volume using a ruler and the associated understanding of the relationship between volume and the separate linear measurements, e.g. volume of a cube = length x height x breadth = (linear dimension of one edge)^3 developed when the child was close to the stage of formal operations.

In the pilot survey we asked children to measure the volume of a block of wood using a ruler and we discovered that very few children were able to do this. Even the majority of the eleven-year-olds simply used any linear measurement in order to give a numerical answer. Often such answers were expressed in centimetres. Sometimes there was evidence that the children were trying to remember a technique of measurement of volume that they had been told. It was observed that a few of the older children did in fact measure three lengths (but not always the right three) and attempted to relate these in some way — usually by adding them together. It was clear that very few children, even at eleven years of age, had an understanding of this principle of measurement of volume.

The numbers of correct results (Table 69) are significantly lower at all ages than for any of the earlier tests on the concept of volume. Earlier items (e.g. item 10) had indicated that children found difficulty in building blocks of similar volumes but different shapes and attempted to do this by matching single dimensions. This item demonstrates that the majority of the children in this age group failed to realize that, to use unit blocks as measurement devices,

Table 69   Results for volume item 16 (average ability)

Answer	7y 5m	7y 11m	8y 5m	8y 11m	9y 5m	9y 11m
	%	%	%	%	%	%
Correct: used unit blocks correctly	12	10	18	19	27	28
Correct use of unit blocks but wrong conclusion	3	2	2	4	2	4
Incorrect: covered surfaces only	53	44	59	42	46	33
Incorrect: measured heights or lengths only	3	3	0	4	2	5
Incorrect: measured perimeters	11	4	0	5	8	5
Incorrect: unable to operate	19	38	22	26	16	25
Sample size (= 100%)	75	72	79	78	79	76

they have to make exactly similar shapes as the volumes to be measured. It can be seen (p. 190) that this test consists of a block (X in the diagram) which can be matched by using a single layer of the unit blocks. Nearly all the children carried out this task successfully, by placing the unit blocks either alongside block X or on top of the upper surface of block X. In other words, it is not clear whether the children were using the unit blocks really to measure length, area of a surface or the volume. When these children were given block Y, very few of them realized the significance of three-dimensional measurements. It could be argued that this was due to manipulation difficulties rather than conceptual ones, but this argument could not be true in this test. The unit blocks and block Y are so designed that the unit blocks can be orientated in any position to make up a block of similar shape to Y. Clearly the concept of measurement of volume by using unit blocks was not understood by the majority of the pupils.

Of the incorrect responses, a few did indeed focus their attention on single linear measurements, e.g. height or perimeter, but most of the children (53% of 7$\frac{1}{2}$ and 33% of 10 year-old children) covered one or more of the surfaces of

the block in order to arrive at a number answer. The reason for this choice
may be due to simple Piagetian centring of attention on any visual aspect that
happens to dominate the situation, but in that case one would expect a more
even distribution of selection of heights or perimeters.

It is interesting to speculate whether the children in our sample had
previously used blocks of this type to cover surfaces in order to measure areas.
A number of books and workcards used by primary school teachers advocate
this approach. If this is true, and the concept of area is taught before the
concept of volume, then such practices could lead to later misconceptions
about volume measurement. One suspects from the results that this may have
happened in our sample. Once more such concept tests indicate possible teaching
approaches. The use of blocks rather than flat surfaces as area measuring units
is, at best, a doubtful practice and could obviously lead to misconceptions
about volume measurement. Further, there appears the question of teaching
sequence. The practice of teaching the concept of area before the concept of
volume may not be justified on concept development grounds. If the interpretation given so far is correct, there is much to be said for introducing suitable
units for both area and volume measurement about the same time. In this way
the children are more likely to realize the significance of, and difference
between, the two types of measurement.

Finally, the proportion of children who were unable to operate at all
should be noticed. These children had no idea how to tackle the problem. By
this time nearly all the children were highly motivated to 'do the puzzle games',
and this complete lack of ability cannot be explained by shyness. They were
quite unable to formulate a procedure in their minds; they neither realized
that two measurements were required before comparisons could be made, nor
understood that the unit blocks were to be used as intermediary measuring
devices. All resorted to simple visual comparisons and many attempted to
match the two blocks by placing one on top of the other. As the blocks were
designed so that such straightforward visual matching was difficult, these
children gave up and did not bother to use the unit blocks at all.

The ability to work out procedures before carrying out an investigation
indicates that the child is moving into the stage of formal operations and the
last item tests for this ability.

Results: item 17

The child is shown two containers and is asked to find out which has the
greater internal volume. To do this he is given a cylinder of greater volume
than the two containers, a pen, bowl and funnel. When the child has obtained
an answer, one of the containers is removed and a third container is introduced.

Once more the child is asked to find the container of greater volume. The container that was common to both measurements is then removed and the first and third containers are placed in front of the child, who is asked to indicate which of these two has the greater volume without carrying out any further practical investigations.

The form of logic that is involved here is of the type: since A is greater than B and B is greater than C, then A *must be* greater than C. In addition to testing this more advanced concreto-logical reasoning, the child is also being required to work out procedures in his mind. However, the task is not completely open-ended in the sense that the tester only presents two containers at a time to the pupil. Further guidance is given with questions designed to encourage the memorization of the important bits of information.

In order to introduce a conflicting visual element into the test, the containers are so designed that, when the final pair is shown to the child, the one which has the least volume is 'taller' than the other. It is argued that strong conservers would ignore this visual aspect and rely on logic in order to arrive at their answers.

Table 70   Results for volume item 17 (average ability)

Answer	7y 5m	7y 11m	8y 5m	8y 11m	9y 5m	9y 11m
	%	%	%	%	%	%
Correct: reasoning correct	5	7	13	15	27	32
Incorrect: conclusions incorrect but separate practical operations correct	9	7	5	10	16	14
Incorrect: unable to operate	85	86	82	76	57	55
Sample size (= 100%)	75	72	79	78	79	76

This task is beyond most of the seven- and eight-year-old children (Table 70). Both the practical procedure and the logical reasoning required exceed their abilities. Many children simply poured water into one container without necessarily filling it. A few were able to work out practical procedures and determine which of *two* containers has the greater volume when they are filled with water. However, these children failed completely to arrive at the correct final solution when the last two containers were placed in front of them and they were asked to work out in their minds which had the greater volume. The logic required was above their heads, and they reverted to arguments based on visual appearances, e.g. 'This has more room inside because it is taller'.

In our pilot survey the proportion of children who fell into this category was, on average, 10% higher than for the quoted sample. Perhaps children in the pilot survey tended to persevere with the separate measurements even though they did not possess the ability to use the separate pieces of information they had gathered.

This test clearly demonstrates that activities involving the working out of procedures and the practice of logic, i.e. the working out of solutions in the mind rather than as a result of direct practical activity, are far more complex in conceptual terms than activities described in earlier test items. Piaget's general pattern of stages is well demonstrated; although this does not allow a teacher to deduce the actual stage reached by an individual according to age, it does allow a teacher witnessing typical misconceptions by a child to plan sequential learning materials which will be meaningful to that child at that stage.

Summary of test results: measurement of volume and use of logic

1. Piaget's general pattern of stages is confirmed; all these tasks proved to be harder for the children.
2. Nevertheless, many of the younger pupils still showed the ability to carry out the tasks successfully.
3. Tests of this type tend to measure manipulation skills and the ability to work out procedures, as well as more advanced logic. It is suggested that many researches do not clearly distinguish between these features when interpretations of test results are made.
4. Measurement of volume proved to be a difficult task, although it is suspected that misconceptions may have arisen because children may have used 'blocks' to measure area in previous class work.
5. Measurement and comparison of volumes by pouring water from one container to the other also proved to be a difficult task for the children. When the task additionally involved the use of logic, the children failed completely.

    This finding is of considerable interest when it is remembered that children are often encouraged to carry out such tasks in the infant classes. In the light of these results, it is extremely doubtful whether such tasks are matched to the developmental level of the child at the infant stage. It would appear that such practical activity would be best carried out some three years later.

For the research worker this section has attempted to probe a stage of conceptual development which is rarely explored in research studies. Most researches on the concept of volume deal exclusively with the idea of conservation, and very few have incorporated test items which examine the children's ability to measure volume, to work out practical activities in their minds, or to use the forms of concreto-logic described by Piaget. Again, the need for further research is pinpointed, and the present study accentuates the need for the careful structuring and designing of suitable test materials.

For the teacher this section questions a number of practices now carried out in the primary school. The need for practice in volume measurement at the primary school stage is obviously indicated, and the present view of teaching the concept of area before that of volume (if volume is taught at all in the primary school) is challenged. The question of sequence is discussed in greater length in the next chapter.

The need for careful structuring of teaching materials is brought out strongly in this section, and the matching of activities to the stage of development of the pupil is concluded to be the most important implication of the results.

8 Comparative study of the order of acquisition of the concepts of weight, area and volume

One of the main objectives of the present research was to examine the same children's responses to similar tests in all three concepts.

The order of acquisition of different concepts has been a topic of considerable interest to Piagetian research workers, and the interpretation of their findings has had some influence on the teaching of these subjects in schools. One of the most common interpretations concerns the order of acquisition of the concepts of weight and volume. It is widely held that the concept of weight is understood before that of volume, and also that the concept of area is easier to understand than that of volume. These conclusions have affected the teaching of these topics in primary schools, and many teachers' guides advocate that the teaching of the concept of weight be carried out at seven or eight years of age, or even earlier, and that volume be left until the final years of the primary school. The concept of area, on the other hand, commonly features in the mathematics curriculum of the 7–11 year-old.

Examination of earlier research on the sequential development of concepts shows that the conclusions were often based on a cross-reference of two different samples, one sample or group experiencing one or two tests on one concept and the other group tests on another concept. These samples were often made up of few children and, in the main, the tests explored the children's understanding of conservation or measurement. More recent researches (e.g. by Beard, Lister, Hyde) have attempted to overcome the obvious weaknesses in these earlier studies and have examined the same children using tests dealing with two or three concepts.

Beard (1963) used five tests in each of the concepts of weight and volume with the same children; Piaget's order of achievement of conservation in the concepts of 'substance' (see earlier note on the concept of substance, p. 142) and weight was not borne out. Commenting on these differences, Beard stressed the importance of relevant practical experience and suggested that success or failure in any one concept seemed to be related to the child's degree of experience in that concept rather than to a natural order of development from one concept to another. In another research (Beard, 1963) concerned with a study of the acquisition of number concepts she suggested that general conclusions on the order of acquisition of different concepts were not so easily deduced (p. 115):

Two points deserve further mention. First, children differed to some degree in the order in which they understood concepts. Some could count fluently to a hundred or more but failed in simple conservation: by contrast, a child who could not count accurately to twenty succeeded in every other item. Secondly, there was a greater variety in the kind of answers given than Piaget describes.

So far, the present research has emphasized the particularity of individual responses in the various test items and, although Piaget's general pattern of development in stages emerges, it is clear that individuals do not necessarily follow such well-defined paths. As such variation had been witnessed, it was wondered to what extent the children would conform to Piaget's pattern of acquisition of concepts, according to which they would tend to understand the concept of weight before area and volume, and their understanding of the concept of volume would prove to be the more difficult.

In order to do this it was necessary to design tests in all three concepts which could be termed 'parallel' items, i.e. having the same basic features and measuring similar conceptual stages, but using different practical materials. The easiest to design of these groups of tests proved to be that concerned with the conservation of weight, area and volume, and the results of this group are considered before those involving the use of concreto-logic and measurement.

In the preceding chapters only the responses of children of average ability (as measured by a non-verbal intelligence test) were considered, but we are now concerned with comparisons between all the children who gave correct responses in the various items; in this chapter, therefore, the figures relate to the total number of children in the sample.

Table 71 presents the results (as percentages) of all the test items in the three concepts which required only the understanding of conservation for their correct solution. Nineteen tests — five for weight, nine for area and five for volume — fell into this category. For each age group the percentage of correct responses as indicated by correct answers and correct verbal explanation is given alongside the number of incorrect responses of the type indicating that the children were basing their conclusions on simple perception or appearances (other incorrect responses are not analysed in this chapter).

Four general points emerge from an examination of this table.

1. With the exception of one or two items, the results all follow the same general trend. It is difficult to conclude that the understanding of conservation in any one concept is more difficult for the children than in

Table 71   Conservation in weight, area and volume

	7y 5m		7y 11m		8y 5m	
	Correct	Incorrect*	Correct	Incorrect*	Correct	Incorrect*
	%	%	%	%	%	%
Weight						
Item 4a	52	28	63	24	66	26
Item 4b	39	37	57	32	60	31
Item 5	41	27	50	19	59	15
Item 6a	59	25	68	17	80	14
Item 6b	68	17	71	17	82	12
. . . .						
Area						
Item 6a	25	47	29	41	43	31
Item 6b	67	19	71	18	85	9
Item 7a	49	38	54	34	71	19
Item 7b	58	29	62	27	75	17
Item 8	8	69	11	70	18	68
Item 9a	58	34	68	24	81	15
Item 9b	70	15	72	18	90	6
Item 9c	61	25	68	17	84	10
Item 10	43	37	43	24	64	18
. . . .						
Volume						
Item 7	51	38	56	28	68	24
Item 8a	43	38	46	32	57	25
Item 8b	35	34	45	29	54	25
Item 9a	51	39	57	33	69	24
Item 9b	52	40	58	28	72	18
. . . .						
Sample size, *N* (= 100%)		146		150		150

* 'Incorrect' refers to incorrect responses due to centring; other incorrect responses are not shown.

8y 11m		9y 5m		9y 11m	
Correct	Incor-rect*	Correct	Incor-rect*	Correct	Incor-rect*
%	%	%	%	%	%
71	19	83	8	80	14
63	25	80	11	77	16
75	6	70	6	74	5
88	7	90	7	84	11
87	6	93	6	91	5
. . . . .	. . . .	. . . .	. . . .	. . . .	. . . .
49	29	63	21	55	25
90	7	87	6	87	8
76	21	78	16	83	15
81	14	85	10	86	9
20	64	21	66	26	66
83	14	90	7	88	9
89	7	93	2	93	2
83	8	90	4	90	5
61	15	69	13	73	9
. . . . .	. . . .	. . . .	. . . .	. . . .	. . . .
71	18	75	20	79	13
62	16	74	11	72	10
63	16	72	15	72	17
70	24	73	24	71	22
75	16	81	12	77	15
. . . . .	. . . .	. . . .	. . . .	. . . .	. . . .
	155		155		149

any of the others. The numbers of fully correct responses range more or less between the same figures from concept to concept. The only clearly observable trend is that fewer children appear to be dominated by visual appearances in the weight tests than in the other two concepts.

2. There is more variation in the numbers of correct responses between similar items in any one concept than can be generally detected between items in different concepts. It should be remembered that, with the exception of the one or two items referred to below, all were carefully designed to be presented in similar fashion. In all these cases the children remained in a passive situation, observing the tester handling the materials. In all these items, too, the children first saw and agreed that the property in question (weight, area or volume) was equal in the two objects. One object was then deformed or rearranged to accentuate a dimension and the children were asked questions of a similar nature to determine whether they understood the concept of conservation.

   Test items using discontinuous objects (weight item 6b; area items 9b and 9c) broken up into separate pieces, rather than objects rearranged into continuous, elongated shapes, produce more correct responses than any other. Other variations in the results are more easily explained in terms of variations between actual items rather than of relative difficulty in understanding one concept (say, weight) rather than another (say, volume).

3. In three or four items the results differ significantly from the general pattern. These differences can be explained in terms of individual design.

   In area item 6 the children did not first see and agree that the two shapes had similar areas. In fact, the two shapes were clearly seen to be different at the beginning of the test and the children were asked, if they thought that they had equal areas. In contrast to all the other items, they were not encouraged, therefore, to use the mental operation of reversibility by any practical procedure on the part of the tester. The children, too, had to manoeuvre the shapes in order to arrive at an answer and this proved to be difficult, especially in item 6a.

   Similarly, in area item 8, the children were given two different shapes and once more asked if they thought the two had similar areas. They had to determine whether they should rely on perception or on arguments based on conservation. The observation that the numbers of correct responses fall dramatically in this item and that the number of reasons based on perception increase correspondingly demonstrates the unstable nature of the children's beliefs and reasoning powers in this age range.

Clearly single tests do not give accurate pictures of children's understanding of a particular concept.

4. The concept of conservation of solid and occupied (space) volume is only marginally more difficult than that of conservation of weight. Indeed, one can perhaps detect that conservation of area is generally better understood than conservation of either weight or volume. This slight difference is perhaps to be expected, as 'area' is commonly taught at this age. Indeed, the conservation of volume is surprisingly well understood, even at $7\frac{1}{2}$ years of age, considering that it is rarely taught directly in the classroom. It would seem that there is very little basis for the supposition that the concept of volume is harder to understand than, say, that of area. From the present results, there is much to be said for the introduction of the concept of conservation in all three topics at about the same time. This question of teaching sequence is referred to again later.

As the results throw considerable doubt on the reliability of earlier research, the analysis has been carried further. Two tests in each concept were selected for closer comparisons. All satisify the three conditions that (i) the children remain in a passive situation; (ii) the children first see and agree that the property in question is the same in the pair of objects; (iii) the children see a dimension changed and are asked whether the property (weight, area or volume) of the objects is still the same, increased or decreased.

Both area test items use shapes that are broken up and reorientated into a continuous form. Weight item 4a is the familiar plasticine ball and sausage test where one ball is elongated. Weight item 6a is similar to the two area items, in that the blocks are broken up and reorientated into a continuous form. This feature is also seen in volume item 7, whereas volume item 8a is the well-known cylinder-conical flask liquid test (here with container and wider beaker, p. 161) and has a slightly more complicated practical procedure than the others in that two other (similar) containers are also used. The results are now presented (Table 72) as actual numbers of children who gave correct responses (percentages are given alongside).

The liquid volume item (8a) is more difficult than any of the others. Conservation of liquid volume does appear to be harder to understand than the conservation of the other properties. Conservation of area is better understood at all ages than even weight. Again this could be explained in terms of practical experience in the classroom rather than in terms of Piagetian sequence. Comparison of the weight items with volume item 7 shows that the figures for correct responses are almost identical at all ages. Above all else, the results clearly demonstrate that over half of even the youngest children, regardless of

Table 72 Correct responses to conservation tasks

	7y 5m		7y 11m		8y 5m		8y 11m		9y 5m		9y 11m	
	No.	%	No.	%	No.	%	No.	%	No.	%	No.	%
Weight												
Item 4a	76	52	95	63	99	66	109	71	130	83	119	80
Item 6a	86	59	102	68	119	80	136	88	139	90	125	84
Area												
Item 7b	85	58	92	62	113	75	125	81	132	85	128	86
Item 9a	85	58	102	68	122	81	128	83	139	90	131	88
Volume												
Item 7	75	51	85	56	101	68	110	71	116	75	117	79
Item 8a	62	43	68	46	86	57	96	62	115	74	108	72
Sample size, N (= 100%)	146		150		150		155		155		149	

their mental ability in intelligence test terms, are able to give correct answers and verbally explain their reasons in all six tests of conservation.

If the property of conservation is more difficult to grasp in, say, volume or area than in weight and this understanding is expressed by children in the concept of weight before the concept of volume, as is so often maintained, then it follows that if children display understanding of conservation in volume, these children should also all display understanding in weight. If the evidence is contrary to this thesis, then an order in the understanding of volume and weight cannot be admitted. To test for this it is necessary to ask: 'Of those children who were correct in the volume tests how many of those same children were correct in the weight tests (and, in turn, in area)?' The results of such an analysis are displayed in Figs I–V on pp. 208–17. The comparisons are made as follows.

Fig. I   Volume 7 with weight 4a : volume 7 with weight 6a.
Fig. II   Volume 8a with weight 4a: volume 8a with weight 6a.
Fig. III   Volume 7 with area 7b : volume 7 with area 9a.
Fig. IV   Volume 8a with area 7b : volume 8a with area 9a.
Fig. V   Area 7b with weight 4a : area 9a with weight 6a.

As an example, of this particular method of display, the number of $7\frac{1}{2}$ year-old children who gave correct answers to volume item 7 is examined to see how many of them also gave correct responses in weight item 4a. Reading left to right, 75 children (23 + 52) out of 146 gave the correct answer to volume item 7; *of these,* 23 (31%) gave the correct answer to this item but *did not* give the correct answer to weight item 4a. The remaining 52 (69%) also gave the correct answer to weight item 4a. Alternatively, reading right to left, 76 children (52 + 24) gave the correct answer to weight item 4a. Of these, 24 (32%) gave the correct answer to this item but *did not* give the right answer to the volume item. Obviously the remaining 52 (68% of weight item 4a correct answers) also gave the correct response to the volume item.

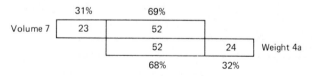

Age: 7y 5m, *N* = 146

(*main text cont. on p. 218*)

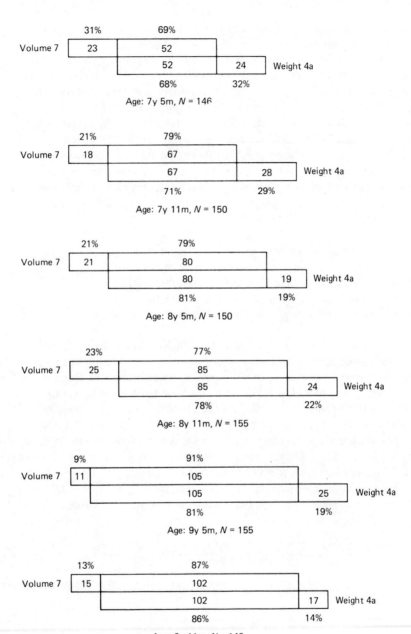

Fig. I

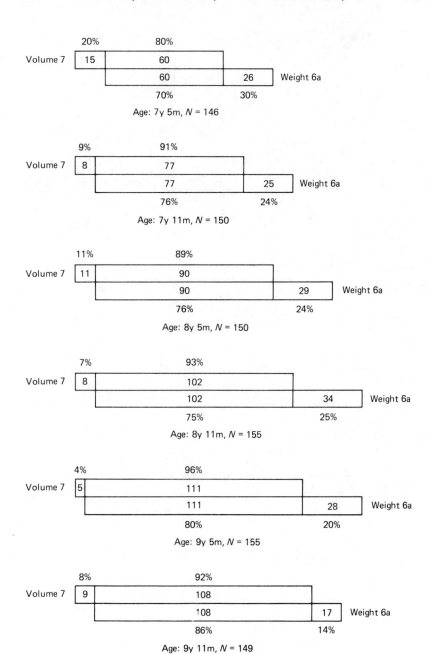

Age: 7y 5m, N = 146

Age: 7y 11m, N = 150

Age: 8y 5m, N = 150

Age: 8y 11m, N = 155

Age: 9y 5m, N = 155

Age: 9y 11m, N = 149

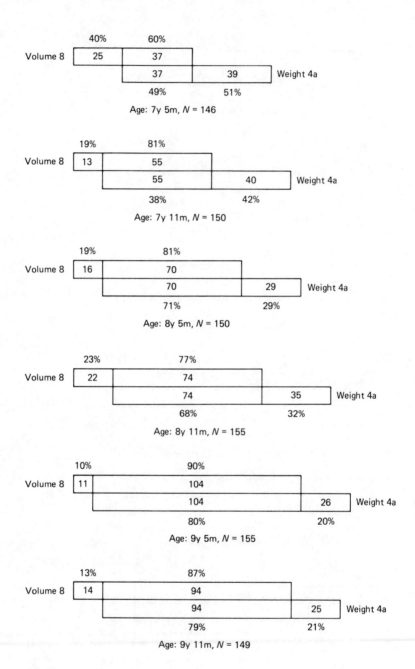

Fig. II

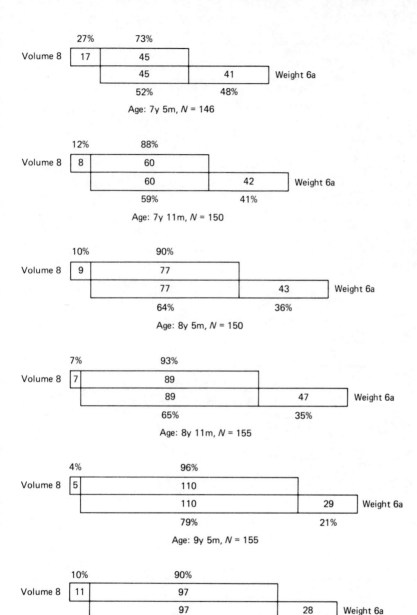

Age: 7y 5m, N = 146

Age: 7y 11m, N = 150

Age: 8y 5m, N = 150

Age: 8y 11m, N = 155

Age: 9y 5m, N = 155

Age: 9y 11m, N = 149

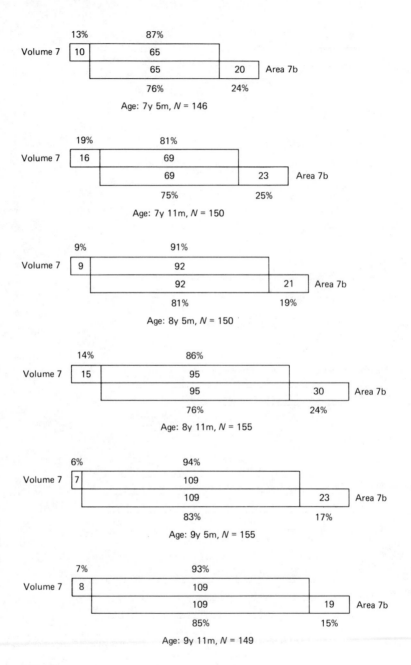

Fig. III

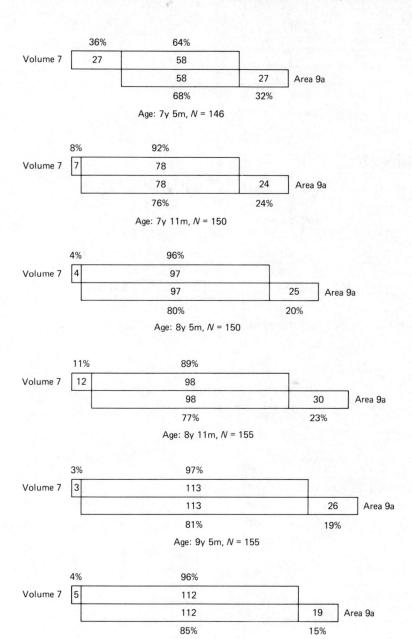

36%   64%
Volume 7 | 27 | 58 |
          | 58 | 27 | Area 9a
68%   32%
Age: 7y 5m, *N* = 146

8%   92%
Volume 7 | 7 | 78 |
          | 78 | 24 | Area 9a
76%   24%
Age: 7y 11m, *N* = 150

4%   96%
Volume 7 | 4 | 97 |
          | 97 | 25 | Area 9a
80%   20%
Age: 8y 5m, *N* = 150

11%   89%
Volume 7 | 12 | 98 |
          | 98 | 30 | Area 9a
77%   23%
Age: 8y 11m, *N* = 155

3%   97%
Volume 7 | 3 | 113 |
          | 113 | 26 | Area 9a
81%   19%
Age: 9y 5m, *N* = 155

4%   96%
Volume 7 | 5 | 112 |
          | 112 | 19 | Area 9a
85%   15%
Age: 9y 11m, *N* = 149

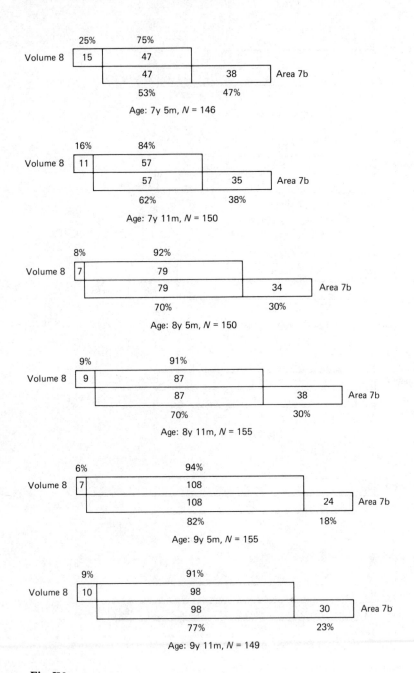

Fig. IV

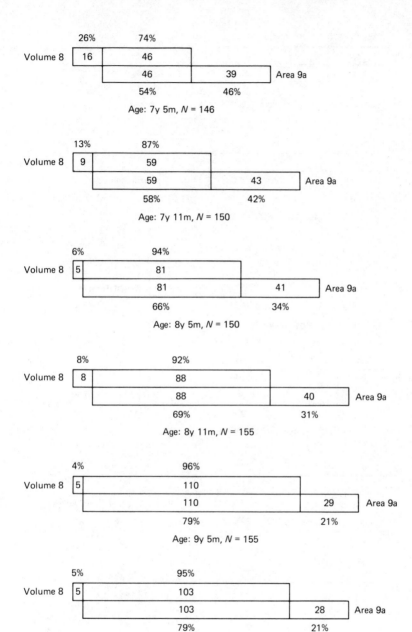

	26%	74%	
Volume 8	16	46	
		46	39	Area 9a
	54%	46%	

Age: 7y 5m, N = 146

	13%	87%	
Volume 8	9	59	
		59	43	Area 9a
	58%	42%	

Age: 7y 11m, N = 150

	6%	94%	
Volume 8	5	81	
		81	41	Area 9a
	66%	34%	

Age: 8y 5m, N = 150

	8%	92%	
Volume 8	8	88	
		88	40	Area 9a
	69%	31%	

Age: 8y 11m, N = 155

	4%	96%	
Volume 8	5	110	
		110	29	Area 9a
	79%	21%	

Age: 9y 5m, N = 155

	5%	95%	
Volume 8	5	103	
		103	28	Area 9a
	79%	21%	

Age: 9y 11m, N = 149

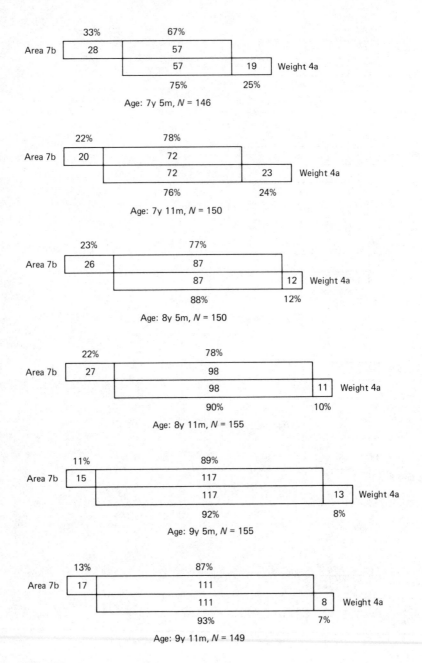

Age: 7y 5m, *N* = 146

Age: 7y 11m, *N* = 150

Age: 8y 5m, *N* = 150

Age: 8y 11m, *N* = 155

Age: 9y 5m, *N* = 155

Age: 9y 11m, *N* = 149

Fig. V

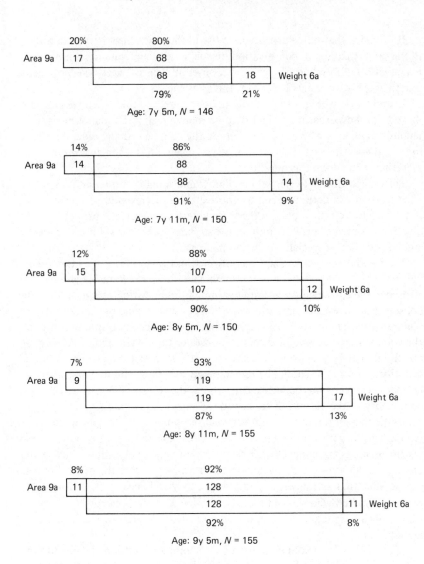

Area 9a

20%   80%
17   68
      68   18   Weight 6a
      79%   21%
Age: 7y 5m, N = 146

Area 9a

14%   86%
14   88
      88   14   Weight 6a
      91%   9%
Age: 7y 11m, N = 150

Area 9a

12%   88%
15   107
      107   12   Weight 6a
      90%   10%
Age: 8y 5m, N = 150

Area 9a

7%   93%
9   119
     119   17   Weight 6a
     87%   13%
Age: 8y 11m, N = 155

Area 9a

8%   92%
11   128
      128   11   Weight 6a
      92%   8%
Age: 9y 5m, N = 155

Area 9a

12%   88%
17   122
      122   3   Weight 6a
      98%   2%
Age: 9y 11m, N = 149

It is argued that only such an analysis will show whether there is an order in the understanding of conservation in weight, area and volume. Simple examination of numbers of correct responses at different ages does not enable one to arrive at firm conclusions on this question.

Examination of Fig. I (volume item 7 compared, in turn, with weight items 4a and 6a) shows that for weight item 4a there are almost equal numbers of children at all ages who conserved *only* in the volume test and who conserved *only* in the weight test. This result is at variance with the conclusions of most Piagetian research on this question.

The comparison between volume item 7 and weight item 6a shows that, at all ages, there is a definite trend for more children to respond correctly only in the weight item than only in the volume test. However, the proportion of children answering correctly only in the supposedly harder volume item is still considerable, especially at the younger ages.

The trend displayed in Fig. I is confirmed in Fig. II, where the more difficult volume item 8a (liquid volume) is compared with weight items 4a and 6a. Although the conservation of liquid volume is more difficult to grasp than the conservation of weight, here too we witness a considerable proportion of children, especially at the lower ages, who gave the correct responses only to the volume item yet gave incorrect responses to the weight items (e.g. 40% of the children at $7\frac{1}{2}$ years who gave the correct responses to the volume item fall into this category). It should be remembered that these children also gave correct reasons for their choices. Once more, the results demonstrate the complexity of the pattern of concept development in children

Whilst there is a trend for more correct responses in the weight items (supporting Piaget's thesis), the conclusion that the concept of conservation of weight precedes the concept of conservation of volume does not follow. Some children, at all ages, grasp one conservation concept before the other, but it is not possible to determine for certain which they will grasp first. Unfortunately, of those children who showed that they understood the concept of conservation in both weight and volume, it is impossible to determine which they grasped first.

The results of two volume items are also compared with the results of two area items (Figs III and IV). At all ages, in all four comparisons, a higher proportion of children gave the correct answers and explanations in the area items without giving correct answers in the volume counterpart items than gave the correct answers in the volume items without giving correct answers in the area counterpart items. However, when one examines this difference at its greatest in all four comparisons, it is noticed that this amounts to 16 (volume 7: area 7b); 23 (volume 7: area 9a); 29 (volume 8a: area 7b) and 36 (volume 8a: area 9a) children out of some 150 in each group. Bearing in mind that the test for conservation of liquid volume (8a) is harder than the other tests, these differences could simply be accounted for by the difference between the children's practical experience in handling area shapes and volumes.

On the other hand, the fact that there were never more children answering correctly only in the volume tests than in the area tests may be taken as evidence for a Piagetian sequence of understanding from conservation in area to conservation in volume. This argument is not favoured here because it is noticed that, at younger ages, the differences between successful answers in one test and successful answers in the other test only are considerably less than at older ages. On Piagetian grounds one would expect the reverse to be true. It seems more reasonable to suppose that the differences increase with age simply because the children gain more experience in carrying out practical exercises dealing with area than they do in the concept of volume. Furthermore, one would not expect any child to grasp the so-called harder concept before the easier concept but in fact a number of children did this. Flavell's (1972, p. 330) point that children 'may exhibit significant asequential features in addition to the obvious sequential ones' is supported by these results.

Figure V compares the results of area item 7b with weight item 4a and area item 9a with weight item 6a. Once more there is a tendency for more children to answer correctly in the area items alone than in the weight items alone but these differences are marginal. On the whole, children are just as likely to conserve in one situation as in another. As these items are probably the best matched in terms of design and method of presentation, they seem to demonstrate that it is not so much the order of conservation across the concepts area and weight and volume that emerges from the results but the variations in the individual's responses according to the exact nature of the task set.

For the research worker this section raises a number of questions relating to Piagetian research design and execution. The type of analysis illustrated is rarely carried out, and it seems obvious that much work still remains to be done before the problem of the rate at which children reach the same conceptual stage in different concepts is resolved.

For the teacher the argument that the concept of volume should be taught after the concept of weight or area is clearly too general to have any practical meaning in the classroom. As far as the idea of conservation is concerned, these results seem to indicate that there is much to be said for introducing this idea at about the same time for all three concepts. Conservation is the common property shared by the three topics, and for the child clearly to understand all three concepts it is necessary to focus his attention on the differences between area, weight and volume as well as on the similarities. It can be argued that, to do this, comparisons must be made, and that children can only have the opportunity to do this if they examine all three topics at the same time.

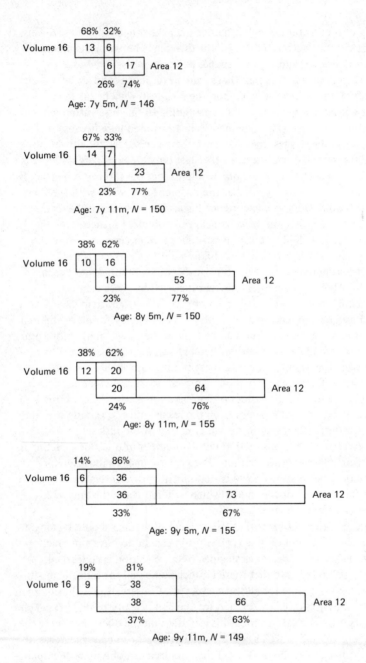

Fig. VI

Perhaps one of the fundamental differences between area and volume is the way each property is measured. Without a clear understanding of methods of measuring area and volume, children can only become more confused in their ideas about the relationship between area and volume and about the more advanced properties of the concepts themselves.

Figure VI compares, in the same manner as before, the responses of the children to items testing for the ability to measure area and volume. Area item 12, which uses the irregular shaped pieces and transparent grids, is compared with volume item 16, which uses the solid blocks and unit blocks. Although a small proportion of children did manage to find the volume of the block without being able to measure area in the other item, the results demonstrate that at all ages children had difficulty in measuring solid volume. At first sight this pattern seems to confirm Piaget's idea that the achievement of the ability to measure area occurs before the ability to measure volume, but a closer inspection reveals a possible alternative reason for the results. At the two youngest age levels the difference between the numbers of children who are able to measure in only one or the other concept is small. In other words, if they have to rely on their basic knowledge about measurement and the properties of area and volume, bearing in mind that at this age their practical experience of actual measuring must be limited in both topics, it is just as likely that they will be able to measure area as to measure volume. It is only as they become older that the differences in ability to measure in the two concepts emerge strongly. An alternative explanation could be that the differences are accounted for in terms of degree of actual practical experience of measurement in the two concepts. The differences could be due to teaching rather than natural conceptual development. From the present results it is impossible to decide which is the correct interpretation.

Finally, to complete this particular form of comparative analysis, five items are selected which test the children's ability to use relatively simple concreto-logic forms of reasoning (Table 73 and Figs VII–IX, pp. 222–7).

Weight item 8 uses the form of logic: since $A = B$ and $B = C$, then A must be equal to C.

Weight item 9 uses the form of logic: since $A > B$ and $B > C$, then $A > C$.

Area item 14 uses the form of logic: since $A + B = C + D$ and $A = C$, then B must be equal to D.

Area item 16 uses the form of logic: since $1A = 3 \times$ units and $1B = 1 \times$ units, then 3B must be equal to 1A.

Volume item 14 uses the form of logic: since $A = C$ and $B = D$ and also $A = B$, then C must be equal to D.

(*main text cont. on p. 228*)

Table 73 Correct responses to tests of concreto-logic

	7y 5m		7y 11m		8y 5m		8y 11m		9y 5m		9y 11m	
	No.	%	No.	%	No.	%	No.	%	No.	%	No.	%
Weight												
Item 8	52	36	65	43	92	61	97	63	115	74	112	75
Item 9	47	32	58	39	80	53	93	60	95	61	101	68
Area												
Item 14	41	28	49	33	82	55	76	49	102	66	97	65
Item 16	27	18	27	18	50	33	57	37	81	52	82	55
Volume												
Item 14	16	11	26	17	35	23	40	26	60	39	59	40
Sample size, N (= 100%)	146		150		150		155		155		149	

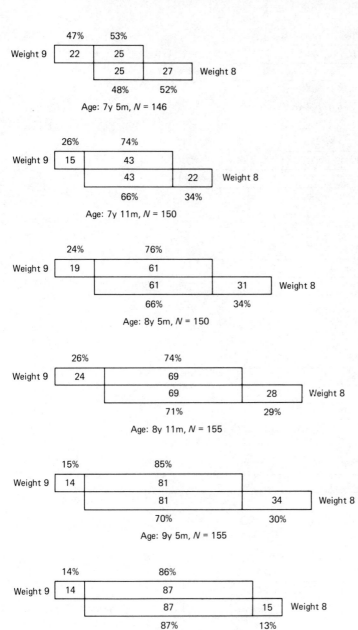

Fig. VII

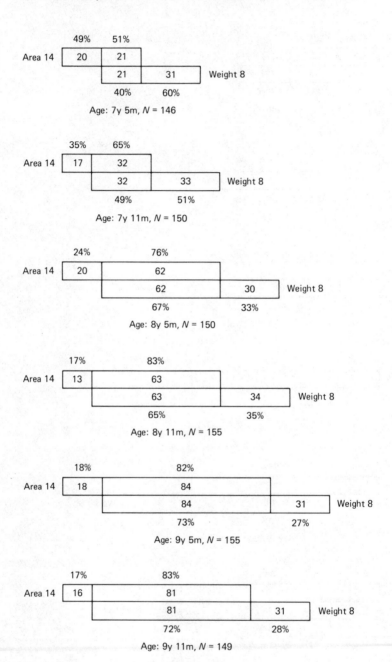

Fig. VIII

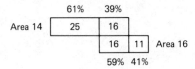

Area 14 — 61% 25 | 39% 16

16 | 11 Area 16

59% 41%

Age: 7y 5m, N = 146

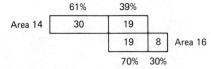

Area 14 — 61% 30 | 39% 19

19 | 8 Area 16

70% 30%

Age: 7y 11m, N = 150

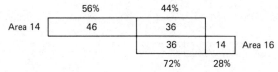

Area 14 — 56% 46 | 44% 36

36 | 14 Area 16

72% 28%

Age: 8y 5m, N = 150

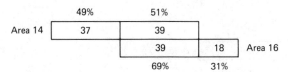

Area 14 — 49% 37 | 51% 39

39 | 18 Area 16

69% 31%

Age: 8y 11m, N = 155

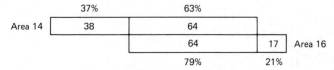

Area 14 — 37% 38 | 63% 64

64 | 17 Area 16

79% 21%

Age: 9y 5m, N = 155

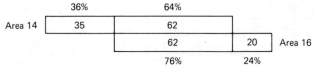

Area 14 — 36% 35 | 64% 62

62 | 20 Area 16

76% 24%

Age: 9y 11m, N = 149

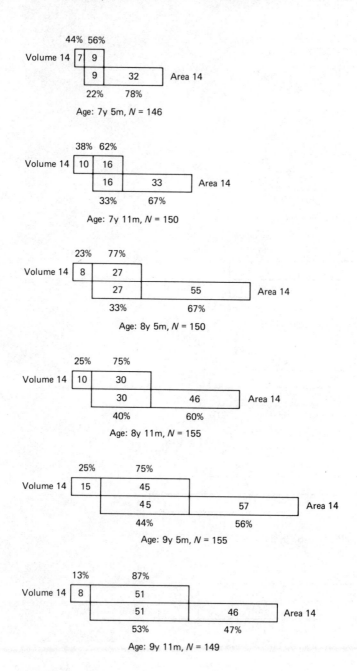

44% 56%
Volume 14 7 9
           9   32   Area 14
          22%   78%
Age: 7y 5m, *N* = 146

38% 62%
Volume 14 10   16
           16   33   Area 14
          33%   67%
Age: 7y 11m, *N* = 150

23%   77%
Volume 14 8   27
           27   55   Area 14
          33%   67%
Age: 8y 5m, *N* = 150

25%   75%
Volume 14 10   30
           30   46   Area 14
          40%   60%
Age: 8y 11m, *N* = 155

25%   75%
Volume 14 15   45
           45   57   Area 14
          44%   56%
Age: 9y 5m, *N* = 155

13%   87%
Volume 14 8   51
           51   46   Area 14
          53%   47%
Age: 9y 11m, *N* = 149

Fig. IX

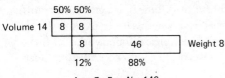

Age: 7y 5m, *N* = 146

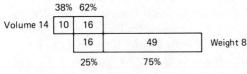

Age: 7y 11m, *N* = 150

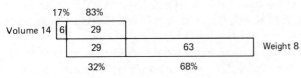

Age: 8y 5m, *N* = 150

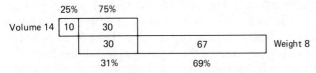

Age: 8y 11m, *N* = 155

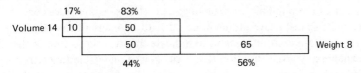

Age: 9y 5m, *N* = 155

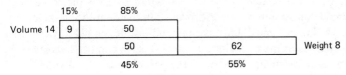

Age: 9y 11m, *N* = 149

If one is to maintain that the concept of volume in general is more difficult to grasp than, say, the concept of weight, it is necessary to explore the children's responses to tests involving similar logical frameworks for their solution as well as their responses to tests dealing with conservation. Such comparisons are rarely carried out.

It is extremely difficult to design practical tests in each of the concepts which examine the same type of logical thinking. In the present study an attempt was made, not so much to design identical tests, but to design tests which used forms of reasoning which Piaget had identified as being typical for the stage of conceptual development likely to have been reached by a number of the children in our sample. Nevertheless, the items are not exactly identical in degree of complexity and, as a result, exact comparisons are difficult to make.

It is maintained that the logic $A = B$, $B = C$, therefore $A = C$ is easier to grasp than the logic $A > B$, $B > C$, therefore $A > C$, and that these in turn are more difficult than the logic $A + B = C + D$ and $A = C$, therefore $B = D$. The first two of these logical forms occur in the weight test items whilst the third occurs in an area test item. Table 73 shows the numbers of correct responses which include only those children who were able to explain correctly the reasons for their choices i.e. they clearly demonstrated the power to use the required form of logical reasoning. The results appear to confirm the order of complexity of the logic outlined above. In all the first three items the children remain in the passive situation. Area item 16 calls upon the children to devise practical procedures before they can use the required logic and they have to carry out practical tasks by themselves. This added feature clearly makes the test more difficult and it is difficult to determine whether or not this factor, rather than the form of logic, caused the fall in the number of correct solutions. In volume item 14 the pupil has to remember and relate separate pieces of information and this test proved to be more difficult than any of the others.

This interpretation, if correct, seems to indicate that it is the nature of the logic applicable in any given situation that is the key to understanding rather than the topic (area, weight or volume) in question. To identify conceptual ability with physical 'concepts' such as weight or area or volume is an over-simplification of the conceptual process. It was wondered how the children in our sample would compare in their performances in the items using these forms of logic. Although time did not permit, and test design did not warrant, an exhaustive analysis of these results, a number of such comparisons are presented here, as all highlight, once more, the particularity of individual responses.

Figure VII compares the results of weight item 9 with weight item 8. The logic of item 8 is easier to understand than the logic of item 9; nevertheless, a considerable proportion of the children used one form of logic without using the other. In other words, although one form of logic is generally shown to be used more often than the other form by more children at a given age the fact that some children are apparently able to use the harder form of logic without demonstrating their ability to use the easier form in the other item complicates the analysis of the conceptual process.

Figures VIII and IX confirm the pattern of results. The logic required in weight item 8 is seen to be easier than that required in area item 14 and this, in turn, is an easier test than area item 16. Volume item 14 proved to be the most difficult of all. In all these figures, however, it is seen that *a considerable proportion of children continued to display an ability to solve the task generally accepted as harder without being able to solve the task accepted as easier.*

It is this asequential feature witnessed in all the results presented in this chapter that emphasizes the need for caution before accepting the principle that *all* children will consistently follow the Piagetian stages of conceptual development. Whilst this study demonstrates that children do display the type of thinking processes described by Piaget, it does not entirely support the interpretation that these processes follow *well-defined* sequential paths. Patterns of performances of groups of children taken together seem to follow Piagetian stages in general but the responses of individual children do not necessarily correspond to such well-defined stages.

This chapter also emphasizes the difficulties encountered when attempting to design tests which allow the research worker to make meaningful comparisons. Very often the introduction of a slightly different practical procedure alters the picture presented to the children to such a degree that their responses vary considerably from one test to another. Research studies which do not include careful analysis of test design are of limited value in Piagetian studies of conceptual development.

9 Intelligence and the acquisition of the concepts of weight, area and volume

Recent researches have examined, on a limited scale, the relationship between mental age or ability and conceptualization. The limitations of these studies have been discussed in Chapter 1. Nevertheless, these studies present a general pattern of relationship between intelligence as measured by some form of intelligence test and the ability to conceptualize. Mealings (1963, p. 204), in a study of problem solving and related teaching methods, wrote: 'We see that the ability to solve scientific problems at the formal level was more closely correlated with mental age than with chronological age'. Carpenter (1955) and Peel (1959), both studying a small sample of children, arrived at similar conclusions whilst, at the adolescent age, Wells (1972, p. 212) commented that 'The progression of the quality of scientific thinking (ability to solve problems etc.) was found to correlate more highly with the mental age of the subjects than with their chronological age'. At younger ages, Hood (1962), again using a relatively small sample, studied Piaget's theory of the development of number in children between the ages of 4y 9m and 8y 7m and arrived at the conclusion that 'It is not mere age, however, but mental stature which is primarily important' in the ability to conceptualize (p. 276).

As Piaget has, indirectly, referred to ages when discussing his stages of development, and as age is commonly related to stages of development by other writers, it appeared that a comparative study between the correct responses in the test items of the present study and intelligence as measured by a standardized intelligence test would be a worthwhile exercise.

It has been pointed out, in the chapters discussing each concept in turn, that age gives little guidance to the ability of the children to conceptualize. It was wondered whether a related study of the children's intelligence would provide a better picture of this ability to understand the concept of area, weight and volume. In order to do this, the children were carefully selected so that there would be almost equal numbers of children in each of four ability bands at each age. This rather unusual procedure was adopted so that meaningful numbers of children could be obtained in the lower and higher ability bands. In this way it was possible to use basic sampling techniques on the data and apply the chi-squared statistic on the resultant sample. Although the analysis is somewhat limited and could obviously be amplified with the available data, it is hoped that the application of this technique to the results from *a number* of the test items in the research gives a far better picture of the relationship between intelligence and conceptualization ability than has been obtained in the majority of studies up to the present time.

Before examining these tables, three points have to be borne in mind.

1. The intelligence tests used in this research were the non-verbal picture tests issued by the National Foundation for Educational Research (1954, 1964) under the titles *Picture Test A* and *Non-verbal Test BD*. Unfortunately, it was not possible to obtain one non-verbal intelligence test that covered the whole age range in the sample and so *Picture Test A* was used with the two seven year-old age range samples (7y 5m and 7y 11m) and *Non-verbal Test BD* with the other four ages (8y 5m to 9y 11m).

   The manifestation of intelligence effectively measured by these tests was the ability of the children to categorize material. Sorting and setting and picking 'the odd one out' in a series of pictures were the essential ingredients. It was argued that, as Piaget refers to the importance of categorizing ability in conceptualization, it was reasonable to expect a relationship between the results of such tests and the performance of the children in the concept assessment items.

2. The sample was selected from a much higher total of children tested with the intelligence tests. Although the selection of children within each ability range from this total sample was not entirely random — practical limitations prevented this — it may reasonably be assumed that, within each ability and age range, the sample is representative of the total population tested within these ranges.

3. A number of test items which at first seemed of interest in this study (e.g. tests on formal logic, manipulative skill, etc.) have not been included in the tables because detailed analysis clearly showed that only children of higher ability were able to solve the problems, i.e. the cell sizes in the statistical frequency tables were too small to justify the use of the chi-squared statistic.

The tables selected, therefore, are those which clearly show a distribution of scores through the chosen ability and age ranges to that the appropriate statistical calculations can be applied. Even so, because of the nature of the test items and the extreme ranges from low ability children aged 7y 5m to

Table 74 Tests of conservation of weight

Item 4a		Ability band ≤89	90—99	100—109	≥110	χ^2	Signif.
7y 5m	P	9	19	21	27	16·62	0·01
	F	25	21	14	10		
7y 11m	P	16	23	23	33	13·72	0·01
	F	22	13	13	7		
8y 5m	P	17	22	27	33	10·85	0·02
	F	14	20	10	7		
8y 11m	P	19	27	29	34	15·37	0·01
	F	19	15	7	5		
9y 5m	P	25	35	35	35	9·64	0·05
	F	12	4	5	4		
9y 11m	P	22	28	36	33	—	—
	F	15	7	5	3		

Item 5							
7y 5m	P	7	16	17	20	9·29	0·05
	F	27	24	18	17		
7y 11m	P	17	15	15	28	8·82	0·05
	F	21	21	21	12		
8y 5m	P	17	21	23	27	2·96	—
	F	14	21	14	13		
8y 11m	P	24	35	28	30	4·66	—
	F	14	7	8	9		
9y 5m	P	18	32	30	28	11·19	0·02
	F	19	7	10	11		
9y 11m	P	22	27	29	32	8·59	0·05
	F	15	8	12	4		

Item 6a							
7y 5m	P	12	21	26	27	14·96	0·01
	F	22	19	9	10		
7y 11m	P	21	22	24	35	10·64	0·02
	F	17	14	12	5		
8y 5m	P	19	32	33	35	10·23	0·02
	F	12	10	4	5		
8y 11m	P	26	40	31	39	—	—
	F	12	2	5	0		
9y 5m	P	30	36	37	36	—	—
	F	7	3	3	3		
9y 11m	P	26	27	37	35	—	—
	F	11	8	4	1		

high ability children aged 9y 11m, it will be observed that some cell sizes fall below 5 in number. When this occurs the chi-squared statistic is not applied, but the results are displayed as the pattern of performances is still clearly apparent.

The tables are displayed in four sections. The letters P and F indicate pass and fail throughout.

SECTION 1: TESTS OF CONSERVATION

Three tests in weight, four in area and three in volume are shown (Tables 74–6). Once more the general similarity of the results may be seen, and in all items there is a clear pattern of relationship between intelligence scores and ability to conserve in the three topics. It is seen that the difference in the proportion of passes between children of high ability and children of low ability is significant at least at the 5% level at all ages, and in many cases at the 1% level. The consistency of the pattern in all ten test items chosen enables us to conclude that a relationship very probably does exist between success in the conservation tests in this research and the ability of the children as measured by the intelligence tests.

There are a number of differences in the individual tests that are worthy of discussion. It can be seen that area item 6b (Table 74) is easier than all the others. However, in this item the children simply had to judge whether two shapes were similar in area, i.e. they did not see any changes made in dimension and were not placed in exactly the same test situation as in the other items.

Many of these items admirably cover the ability range of the children. In the majority of items few children of low ability at the youngest age solved the problem successfully whilst, on the other hand, few of the children of high ability at the oldest age failed.

It appears that the ability to conserve is a gradual development throughout the age range under study and this picture reinforces the earlier conclusion that age provides little guidance as a measure for this ability.

SECTION 2: TESTS OF THE ABILITY TO USE CONCRETO-LOGIC

The relative difficulty of the forms of logic used in these tests was discussed in the previous chapter and the order of presentation which follows conforms to this suggested sequence, e.g.

Weight item 8 uses the logic A = B, B = C, therefore A = C.
Weight item 9 uses the logic A > B, B > C, therefore A > C, etc.

Table 75   Tests of conservation of area

Item 6b		Ability band ≤89	90–99	100–109	≥110	χ^2	Signif.
7y 5m	P	18	26	23	31	7·86	0·05
	F	16	14	12	6		
7y 11m	P	24	22	26	35	8·22	0·05
	F	14	14	10	5		
8y 5m	P	25	35	31	36	1·34	–
	F	6	7	6	4		
8y 11m	P	29	39	34	37	–	–
	F	9	3	2	2		
9y 5m	P	29	32	36	38	–	–
	F	8	7	4	1		
9y 11m	P	30	31	37	32	–	–
	F	7	4	4	4		

. . . .

Item 7b

		≤89	90–99	100–109	≥110	χ^2	Signif.
7y 5m	P	11	22	23	29	14·4	0·01
	F	23	18	12	10		
7y 11m	P	18	18	21	35	16·7	0·01
	F	20	18	15	5		
8y 5m	P	13	29	34	37	–	–
	F	18	13	3	3		
8y 11m	P	25	33	30	37	–	–
	F	13	9	6	2		
9y 5m	P	25	34	35	38	–	–
	F	12	5	5	1		
9y 11m	P	24	32	37	35	–	–
	F	13	3	4	1		

. . . .

From the results (Tables 77–8) it can be seen that there is a general pattern of difficulty in these forms of logic but the differences are not so marked when one examines the performances at the various ability levels as was the case when the total results at the different ages were examined. Once more there is a clear relationship between ability to solve these conceptual problems and intelligence. Indeed, a significant relationship at the 1% level occurs in nearly

Item 9a		Ability band				χ^2	Signif.
		≤89	90–99	100–109	≥110		
7y 5m	P	13	23	23	26	8·59	0·05
	F	21	17	12	11		
7y 11m	P	20	24	24	34	9·49	0·05
	F	18	12	12	6		
8y 5m	P	20	32	33	37	12·21	0·01
	F	11	10	4	3		
8y 11m	P	23	36	32	37	—	—
	F	15	6	4	2		
9y 5m	P	27	35	38	39	—	—
	F	10	4	2	0		
9y 11m	P	25	31	39	36	—	—
	F	12	4	2	0		

. . . .

Item 10							
7y 5m	P	8	20	15	20	7·9	0·05
	F	26	20	20	17		
7y 11m	P	12	17	9	26	14·97	0·01
	F	26	19	27	30		
8y 5m	P	12	27	27	30	11·98	0·01
	F	19	15	10	10		
8y 11m	P	20	26	19	30	7·86	0·05
	F	18	16	17	9		
9y 5m	P	18	29	30	29	8·76	0·05
	F	19	10	10	10		
9y 11m	P	18	27	35	30	16·84	0·01
	F	19	8	6	6		

every case. It will be remembered that some of these items test the ability of
the children to work out procedures in their minds before carrying out the
practical tasks and the related logic. In all examples the general patterns of

(main text cont. on p. 239)

Table 76   Tests of conservation of volume

Item 7		Ability band				χ^2	Signif.
		⩽89	90—99	100—109	⩾110		
7y 5m	P	9	12	24	30	33·0	0·01
	F	25	28	11	7		
7y 11m	P	15	20	20	30	10·08	0·02
	F	23	16	16	10		
8y 5m	P	15	26	26	34	11·44	0·01
	F	16	16	11	6		
8y 11m	P	23	29	27	31	4·34	—
	F	15	13	9	8		
9y 5m	P	20	30	35	33	14·34	0·01
	F	17	9	5	6		
9y 11m	P	23	26	34	34	—	—
	F	14	9	7	2		

. . . .

Item 8a							
7y 5m	P	2	13	19	28	38·97	0·01
	F	32	27	16	9		
7y 11m	P	2	16	16	27	15·15	0·01
	F	29	20	20	13		
8y 5m	P	9	21	28	28	13·97	0·01
	F	22	21	9	12		
8y 11m	P	18	24	24	30	7·89	0·05
	F	20	18	12	9		
9y 5m	P	17	31	33	34	20·85	0·01
	F	20	8	7	5		
9y 11m	P	14	27	35	32	—	—
	F	23	8	6	4		

. . . .

Item 9a							
7y 5m	P	6	20	21	27	23·41	0·01
	F	28	20	14	10		
7y 11m	P	16	16	21	33	16·40	0·01
	F	22	20	15	7		
8y 5m	P	15	29	27	33	9·88	0·02
	F	16	13	10	7		
8y 11m	P	21	28	25	34	9·56	0·05
	F	17	14	11	5		
9y 5m	P	16	28	35	34	—	—
	F	21	11	5	5		
9y 11m	P	18	24	32	32	—	—
	F	19	11	9	4		

Table 77   Tests of concreto-logic: weight

Item 8		Ability band ≤89	90–99	100–109	≥110	χ^2	Signif.
7y 5m	P	5	13	16	18	10·94	0·02
	F	29	27	19	19		
7y 11m	P	11	11	13	30	22·7	0·01
	F	27	25	23	10		
8y 5m	P	12	20	26	34	20·71	0·01
	F	19	22	11	6		
8y 11m	P	15	26	23	33	16·74	0·01
	F	23	16	13	6		
9y 5m	P	17	31	34	33	20·70	0·01
	F	20	8	6	6		
9y 11m	P	18	26	38	30	–	–
	F	19	9	3	6		
Item 9							
7y 5m	P	3	11	12	21	–	–
	F	31	29	23	16		
7y 11m	P	10	8	15	25	16·27	0·01
	F	28	28	21	15		
8y 5m	P	9	22	20	28	11·81	0·01
	F	22	20	17	12		
8y 11m	P	21	23	20	28	4·59	–
	F	17	9	16	11		
9y 5m	P	15	25	27	30	11·55	0·01
	F	22	14	13	9		
9y 11m	P	17	21	33	30	16·06	0·01
	F	20	14	8	6		
Item 12							
7y 5m	P	7	10	15	20	11·6	0·01
	F	27	30	20	17		
7y 11m	P	8	14	12	25	14·88	0·01
	F	30	22	24	15		
8y 5m	P	10	18	26	33	24·53	0·01
	F	21	24	11	7		
8y 11m	P	16	20	30	34	27·9	0·01
	F	22	22	6	5		
9y 5m	P	17	30	33	33	18·49	0·01
	F	20	9	7	6		
9y 11m	P	21	25	33	33	–	–
	F	16	10	8	3		

Table 78   Tests of concreto-logic: area

Item 14		Ability band ≤89	90–99	100–109	≥110	χ^2	Signif.
7y 5m	P	4	12	13	12	–	–
	F	30	28	22	25		
7y 11m	P	8	9	12	20	8·76	0·05
	F	30	27	24	20		
8y 5m	P	10	19	24	29	14·49	0·01
	F	21	23	13	11		
8y 11m	P	8	22	17	29	22·09	0·01
	F	30	20	19	10		
9y 5m	P	14	28	27	33	19·67	0·01
	F	23	11	13	6		
9y 11m	P	12	29	27	29	26·01	0·01
	F	25	6	14	7		

. . . .

Item 15							
7y 5m	P	2	3	6	8	–	–
	F	32	37	29	29		
7y 11m	P	2	6	12	22	–	–
	F	36	30	24	18		
8y 5m	P	9	21	15	24	7·45	–
	F	22	21	22	16		
8y 11m	P	17	20	23	27	6·01	–
	F	21	22	13	12		
9y 5m	P	16	24	28	30	10·32	0·05
	F	21	15	12	9		
9y 11m	P	12	22	27	36	–	–
	F	25	13	14	0		

. . . .

Item 16							
7y 5m	P	0	6	6	15	–	–
	F	34	34	29	22		
7y 11m	P	1	2	7	17	–	–
	F	37	34	29	23		
8y 5m	P	5	11	17	17	9·25	0·05
	F	26	31	20	23		
8y 11m	P	9	14	13	21	9·18	0·05
	F	29	28	23	18		
9y 5m	P	6	21	26	28	27·8	0·01
	F	31	18	14	11		
9y 11m	P	12	14	29	27	20·7	0·01
	F	25	21	12	9		

performances which emerge are noteworthy for their similarities.

Also important is the evidence that tasks in this section are clearly more difficult than those on conservation, confirming Piaget's general pattern of stages once more. These results, above all else, pinpoint with some clarity the variation of individual responses throughout the age range under study.

It will be noticed that no test items concerning the topic of volume are included in this section. If one examines the results for such tests in Chapter 7, it will be seen that the numbers of correct responses were low at all ages. When the ability ranges were also considered it was observed that the children who gave these correct answers all fell into the higher ability ranges.

Table 79 Tests of displaced volume

Item 11		Ability band				χ^2	Signif.
		≤89	90–99	100–109	≥110		
7y 5m	P	3	5	10	9	–	–
	F	31	35	25	28		
7y 11m	P	5	15	11	19	11·8	0·01
	F	33	21	25	21		
8y 5m	P	9	10	15	19	6·05	–
	F	22	32	22	21		
8y 11m	P	16	16	20	22	4·11	–
	F	22	26	16	17		
9y 5m	P	7	21	22	26	19·20	0·01
	F	30	18	18	13		
9y 11m	P	12	22	24	29	17·62	0·01
	F	25	13	17	7		
Item 13							
7y 5m	P	3	10	1	2	–	–
	F	31	30	34	35		
7y 11m	P	4	1	7	4	–	–
	F	34	35	29	36		
8y 5m	P	2	3	12	9	–	–
	F	29	39	25	31		
8y 11m	P	6	2	5	7	–	–
	F	32	40	31	32		
9y 5m	P	5	9	8	13	–	–
	F	32	30	32	26		
9y 11m	P	3	8	12	13	–	–
	F	34	27	29	23		

SECTION 3: TESTS OF DISPLACED VOLUME

The picture is not so clear in this section. Although there is a trend (Table 79) for the children of high ability to do better than their fellows at all ages, the relationship is not so well marked. It may well be that understanding displaced volume depends to a great extent on the degree of practical experience that the children may have had. As it is doubtful whether the children in our sample had experienced such activities, the resultant pattern of performance may reflect this to a certain degree. Even so, the two tests once more cover the ability range of the children in a satisfactory manner and the trends of the previous tables can be seen once more.

SECTION 4: TESTS OF MEASUREMENT OF AREA AND VOLUME

Table 80, perhaps more than any of the others, displays the relative poor performances of the less intelligent pupils. The area item is particularly interesting in this respect. It was expected that most children would have been able to carry out this measuring task, as it was known that such activities are commonplace in the modern primary school. It is difficult, therefore, to explain the consistent poor performances of the less intelligent pupils and one is led to reflect on their eventual level of understanding of such measurements when older. Perhaps these children never grasp the concept of measurement of either area or volume; certainly any teaching of the topic that had occurred during the $2\frac{1}{2}$ years covered by this cross-sectional survey had little effect on these low ability children.

In conclusion, it would appear from this analysis that Piaget is correct in maintaining that the ability to categorize material and data is of considerable importance in the process of conceptualization. For the research worker this section indicates the need for further study of the relationship between mental age or intelligence and the ability to understand basic concepts. For the teacher the need for careful and continuous evaluation of children's understanding of the work that they carry out in class is emphasized once more. Once again, too, the range of performance throughout the age range 7–10 years is observed, and this would seem to indicate the need for careful and structured planning of the teaching of these topics for the whole age range.

Table 80   Tests of measurement in area and volume

Area Item 12		Ability band ≤89	90–99	100–109	≥110	χ^2	Signif.
7y 5m	P	0	2	5	8	–	–
	F	34	38	30	29		
7y 11m	P	0	0	2	12	–	–
	F	38	36	34	28		
8y 5m	P	5	9	11	19	4·46	–
	F	26	33	26	21		
8y 11m	P	6	12	12	25	21·26	0·01
	F	32	30	24	14		
9y 5m	P	3	20	27	25	32·8	0·01
	F	34	17	13	14		
9y 11m	P	5	12	25	24	27·52	0·01
	F	32	23	16	12		

. . . .

Volume Item 16		≤89	90–99	100–109	≥110	χ^2	Signif.
7y 5m	P	1	3	6	9	–	–
	F	33	37	29	28		
7y 11m	P	3	3	4	11	–	–
	F	35	33	32	29		
8y 5m	P	2	6	8	10	–	–
	F	29	36	29	30		
8y 11m	P	3	9	6	14	–	–
	F	35	33	30	25		
9y 5m	P	3	8	13	18	–	–
	F	34	31	27	21		
9y 11m	P	7	8	13	19	11·48	0·01
	F	30	27	28	17		

10 Summary and conclusions

> I cannot reach it; and my striving eye
> Dazzles at it, as at eternity.
>
> . . . And yet the practice wordlings call
> Business, and weighty action all,
> Checking the poor child for his play,
> But gravely cast themselves away
>
> . . . How do I study now, and scan
> Thee more than e'er I studied man,
> And only see through a long night
> Thy edges and thy bordering light!
> O for thy centre and midday!
> For sure that is the narrow way!
>
> Henry Vaughan (1622–95), 'Childhood'

1. This research has not disproved Piaget's main thesis that the conceptual process follows stages of development. It would seem that, when examining groups of children, this framework provides a more than useful guide for teacher and research worker alike. However, the results of this study emphasize the particularity of the individual and that it is a doubtful practice to categorize the performances of individual children within a rigid framework of stages.

2. Children at younger ages (7y 5m) do not, in the main, display the ability to use concreto-logic forms of reasoning but, on the other hand, more children at the age of ten do display this ability. This finding agrees with Piaget's thesis.

   All children tend to rely on perception and the immediate appearances of changes and, if presented with unfamiliar problems, tend to use such observations as a basis for conclusions. This is true even if the same children have earlier displayed the ability to use forms of concreto-logic. This observation emphasizes the improbability of ever witnessing the true conceptual ability of children through the use of single test items.

3. Many of the seven-year-old children were able to use concreto-logical forms of reasoning, whereas many of the ten-year-olds never displayed such ability. This finding suggests that ages should not be used as fine indicators of children's conceptual ability.

4. The relative difficulty of understanding the topics of area, weight and volume is a factor which governs the teaching of these topics in school. As far as the concepts of conservation and use of logic were concerned, the results show that there is little difference in the degree of difficulty of understanding between the three topics. It would appear that the nature of the thinking processes involved at the various levels of achievement within the three topics is more important in conceptualization than the general nature of the topics themselves.

5. The majority of the children in this research did not fit neatly into one or other of the stages described by Piaget. Most were in a transitional stage. Even those who displayed the ability to use concreto-logical forms of reasoning (e.g. reversibility) often reverted to reasons based on perception when presented with test materials likely to produce conflict in the child's mind between choices based on perception and those based on concreto-logic. (Contrast the results of area item 8 with earlier items testing for conservation and reversibility.)

   It is concluded that a high proportion of the children of average ability in this sample used alternative forms of thinking depending on how they perceived the problem. These children do not fall neatly into one stage or another in *all* situations, although they may appear to do so if the evidence is based on single test items. By its very nature the learning process is transitory, and the children conform to this dynamic principle.

6. It is concluded that there is a relationship between the mental ability of children as measured by a non-verbal intelligence test and their ability to understand the concept of conservation of area, weight and volume as well as their ability to use concreto-logical forms of reasoning.

7. The study has highlighted some of the problems that need to be taken into account when designing Piagetian research. Many of these difficulties were not resolved and, in particular, the problem of measuring the conceptual process through the use of verbal forms of communication remains a fundamental issue in this form of research. It is believed, however, that the results presented here do give good measures of the understandings and misunderstandings of children between the ages of seven and eleven in the concepts of area, weight and volume.

Many of the results of this inquiry raise issues for further research. An attempt was made to standardize Piagetian testing procedures and to avoid pitfalls caused by ambiguous questions and statements. Nevertheless, the form of the communication between pupil and teacher or tester remains the weakest link in the data-gathering chain. Words or terms conveying real world images in the pupil's mind (e.g. 'grass in a field' to denote area) produced more right answers than when abstract terms ('amount of surface' or 'area') were used. The linguistic form of the question and its relationship to the task set often confused the children so that a slight variation in the wording of the question or in the stress laid on certain words, or even of the practical objects themselves, generated different interpretations of the question by the same children.

Furthermore, a number of children, especially the younger ones, were able to make choices (often correct ones) in the tests and were obviously thinking about the tasks but were quite unable to give reasons for their choices. In other words, their ability to communicate in oral terms was not matched to their conceptual ability. Curiously little reference is made in previous research to such groups of children. There is a need for more research on this problem. It is wondered if there is a relationship between stages of conceptualization and stages of understanding terms and phrases.

All the test items — in common with other Piagetian researches — called upon the children to listen with understanding, to interpret and respond according to their conceptual powers and to communicate orally their reasons for their responses. It seems clear that these abilities may not be equally well developed in an individual at any given time. Lack of these communication skills obviously masks the true level of conceptualization of the child.

Even Piaget seems to neglect this problem and all researchers in the field should heed Donaldson's recent comment (1978, p. 61) that 'When [Piaget] does talk about [language learning] he is much more sensitive to differences between what language has become for the adult and what language is for the child in the early stages. However, when he himself, as an experimeter, *uses* language as part of his method of studying children's thinking, he appears to lose sight of the significance of this issue.'

It seems to be clear, too, that further research in this field should incorporate in its design a number of similar or parallel tests. Many earlier researchers relied on the data gathered from one or two items and the reliability of the ensuing interpretations is open to question. More rigorous techniques need to be developed so that experiments not only test the plausibility of a *particular* hypothesis or explanation but also eliminate all other possible explanations. Recent experiments by Bryant (1974), admittedly in a limited field, have highlighted the necessity for this feature of test design, and this particular study also emphasizes the importance of examining variables other than, say, age when studying conceptualization. Mental ability, as measured by a non-verbal intelligence test, appears to be closely related to stages in conceptual ability, and further research needs to be developed in this area.

For the teacher the present research has accentuated the need to use practical materials with young children and, above all else, to structure the resulting activities carefully. A course aiming at developing clear thinking and conceptualization needs to be related from one school year to the next and calls for close co-operation on the part of the teachers. Primary school teachers have many schemes in mathematics and science at their disposal, and this study indicates that guidance for teachers on the planning of curricula in a structured fashion together with guidance on the evaluation of individual pupils' progress should now be the main objective of curriculum planners over the next decade. (See the Schools Council Progress in Learning Science Project (1977), directed by Wynne Harlen, for recent work in this field.)

Throughout, the variation in the responses of individuals has emerged as the principal observation, and this hinders us from producing a neat and rigid framework for the conceptual powers of our children. Nevertheless, the ability to deviate from the average, from the expected behaviour, is the mark of the intelligent man. It can be maintained that it is only by such deviation, together with the ability to move from thinking about the visual to thinking in terms of mental images, that adults and particularly children can form new ideas and understand the various concepts presented to them.

The measurement of the average ability of an age group or a group of pupils does not supply information of any great worth. Such measurements create a restrictive view of the performances of individuals within a group and tell us nothing about the capabilities of, or the difficulties experienced by, individuals within the group. The strength of Piagetian research lies not in the measurement of average performances but in the recording and measurement of individual responses.

Knowledge is not a loose-leaf notebook of facts – The commonplace of the schoolbooks of tomorrow is the adventure of today, and that is what we are engaged in.

J. Bronowski (1973), *The Ascent of Man*

The project team and consultative committee

Project team

Joseph Rogers (director)
Eryl Rothwell Hughes
Diana Bell
Meriel Williams (assistant)

Ann Scott (assistant)
Enid Griffiths (secretary)
Sally Pritchard (Secretary)

Consultative committee

Professor J. R. Webster (chairman): *Head of Dept of Education, University College of North Wales, Bangor*

Professor W. J. G. Beynon: *Head of Dept of Physics, University College of North Wales, Aberystwyth and Chairman, Schools Council Committee for Wales*

John Broom: *Member of Schools Council Committee for Wales Primary Sub-committee*

F. E. Clegg: *Principal, St Mary's College of Education, Bangor*

G. Llewelyn Evans: *Vice-Principal, Normal College of Education, Bangor*

H. I. Evans: *Principal, Cartrefle College of Education, Wrexham*

Eric Finney: *Chief Curriculum Adviser, Monmouthshire*

R. Hurley: *Assistant Education Officer, Glamorgan*

Dennis Jones: *Primary Schools Adviser, Anglesey*

† W. E. Jones: *Director of Education, Merionethshire*

E. J. Machin: *Inspector of Schools, Birmingham*

Professor E. Mendoza: *Head of Dept of Physics, University College of North Wales, Bangor*

† Vincent H. Timothy: *Headmaster, Ysgol Llywelyn County Primary School, Rhyl*

Note: Names of colleges and local education authorities are those at the time the project ended.

Participating schools

Pilot survey

Anglesey

Bryngwran
Cemaes
Park, Holyhead
Llanffaethlu
Llanfairpwll
Llanfechell
Llanrhuddlad
Llangaffo

Caernarvonshire

Pwllheli
Portmadoc
Glanadda
Rhosgadfan

Denbighshire

Bod Alaw
Colwyn Bay
Pentrefoelas
Frongoch, Denbigh
Old Colwyn
Rhosddu, Wrexham
Ceiriog, Chirk
Llangollen

Flintshire

Bryn Deva
Connah's Quay
Holywell Welsh
Meliden
Northop Hall
Overton-on-Dee
Penley
Mynydd Isa

Merionethshire

Glyndyfrdwy
Llanuwchllyn
Manod, Blaenau Ffestiniog
Parc, Bala

Montgomeryshire

Llandysilio
Machynlleth
Trefeglwys
Newtown

Note: Names of authorities predate the 1974 reorganization.

247

Main survey

Cheshire

West Kirby Black Horse Hill
Upton Westlea County Primary
Neston Willaston Primary.
Oldfield County Junior
Brookhurst County Primary
Huntington County Primary
Parklands County Junior
Woodfall County Junior
Woodlands County Junior
Sutton Way County Junior

Glamorgan

Betws County Junior
Croesty County Primary
Litchard County Junior
Llangewydd County Junior
Mynydd Cynffig Junior
Oldcastle County Junior
Pencoed County Junior
Penybont County Primary
Tondu County Junior
St Mary's Roman Catholic Primary

Lancashire (Blackpool)

Hawes Side Junior and Infant
Devonshire Junior
Revoe Junior
Baines Endowed Church of England
St John Vianney Roman Catholic
Norbreck Junior and Infant
Holy Family Roman Catholic
St John's Church of England
Roseacre Junior
Moor Park Junior
Claremont Junior

Lancashire (Lancaster)

Garstang County Primary
Skerton County Junior
Ryelands County Primary
West End County Junior
Dallas Road County Junior
Bowerham County Junior
Torrisholme County Primary
St Peter's Church of England Junior
St Mary's Roman Catholic Junior

Manchester

Old Moat Junior
Greenheys Junior
St Phillips Church of England Primary
St Augustine's Rom n Catholic Primary
Claremont Road Junior
Briscoe Lane Junior
All Saints Church of England Primary
New Moston Junior
St Chrysostom's Primary
St Wilfrid's Junior
Teachers' Centre, Barlow Moor Road

Monmouthshire

Trinant Junior
Blackwood Junior
Cefn Fforest Junior
Pontllanfraith Junior
Aberbargoed Junior
Upper Rhymney Junior
Earl Street Junior
Georgetown Junior
Dukestown Junior
Rhiw-Syr Dafydd Junior

Newport

Malpas Church in Wales
Eveswell Junior
Durham Road Junior
Crindau Junior
St Michael's
Monnow Junior
St David Lewis Roman Catholic Primary
Glasllwch Primary
Maindee Junior
St Andrew's Junior

Shropshire

Market Drayton County Primary
Shawbury County Primary
St Mary's Church of England
Pool Hill County Junior
Dothill County Primary
St George's Church of England Junior
Ercall County Junior
Gobowen County Primary
Longlands County Primary
St Mary's Church of England

Wiltshire

Ivy Lane County Junior
Monkton Park County Primary
St Mary's Roman Catholic Aided Primary
Southbroom Church of England Controlled Junior
Lyneham County Junior
Malesbury Church of England Controlled Primary
Newtown County Junior
Parochial Controlled Junior
St Bartholomew's Church of England Controlled

References

Almy, M. C., et al. (1966). *Young Children's Thinking: Studies of Some Aspects of Piaget's Theory* (foreword by Jean Piaget). New York: Teachers' College, Columbia University.

Association of Teachers of Mathematics (1963). *Piaget's Researches into Mathematical Concepts.* Pamphlet of articles reprinted from the Association's bulletin, *Mathematics Teaching* (now out of print).

Ausubel, D. P. (1965a). 'Stages of intellectual development and their implications of early childhood education', in *Concepts of Development in Early Childhood Education,* ed. P. B. Neubauer (proceedings of an institute sponsored by the Child Development Center, New York). Springfield, Ill.: C. C. Thomas.

——(1965b). 'Cognitive structure and the facilitation of meaningful verbal learning', in *Readings in the Psychology of Cognition*, ed. R. C. Anderson and D. P. Ausubel. New York: Holt, Rinehart.

—— (1968). *Educational Psychology: a Cognitive View*. New York: Holt, Rinehart.

Barnes, D., Britton, J. and Rosen, H., for London Association for the Teaching of English (1969, rev. ed. 1971). *Language, the Learner and the School.* Penguin.

Beard, R. M. (1960). 'The nature and development of concepts', II, *Educational Review* **13** (1960–61), 12–26.

——(1962). 'Children's reasoning: a repetition of some of Piaget's experiments by members of the A.T.M.', *Mathematics Teaching* **21** (winter), 33–9.

——(1963). 'The order of concept development studies in two fields', I and II, *Educational Review* **15** (1962–63), 105–17 and 228–37.

——(1964). 'Further studies in concept development', *Educational Review* **17** (1964–65), 41–58.

——(1969). *An Outline of Piaget's Developmental Psychology for Students and Teachers.* Routledge.

Berlyne, D. E. (1957). 'Recent developments in Piaget's work', *British Journal of Educational Psychology* **27** (1), 1–12.

Board of Education Consultative Committee (1931). *The Primary School.* HMSO.

Braine, M. D. S. (1959). 'The ontogeny of certain logical operations: Piaget's formulation examined by nonverbal methods', *Psychological Monographs: General and Applied* **73** (5) (whole no. 475).

—— (1962). 'Piaget on reasoning: a methodological critique and alternative proposals', in Kessen and Kuhlman (1962), 41–61.

Brown, G., and Desforges, C. (1977). 'Piagetian psychology and education: time for revision', *British Journal of Educational Psychology* **47** (1), 7–17.

Bruner, J. S. (1959). 'Inhelder and Piaget's *The Growth of Logical Thinking*: I. A psychologist's viewpoint', *British Journal of Psychology* **50** (4), 363–70.

—— (1960). *The Process of Education.* Oxford University Press.

—— (1966). *Toward a Theory of Instruction.* Cambridge, Mass.: Harvard University Press (Belknap Press).

Bruner, J. S., Goodnow, J. A. and Austin, G. A. (1956). *A Study of Thinking.* Chapman & Hall.

Bryant, P. E. (1971a). 'Cognitive development', *British Medical Bulletin (Cognitive Psychology)* **27** (3), 200–5.

—— (1971b). Paper to the Annual Meeting of the British Association, Swansea (unpublished).

—— (1972a). 'Bryant replies on Piaget', *Times Educational Supplement,* 25 February, p. 4.

—— (1972b). 'The understanding of invariance by very young children', *Canadian Journal of Psychology* **26** (1), 78–96.

—— (1974). *Perception and Understanding in Young Children.* Methuen.

Carpenter, T. E. (1955). 'A pilot study for a quantitative investigation of Piaget's original work on concept formation', *Educational Review* **7** (1954–55), 142–9.

Churchill, E. M. (1958). 'The number concepts of young children'. Unpublished M.Ed thesis, University of Leicester.

—— (1961). *Piaget's Findings and the Teacher.* London: National Froebel Union.

Cockcroft, W. H. (1968). *Your Child and Mathematics* (Nuffield Mathematics Project). Edinburgh: W. & R. Chambers.

Dienes, Z. P. (1959). 'The growth of mathematical concepts in children through experience', *Educational Research* **2** (1959–60), 9–28.

Dodwell, P. C. (1960). 'Children's understanding of number and related concepts', *Canadian Journal of Psychology* **14** (3), 191–205.

———(1961). 'Children's understanding of number concepts: characteristics of an individual and of a group test', *Canadian Journal of Psychology* **15** (1), 29–36.

———(1963). 'Children's understanding of spatial concepts', *Canadian Journal of Psychology* **17** (1), 141–61.

Donaldson, M. (1978). *Children's Minds.* Fontana (Collins).

Elkind, D. (1961a). 'The development of quantitative thinking: a systematic replication of Piaget's studies', *Journal of Genetic Psychology* **98** (1), 37–46.

———(1961b). 'Children's discovery of the conservation of mass, weight and volume: Piaget replication study II', *Journal of Genetic Psychology* **98** (2), 279–87.

———(1962). 'Quantity conceptions in college students', *Journal of Social Psychology* **57** (2), 459–65.

———(1967). 'Piaget's conservation problems', *Child Development* **38** (1), 15–27.

———(1970). *Children and Adolescents.* Oxford University Press.

Elkind, D. and Flavell, J. H., eds (1969). *Studies in Cognitive Development: Essays in Honor of Jean Piaget.* Oxford University Press.

Flavell, J. H. (1962). 'Historical and bibliographical note', in Kessen and Kuhlman (1962), 5–18.

———(1963a). *The Developmental Psychology of Jean Piaget.* Princeton, NJ: Van Nostrand.

———(1963b). 'Piaget's contributions to the study of cognitive development', *Young Children* **21**, 164–77.

———(1971). 'Concept development', in *Carmichael's Manual of Child Psychology*, ed. P. H. Musson. 3rd ed. Wiley. 983–1059.

———(1972). 'An analysis of cognitive-developmental sequences', *Psychological Monographs: General and Applied* **86**, 279–350.

———(1975). 'The concept of stage: stage-related properties of cognitive development', in *Basic and Contemporary Issues in Developmental Psychology*, ed. P. H. Musson et al. New ed. New York: Harper & Row. 6–17.

Fogelman, K. R. (1969). 'Difficulties of using Piagetian tests in the classroom', I, *Educational Research* **12** (1969–70), 36–40.

———(1970). *Piagetian Tests for the Primary School.* Slough: NFER Publishing Co.

Fournier, E. (1967). 'Un apprentissage de la conservation des quantités continues par une technique d'exercices opératoires'. Unpublished doctoral dissertation, Montreal University (cited in Modgil, 1974).

Gelman, R. (1969). 'Conservation acquisition: a problem of learning to attend to relevant attributes', *Journal of Experimental Child Psychology* **7** (2), 167–87.

Goldschmid, M. L. (1967). 'Different types of conservation and nonconservation and their relation to age, sex, IQ, MA and vocabulary', *Child Development* **38**, 1229–46.

Harlen, W. (1968). 'The development of scientific concepts in young children', *Educational Research* **11** (1968–69), 4–13

—— (1975). *Science 5–13: a Formative Evaluation* (Schools Council Research Studies). Macmillan Education.

Holloway, G. E. T. (1967). *An Introduction to 'The Child's Conception of Geometry'*. New ed. Routledge/National Froebel Foundation.

Hood, H. B. (1962). 'An experimental study of Piaget's theory of the development of number in children', *British Journal of Psychology* **53** (3), 273–86.

Hooper, F. H. (1968). 'Piagetian research and education', in Sigel and Hooper (1968), 423–35.

—— (1969). 'Piaget's conservation tasks: the logical and developmental priority of identity conservation', *Journal of Experimental Child Psychology* **8** (2), 234–49.

Hunt, J. McV. (1961). *Intelligence and Experience*. New York: Ronald Press.

—— (1969). 'The impact and limitations of the giant of developmental psychology', cited in Elkind and Flavell (1969).

Hyde, D. M. G. (1959). 'An investigation of Piaget's theories of the development of the concept of number'. Unpublished doctoral thesis, University of London.

—— (1970). *Piaget and Conceptual Development: with a Cross-Cultural Study of Number and Quantity*. London: Holt, Rinehart.

Inhelder, B. (1954). 'Patterns of inductive thinking', *Proceedings* of the Fourteenth International Congress on Psychology, 217–48.

—— (1957). 'Developmental psychology', *Annual Review of Psychology* **8**, 139–62.

—— (1962). 'Some aspects of Piaget's genetic approach to cognition', in Kessen and Kuhlman (1962), 19–34.

—— (1969). 'Memory and intelligence', in Elkind and Flavell (1969), 337–64.

Inhelder, B. and Piaget, J. (1955: Eng. 1958, reprinted 1968). *The Growth of Logical Thinking from Childhood to Adolescence: an Essay on the Construction of Formal Operational Structures*. Trans. A. Parsons and S. Milgram. Routledge.

Inhelder, B. and Piaget, J. (1959: Eng. 1964, reprinted 1970). *The Early Growth of Logic in the Child: Classification and Seriation*. Trans. E. A. Lunzer and D. Papert. Routledge.

Keasey, C. T. and Charles, D. C. (1967). 'Conservation of substance in normal and mentally retarded children', *Journal of Genetic Psychology* **111**, 271–9.

Kessen, W. (1962). ' "Stage" and "structure" in the study of children', in
    Kessen and Kuhlman (1962), 65–82.
Kessen, W. and Kuhlman, C., eds (1962). *Thought in the Young Child* (report
    of a conference on intellective development with particular attention to the
    work of Piaget), *Monographs of the Society for Research in Child Develop-
    ment* **27** (2) (serial no. 83).
Laurendeau, M. and Pinard, A. (1970). *The Development of the Concept of
    Space in the Child.* New York: International Universities Press.
Lister, C. M. (1969). 'The development of a concept of weight conservation
    in E.S.N. children', *British Journal of Educational Psychology* **39** (3),
    245–52.
—— (1970). 'The development of a concept of volume conservation in ESN
    children', *British Journal of Educational Psychology* **40** (1), 55–64.
—— (1972). 'The development of ESN children's understanding of conserva-
    tion in a range of attribute situations', *British Journal of Educational
    Psychology* **42** (1), 14–22.
Lovell, K. (1959). 'A follow-up study of some aspects of the work of Piaget
    and Inhelder on the child's conception of space', *British Journal of
    Educational Psychology* **29** (2), 104–17.
—— (1961a). *The Growth of Basic Mathematical and Scientific Concepts in
    Children.* University of London Press.
—— (1961b). 'A follow-up study of Inhelder and Piaget's *The Growth of
    Logical Thinking*', *British Journal of Psychology* **52** (2), 143–53.
Lovell, K. and Ogilvie, E. (1960). 'A study of the conservation of substance
    in the junior school child', *British Journal of Educational Psychology* **30**
    (2), 109–18.
—— (1961a). 'A study of the conservation of weight in the junior school
    child', *British Journal of Educational Psychology* **31** (2), 138–44.
—— (1961b). 'The growth of the concept of volume in junior school
    children', *Journal of Child Psychology and Psychiatry* **2** (2), 118–26.
Lunzer, E. A. (1960a, new ed. 1973). *Recent Studies in Britain Based on the
    Work of Jean Piaget.* Slough: NFER Publishing Co.
—— (1960b). 'Some points of Piagetian theory in the light of experimental
    criticism', *Journal of Child Psychology and Psychiatry* **1** (1960–61) (1),
    191–202.
—— (1972) 'The Piaget controversy', *Times Educational Supplement*, 11
    February, p. 18.
Mays, W. (1953). Introduction to Piaget's logic, in Piaget (1953).
Mealings, R. J. (1963). 'Problem-solving and science teaching', *Educational
    Review* **15** (1962–63), 194–207.
Modgil, S. (1974). *Piagetian Research: a Handbook of Recent Studies.* Slough:

NFER Publishing Co.

National Foundation for Educational Research (1954). *Picture Test A* (by J. E. Stuart). For age range 7.00–8.01. Slough: NFER Publishing Co. (test 42, restandardized 1974).

——— (1964). *Non-verbal Test BD* (by D. A. Pidgeon). For age range 8.00–11.00. Slough: NFER Publishing Co. (test 28, 1964 restandardization).

Peel, E. A. (1959). 'Experimental examination of some of Piaget's schemata concerning children's perception and thinking and a discussion of their educational significance', *British Journal of Educational Psychology* **29** (2), 89–103.

——— (1960). *The Pupil's Thinking.* Oldbourne Press.

Piaget, J. (1923; Eng. 1926, 3rd ed. 1967). *The Language and Thought of the Child.* Trans. M. Warden. Preface by E. Claparède. Routledge.

———, with collaborators (1924: Eng. 1928, reprinted 1969). *Judgement and Reasoning in the Child.* Trans. M. Warden. Routledge.

——— (1927: Eng. 1930, reprinted 1970). *The Child's Conception of Physical Causality.* Trans. M. Gabain. Routledge.

——— (1936: Eng. 1953). *The Origin of Intelligence in the Child.* Trans. M. Cook. Routledge.

——— (1937: Eng. 1955, reprinted 1976). *The Child's Construction of Reality.* Trans. M. Cook. Routledge.

——— (1941: Eng. 1952, reprinted 1964). *The Child's Conception of Number.* Trans. C. Gattegno and F. M. Hodgson. Routledge.

——— (1947: Eng. 1950). *The Psychology of Intelligence.* Trans. M. Piercy and D. E. Berlyne. Routledge.

——— (1952 lectures: Eng. 1953). *Logic and Psychology.* Trans. W. Mays and F. Whitehead. Manchester University Press.

——— (1964a: Eng. 1969). *Six Psychological Studies.* Trans. A. Tenzer and D. Elkind. University of London Press.

——— (1964b). 'Cognitive development in children', *Journal of Research in Science Teaching* **2**, 176–86.

——— (1969: Eng. 1971). *Science of Education and the Psychology of the Child.* Trans. D. Coltman. Longman.

——— (1972: Eng. 1974). *The Child and Reality: Problems of Genetic Psychology.* Trans. A. Rosin. Muller.

Piaget, J. and Inhelder, B. (1941: Eng. 1974). *The Child's Construction of Quantities: Conservation and Atomism.* Trans. A. J. Pomerans. Routledge.

——— (1948: Eng. 1956). *The Child's Conception of Space.* Trans. F. J. Langdon and J. L. Lunzer. Routledge.

——— (1966: Eng. 1969, reprinted 1975). *The Psychology of the Child.* Trans. H. Weaver. Routledge.

Piaget, J. and Szeminska, A. (1941) – *see* Piaget (1941).

Piaget, J., Inhelder, B. and Szeminska, A. (1948: Eng. 1960, reprinted 1966). *The Child's Conception of Geometry.* Trans. E. A. Lunzer. Routledge.

Pinard, A. and Laurendeau, M. (1969). ' "Stage" in Piaget's cognitive development theory', in Elkind and Flavell (1969), 121–70.

Plowden Report (1967). *Children and Their Primary Schools* (a report of the Central Advisory Council for Education (England)). 2 vols. HMSO.

Rosskopf, M. F., Steffe, L. P., and Taback, S., eds (1971). *Piagetian Cognitive Development Research and Mathematical Education.* Report of conference held at Columbia University, 1970. Reston, Virginia: National Council of Teachers of Mathematics.

Schools Council Progress in Learning Science Project. *Match and Mismatch.* In-service training materials for teachers of science to 5–13 year-olds, comprising: *Raising Questions* and *Finding Answers* (books for teachers); *Leader's Guide* (for group leaders, incl. *Raising Questions*); audiovisual materials. Edinburgh: Oliver & Boyd.

Siegel, L. S. (1971). 'The development of the understanding of certain number concepts', *Developmental Psychology* **5** (2), 362–3.

——(1972). 'Development of the concept of seriation', *Developmental Psychology* **6** (1), 135–7.

Sigel, I. E. and Hooper, F. H., eds (1968). *Logical Thinking in Children.* New York: Holt, Rinehart.

Smedslund, J. (1961–2). 'The acquisition of conservation of substance and weight in children', I–VI, *Scandinavian Journal of Psychology* **2**, 11–20, 71–84, 85–7, 153–5, 156–60, 203–10; VII, *Scandinavian Journal of Psychology* **3**, 69–77.

——(1963). 'Patterns of experience and the acquisition of concrete transitivity of weight in eight-year-old children', *Scandinavian Journal of Psychology* **4**, 251–6.

——(1964). 'Concrete reasoning: a study of intellectual development', *Monographs of the Society for Research in Child Development* **29** (2) (serial no. 93), 3–39.

——(1977). 'Symposium: practical and theoretical issues in Piagetian psychology – III: Piaget's psychology in practice', *British Journal of Educational Psychology* **47** (1), 1–6.

Uzgiris, I. C. (1964). 'Situational generality of conservation', *Child Development* **35** (3), 831–41.

Vernon, P. E. (1965). 'Environmental handicaps and intellectual development', *British Journal of Educational Psychology* **35** (1), 9–20.

Vygotsky, L. S. (1962, new ed. 1965). *Thought and Language.* Trans. E. Hanfmann and G. Vakar. Cambridge, Mass.: MIT Press.

Wallace, J. G. (1965). *Concept Growth and Education of the Child.* Slough: NFER Publishing Co.

—— (1972). *Stages and Transition in Conceptual Development.* Slough: NFER Publishing Co.

Wells, J. (1972). 'Some aspects of adolescent thinking in science', *Educational Review* 24 (1971–72), 212.

Wohlwill, J. F. (1962). 'From perception to inference: a dimension of cognitive development', in Kessen and Kuhlman (1962), 87–107.

—— (1968). 'Piaget's system as a source of empirical research', in Sigel and Hooper (1968), 438–46.

Woodward, M. (1962). 'Concepts of space in mentally subnormal studied by Piaget's method', *British Journal of Social and Clinical Psychology* 1, 25–37.

Index